HATING GIRLS

Studies in Critical Social Sciences Book Series

Haymarket Books is proud to be working with Brill Academic Publishers (www.brill.nl) to republish the *Studies in Critical Social Sciences* book series in paperback editions. This peer-reviewed book series offers insights into our current reality by exploring the content and consequences of power relationships under capitalism, and by considering the spaces of opposition and resistance to these changes that have been defining our new age. Our full catalog of *SCSS* volumes can be viewed at https://www.haymarketbooks.org/series_collections/4-studies-in-critical-social-sciences.

HATING GIRLS

An Intersectional Survey of Misogyny

EDITED BY
DEBRA MEYERS
MARY SUE BARNETT

Haymarket Books
Chicago, IL

First published in 2021 by Brill Academic Publishers, The Netherlands
© 2021 Koninklijke Brill NV, Leiden, The Netherlands

Published in paperback in 2022 by
Haymarket Books
P.O. Box 180165
Chicago, IL 60618
773-583-7884
www.haymarketbooks.org

ISBN: 978-1-64259-774-5

Distributed to the trade in the US through Consortium Book Sales and
Distribution (www.cbsd.com) and internationally through Ingram Publisher
Services International (www.ingramcontent.com).

This book was published with the generous support of Lannan Foundation and
Wallace Action Fund.

Special discounts are available for bulk purchases by organizations and
institutions. Please call 773-583-7884 or email info@haymarketbooks.org for more
information.

Cover design by Jamie Kerry and Ragina Johnson.

Printed in the United States.

10 9 8 7 6 5 4 3 2 1

Library of Congress Cataloging-in-Publication data is available.

Contents

Notes on Contributors

Portia Allie-Turco
is a doctoral student in the School of Social and Behavioral Sciences at University of the Cumberlands. Her professional experience includes the roles of: Licensed Mental Health Counselor, counseling clinic director, college lecturer, chief diversity officer and clinical consultant. Her research, and clinical focus, is on healing generational, historical and racial trauma.

Mary Sue Barnett
is a Catholic woman priest, ordained by the Association of Roman Catholic Women Priests. She is founder and president of the Louisville Coalition for CEDAW (Convention on the Elimination of all Forms of Discrimination Against Women) a grassroots nongovernmental organization that seeks to implement the rights and principles of this United Nations women's treaty on the local level. She also serves as a chaplain at a psychiatric hospital. Barnett recently published *Crisis and Challenge in the Roman Catholic Church* (2020).

Melissa Brennan
is currently completing her PhD in Counselor Education and Supervision at University of the Cumberlands. Her areas of interest include school counseling, social justice, gender studies, diversity and equality, child and adolescent counseling, and online teaching and counseling.

Angela Cowser
earned her PhD at Vanderbilt University and is currently Associate Dean of Black Church Studies and Doctor of Ministry programs at Louisville Presbyterian Theological Seminary in Kentucky. She previously served as Director of the Center for the Church and the Black Experience and Assistant Professor of Sociology of Religion at Garrett-Evangelical Theological Seminary (Chicago, Illinois). She was ordained as a Presbyterian Church (U.S.A.) Minister of Word and Sacrament in 2006. Her publications include *Radicalizing Women-Centered Organizing and Power in Post-Conflict Namibia: A Case Study of the Shack Dwellers Federation of Namibia* (Saarbrucken: Scholars Press, 2013), "Leadership Amidst Poverty: A Mixed Methodological Analysis of the Shack Dwellers Federation of Namibia" (*Journal of African American Studies*, 2017), and other articles. She is a member of the Association of Black Sociologists, the National Center for Faculty Development and Diversity, the American Academy of Religion, and the Chicago Organizers Guild.

Diane Dougherty

is an ordained priest in the Association of Roman Catholic Women Priests. She is a lifelong Catholic, former religious sister of 23 years, lay minister of education in Catholic schools, and former Director of Catechesis for the Archdiocese of Atlanta. She is an activist working to promote equality for women and those marginalized by unjust systems in the home, on the street, and in the state.

Dorislee Gilbert

is the Executive Director of the Mary Byron Project, where she leads a legal program dedicated to enhancing justice to end intimate partner violence. At the Mary Byron Project, she provides legal assistance to victims of intimate partner violence, consults with other attorneys doing the same, and provides training to justice-system participants about intimate partner violence and the law. Before joining the Mary Byron Project, she was a felony prosecutor for 15 years in Louisville, Kentucky, specializing in appeals and domestic violence and child abuse prosecutions. In 2019, she was named Assistant Commonwealth's Attorney of the Year. She has engaged with, represented, and presented the cases of hundreds of victims in her career. Gilbert graduated from Kentucky State University and Chicago-Kent College of Law at the Illinois Institute of Technology.

Kristi Gray

is an Assistant Commonwealth's Attorney in Louisville and has been with that office since June 2004. She is currently assigned to the Special Victims Unit. She received her Bachelor of Arts in Criminology from Ohio State University in 1991, and her Juris Doctor from Capital University Law School in 1994. From 1994 until 2004, she served as a Staff Attorney and Directing Attorney for the Department of Public Advocacy in Pikeville and Paintsville. Gray currently serves as the Sexual Assault Liaison and is the point of contact for Human Trafficking cases within the Office of the Commonwealth's Attorney. In addition, she is a member of the Louisville Human Trafficking Task Force and the Louisville Sexual Assault Response Team. She also serves on the Kentucky Sexual Assault Kit Initiative Task Force and has been involved in the implementation of policies and procedures to address the rape kit backlog in Kentucky. She regularly provides training to law enforcement agencies and other criminal justice professionals in the areas of sexual assault and human trafficking.

Tammy Hatfield

serves as a Professor in the School of Social and Behavioral Sciences at University of the Cumberlands. Her areas of expertise and interest include online teaching, intersectional feminist pedagogy, diversity, equity, inclusion, social justice, feminist therapy, gender studies, body image, identity development, first generation students, and Appalachian culture.

Sarah E. Johansson

is a middle school counselor and associate professional counselor, and has worked as a K-12 school counselor for over a decade. With a strong interest in student advocacy, her specific experience and interests include LGBTQ+, poverty, equity, and inclusion.

Sandy Phillips Kirkham

is the author of *Let Me Prey Upon You*, and currently serves on the board of the Council Against Child Abuse. She has spoken before the Ohio Senate, a Maryland court, and appeared on a Boston television show. Her story, "Stolen Innocence," was told in a documentary produced by the Hope of Survivors. Phillips Kirkham works with survivors of sexual abuse and has participated on SNAP (Survivors Network of those Abused by Priests) conference panels, sharing her perspective from the non-Catholic perspective.

Francoise Knox-Kazimierczuk

earned her Ph.D. from Miami University and is an assistant professor at the University of Cincinnati in the College of Allied Health Sciences. She is an experienced clinician with over fifteen years of clinical dietetics experience focusing on chronic disease management. Knox-Kazimierczuk is trained in mix methods and the principles of Community Based Participatory Research (CBPR) to address racial health disparities through a critical race theory lens. Knox-Kazimierczuk is a trained Qualified Administrator for the Intercultural Competence Development Inventory (IDI) and has eleven years of experience facilitating Diversity, Equity, & Inclusion (DE&I) workshops. She has two funded studies focused on addressing racial health disparities.

Debra Meyers

received her Ph.D. from the University of Rochester and is a full professor at Northern Kentucky University teaching a variety of courses in gender studies, history, and religious studies. Meyers has published eight books and dozens of scholarly journal articles and encyclopedia entries. She recently published *Crisis and Challenge in the Roman Catholic Church* (Rowman and Littlefield, 2020) and is currently working on her next book, *Gender, Love, and Religion in the Early Chesapeake*. Meyers earned the distinguished Milburn Outstanding

Professor award at Northern Kentucky University in 2019 for her distinguished service, exceptional scholarship, and excellence in teaching.

Donna Pollard

successfully advocated for improved legislation in Kentucky and other states putting an end to child marriage through parental consent. She continues her advocacy both nationally and internationally, most recently having traveled to Finland as the keynote speaker for the *Zonta International Centennial Conference*, highlighting the devastating implications of child marriage and critically needed global reform. As a survivor herself, Pollard realizes the need for healing and support for victims. She founded *Survivors' Corner*, a nonprofit that provides this connection and empowerment. Her personal journey can be accessed through the A&E Documentary, *"I Was a Child Bride,"* and interviews in *Glamour*, NPR, *US News and World Report*, PBS, CBS News, and many other outlets. She is a frequent panelist and presenter and has given numerous keynote speeches and testimony before legislative committees.

Meredith Shockley-Smith

received her PhD from the University of Cincinnati in Educational Studies. She is an assistant field professor at the University of Cincinnati Medical School focused on building stronger and more equitable relationships in the community. As the Director of Diversity, Equity, Inclusion and Community Strategies at Cradle Cincinnati and Queens Village, Shockley-Smith seeks to work with Black women to co-create sustainable communities that help to reduce stress and in turn lower infant mortality in Cincinnati communities.

Tara M. Tuttle

is the Assistant Dean for Diversity, Equity, and Inclusion of the Lewis Honors College with a secondary appointment as Assistant Professor of Gender and Women's Studies at the University of Kentucky. She is also an affiliate faculty of the University of Kentucky's Center for Equality and Social Justice. Her research examines the intersections of religious belief and female sexuality in contemporary American culture and the deployment of scriptural rhetoric to challenge oppression. Her work has appeared in *The Journal of Religion and Popular Culture, Studies in Popular Culture,* and *The Journal of Catholic Higher Education.*

Johanna W.H. van Wijk-Bos

is Professor Emerita of Louisville Presbyterian Theological Seminary in Louisville, KY, where she served for 40 years as Dora Pierce Professor of Bible

and Faculty Liaison for the Women's Center. She received her PhD in Hebrew
Bible in 1976 from Union Theological Seminary in New York and was ordained
to the Presbyterian ministry in the Downtown United Presbyterian Church of
Rochester, New York in 1977. Van Wijk-Bos is the author of eleven books and
many articles, her most recent books are three volumes in the trilogy *A People
and a Land; The End of the Beginning: Joshua and Judges; The Road to Kingship: 1-
2 Samuel; The Land and its Kings: 1-2 Kings;* with William B. Eerdmans in Grand
Rapids, 2020. She is currently writing a commentary on Deuteronomy in the
Wisdom series, edited by Barbara Reid, to be published by the Liturgical Press,
Collegeville, Minnesota.

Stephanie A. Welsh
is an ordained elder in the Christian Methodist Episcopal Church, where she
served as a pastor in the Gary District from 2010–2018. She is a Board-Certified
Chaplain serving as a staff chaplain at the University of Chicago Medicine. She
supports the critical care and trauma patient population. Welsh is pursuing a
Doctor of Ministry degree from Louisville Presbyterian Theological Seminary.
She holds a Master of Divinity degree from Garrett-Evangelical Theological
Seminary, a Master of Business Administration from Benedictine University,
and a Bachelor of Arts degree from the University of Wisconsin-Milwaukee.
Welsh is featured in the CNN article, "Hospital chaplains are bridging the gap
between patients and grieving families who can't stay by their bedside during
the coronavirus pandemic" (April 26, 2020). She was also featured in the Crain's
Chicago Business, "Crain's 2020 Notable Health Care Heroes" (June 29, 2020).
Welsh is committed to justice, equality, and uplifting the voices of women and
the disenfranchised.

Introduction

Debra Meyers and Mary Sue Barnett

In the 2015 documentary film, *The Hunting Ground*, clinical psychologist David Lisak reports that the problem of sexual assault on college campuses in the United States is out of control. Caroline Heldman shines additional light on the widespread trauma caused by these sexual assaults stating, "There's a lot of victim blaming with this crime which has a silencing effect on survivors."[1] Various students from universities across the country were interviewed after their sexual assaults on or near their campuses by male students. Female students report having heads slammed into walls and having faces pushed into the bathroom tile during rape assaults. In addition to a crime of violence against their intimate, sexual selves, it seems the rapists also aimed to assault their minds, deface them, and rob them of any agency they possessed.

Rachel Hudack, a Saint Mary's College student who was raped by a Notre Dame student in his dorm room, describes how she became isolative and felt "completely changed as a person."[2] Upon reporting the assault, Hudak's distress deepened with the dismissive response of Saint Mary's College president Dr. Carol Ann Mooney. The film argues that perpetrators, college administrators, coaches, and the fraternity system want survivors silenced. Yet, the young women in this film told their truths with boldness. In the face of re-traumatization and death threats, they persevered in their healing and emerged as advocates in solidarity with one another. While still students at UNC Chapel Hill, campus sexual assault survivors Andrea Pino and Annie Clark became advocates for other survivors, traveling across the country to hear stories and to share findings of their Title IX research initiative. They formed alliances with survivors on many campuses to force universities to address sexual assault more rigorously.

Despite the efforts of activists to promote justice for sexual assault survivors, the hyper sexualization and objectification of girls throughout our society allows our rape culture to thrive. Gail Dines, in her 2010 book *Pornland: How Porn Has Hacked Our Sexuality*, describes the hypersexualized U.S. culture in which girls and women are inundated with images and messages that prioritize sex and de-emphasize other aspects of life experience and personal identity. She says that sexualized pop culture *grooms* females like a predator,

---

1   *The Hunting Ground.* Kirby Dick. (United State: Radius-TWC, 2015).
2   Ibid.

stripping them of self-esteem and a full sense of their humanity. She points out that the American Psychological Association's landmark study describes how the sexualization of girls affects them negatively in "cognitive functioning, physical and mental health, and attitudes and beliefs."[3] This often leads to eating disorders, depression, and low self-esteem, all of which are symptoms experienced by females who have been sexually assaulted. Dines argues that, "we appear to be turning out a generation of girls who have been 'assaulted' by the very culture they live in."[4] Similarly Kate Manne suggests that understanding misogyny means understanding the hostility that girls and women face. What we need to know, she contends, is that a girl or a woman faces "gendered, hostile treatment because she is a *woman in a man's world.*"[5] But this misogyny is not limited to our culture.

In recognition of the United Nations International Day of the Girl, the UN Women website published a video of Sore Agbaje performing her poem, "We Do Not Wait Tomorrow," in which she briefly closes her eyes while gently placing her hands to her chest and speaks the names of diverse feminist icons so that the women fill the rooms, "until we keep the promises of the Beijing Declaration, until consent is everyone's first language."[6] From this global platform dedicated to the empowerment of girls around the world, Agbaje embraces global sisterhood in highlighting the importance of fulfilling the objectives set out in the Beijing Declaration and Platform for Action from the 1995 Fourth World Conference on Women in Beijing, China. It was the most progressive blueprint ever produced for advancing women's human rights. Devoted to the safety and flourishing of girls around the world, Section L of the Declaration calls for the elimination of all forms of discrimination against girls, stating that girls are often treated as inferior and are socialized to put themselves last. It calls for the elimination of all negative cultural attitudes and gender-stereotyping that work against girls achieving their highest potential. And it calls for the eradication of egregious forms of violence against girls including child marriage, rape, and female genital mutilation.

In 2011, the United Nations General Assembly adopted Resolution 66/170 to declare October 11 as the International Day of the Girl Child. It is a day for organizations all over the world to provide platforms for girls to assert their power, to mobilize as change agents, to share their visions for the future, and to

3   Gail Dines, *Pornland: How Porn Has Hijacked Our Sexuality*, (Boston: Beacon Press, 2010) 118.
4   Dines, *Pornland*, 118.
5   Kate Manne, *Entitled: How Male Privilege Hurts Women*, (New York: Crown, 2020) 9.
6   UN Women, "#GenerationEquality: We Do Not Wait Tomorrow," unwomen.org, October 11, 2020.

connect with one another across the globe. It is also an opportunity for adults to encourage girls and to listen to them. On International Day of the Girl 2020, United Nations Deputy Secretary-General Amina Mohammed told girls, "Be bold in your demands and be confident in the steps you are taking." She added, "your solutions and ideas are essential to step up the pace of progress."[7] This charge is applicable to all of us who advocate for safety, peace, and justice for girls in the world today. As adults, we too must be bold. Our visions, words, and actions on behalf of girls everywhere must be formidable and unrelenting in resistance to the misogynist barriers and traps that cause them great harm.

Toward that end, *Hating Girls* is a collection of cutting-edge essays addressing the pervasive problem of misogyny from an intersectional framework, particularly focused on identities of gender, race, class, sexuality, and religion. Scholars, activist reformers, and social justice practitioners offer multiple perspectives of the misogyny that dominates our culture, providing both macro-views as well as case studies in the United States. This interdisciplinary analysis exposes the destructive, oppressive beliefs and practices inherent in our society and offers a progressive, equitable way forward.

Kristi Gray and Dorislee Gilbert open with a disturbing overview of the current state of criminal justice for sexual assault victims. They argue that we desperately need a true culture shift in order to change the hearts and minds of juries, prosecutors, police, and judges in order to bring about real justice for sexual assault victims. In chapter two, Tammy Hatfield, Portia Allie-Turco, Sarah E. Johansson, and Melissa Brennan provide a pathway forward to creating a pedagogical social justice practice that promises to bring about the cultural shift needed in order to extinguish misogyny. Tara M. Tuttle, in chapter three, introduces readers to the profound dangers inherent in the purity culture movement espoused by many religious groups. Shockingly, this movement has actually contributed to our rape culture rather than offer a way forward.

Chapter four offers us a case study illustrating the devastating impact of the objectification and sexualization of girls in the middle of the last century through the lens of divorce, birth control, domestic violence, and rape. Rather than laying the blame with the objectification and sexualization of girls with the media, Debra Meyers suggests that Christianity may have played a larger role in creating our society's rape culture. Johanna W. H. van Wijk-Bos, in chapter five, argues that the objectification and sexualization of girls begins very early on in human history with patriarchy's erasure of women from the earliest religious texts and traditions. Chapter six investigates the psychological impact

---

7   UN Web TV, The United Nations Live & On Demand, webtv.un.org, October 9, 2020.

of victims of sexual assault, and Mary Sue Barnett offers some suggestions for a pathway forward by challenging the male-dominant Christianity that supports our rape culture today.

Donna Pollard, in chapter seven, lays bare her personal experience of sexual assault, child marriage, and the inadequate institutions that should protect girls from sexual predators. Her social status, age, physical health, and limited family resources all acted against her ability to reach her potential. Pollard works to prevent child marriages in every state so that others might escape the nightmare she endured. Sandy Phillips Kirkham's childhood experiences have also prompted her to be an active agent for social change. Chapter eight highlights her sexual objectification and sexualization at the hands of a minister she trusted. Her rapist was protected and excused by the entire institutionalized church that she thought was supposed to love and protect her. In chapter nine, Diane Dougherty helps us to better understand how misogyny has been embedded in Christianity that creates rape culture by outlining the role of several patriarchal right-wing institutions within the Roman Catholic church. Similarly, Angela Cowser, in chapter ten, details the destructive power of patriarchy in African-American religious institutions. And Stephanie A. Welsh digs deeper into this religiously sanctioned misogyny in her case studies of Black Methodist Episcopal church clergywomen in chapter eleven. We complete our survey of misogyny with Francoise Knox Kazimierczuk and Meredith Shockley-Smith's research into how our rape culture continues to impact Black women's health and safety. In this chapter, quantitative data details the problem of maternal and infant mortality, alongside qualitative data giving voice to the experience of Black women as they confront racism, sexism, and classism during pregnancy and birth.

Collectively, these chapters in *Hating Girls* provide a cutting-edge intersectional perspective that deconstructs the pervasive misogynies and gender-based violence against females and gender non-conforming people today. And while the interdisciplinary analysis in this volume exposes the destructive, oppressive beliefs and practices inherent in our society, it also provides a progressive, equitable way forward much like the United Nations' Girl Declaration. The Girl Declaration was delivered by a delegation of girls to the United Nations on International Day of the Girl in 2013. Endorsed by Malala Yousafzi and Archbishop Desmond Tutu, it proclaims the hopes and ambitions of five hundred girls in fourteen countries across four continents. A global anthem of empowerment, the girls' voices insist that they are not invisible, and they want their dreams recognized. They locate their enormous hopes in the present moment, not the distant future, through repetition of the words *this moment*—so pressing is their safety, their health, their education, their rising out of the confines of poverty, violence, and stigma. Heralding the powerful immediacy of *now,* with both tenderness and unapologetic fierceness, they proclaim, "This is the moment when my rising no longer scares you, and this is the moment when being a girl became my strength, my sanctuary, not my pain."[8] The Girl Declaration is a manifesto calling for the global rising of girls in a future where the feminine is no longer imprisoned and ravaged. The contributors in this volume, each writing from her expertise, vision, and solidarity, are heeding the voices of girls by doing the invaluable work of exposing misogyny to help clear the path for diverse girls to live their lives on their own terms.

8   The Girl Effect Team, "The Girl Declaration: Making Girls Heard by The World," (October 12, 2016). Retrieved from https://global.girleffect.org/stories/girl-declaration-making-girls-heard-world/.

CHAPTER 1

Sexual Assault Prosecutions

Kristi Gray and Dorislee Gilbert

Women and girls are disproportionately affected by sexual assault. One in five women will experience a completed or attempted rape during their lifetime; while one in fourteen men will be made to either attempt or complete penetration of someone else during their lifetime.[1] Nearly 52.2 million women or 43.5% of women in the United States experienced some form of contact sexual violence in their lifetime.[2] Nearly one fourth (24.8%) of men or 27.6 million men in the United States experienced some form of sexual violence in their lifetime.[3]

Of course, not all sexual assaults are reported to police. Victims may choose not to report for many reasons, including shame, fear of or retribution from perpetrators, and belief that the justice system will not help them.[4] In 2018, for example, only 25% of rape or sexual-assault victimizations were reported to police; this was down from 40% in 2017.[5] This means about three out of every four sexual assaults is not reported. The majority of reported cases involve female victims and male perpetrators. According to RAINN (Rape, Abuse & Incest National Network), the United States' largest anti-sexual violence organization, 955 of every 1000 sexual assault perpetrators will walk free.[6] Approximately 230 of every 1000 cases are reported to police; 46 of those reports lead to an arrest; 9 of those cases are referred to a prosecutor; 5 of those cases will result in a felony conviction; and less than 5 perpetrators will be

1   Sharon G. Smith, et al., *The National Intimate Partner and Sexual Violence Survey (NISVS): 2015 Data Brief-Updated Release* (Atlanta, GA: National Center for Injury Prevention and Control, Centers for Disease Control and Prevention, 2018), 1.

2   Smith, et al., *NISVS: 2015 Data Brief-Updated Release*, 2.

3   Smith, et al., *NISVS: 2015 Data Brief-Updated Release*, 3.

4   Sharon G. Smith, et al., *The National Intimate Partner and Sexual Violence Survey (NISVS): 2010–2012 State Report* (Atlanta, GA: National Center for Injury Prevention and Control, Centers for Disease Control and Prevention, 2017), 6.

5   Rachel E. Morgan and Barbara A. Oudekerk, *Criminal Victimization, 2018* (Washington D.C.: U.S. Department of Justice, Bureau of Justice Statistics, September 2019), page 8, https://www.bjs.gov/content/pub/pdf/cv18.pdf.

6   "The Criminal Justice System: Statistics," RAINN, accessed August 26, 2020, https://www.rainn.org/statistics/criminal-justice-system.

incarcerated for the sexual assault.[7] With such low accountability through the criminal justice system, it is no wonder that more victims do not report, especially when the specifics of their journeys through the criminal justice system are considered.

But sexual assault is not just a legal system issue, it is also a public health issue. Victims face numerous physical and psychological consequences. Women who have a history of violence victimization, including contact sexual violence, stalking, or physical violence by an intimate partner have a statistically significant increased prevalence of asthma, irritable bowel syndrome, frequent headaches, chronic pain, difficulty sleeping, activity limitations, overall poor physical health, and poor mental health than women who have no history of these types of violence.[8] A study conducted by the Centers for Disease Control suggests that the estimated lifetime cost of rape is $122,461 per victim.[9] The study examined a comprehensive analysis of the costs and includes criminal justice-related expenditures such as investigation, adjudication and incarceration. It also includes the cost of health care and mental health care for the victim, as well as factors such as lost work productivity. The economic cost to society is significant. Deterrence and prevention of sexual assault are vital to halting this public health crisis. Those goals require accountability through a justice system that treats victims with respect and dignity and with willingness to listen, investigate, and judge their claims fairly. They require a system and system-participants who are not eager to blame victims and who are not prone to believe anything besides sexual assault because the idea of real sexual assault is so intrusive, personal, and unpredictable that the thought that it could happen even to "good people" is unfathomable. These goals require retraining our minds to recognize biases, prejudices, and fears we have that prevent the legal system from being a safe place where victims can turn for protection, reparation, and justice.

Many people have preconceived notions about the nature of sexual assaults, both about who is likely to commit such offenses and how they are likely to commit them. If you asked an average citizen to imagine what a rapist looks like, they would likely envision something like what is commonly seen on television. A masked intruder or a man who drives a van with no windows. A stranger to the victim. Someone who "looks creepy" and has an untreated

7   RAINN, "The Criminal Justice System: Statistics."
8   Smith, et al., *NISVS: 2010–2012 State Report*, 180.
9   Cora Peterson, Sarah DeGue, Curtis Florence, and Colby N. Lokey. "Lifetime Economic Burden of Rape Among U.S. Adults," *American Journal Preventive Medicine* 55, no. 6 (June 1, 2017): 697. https://doi.org/10.1016/j.amepre.2016.11.014.

severe mental illness or, at a minimum, severely compromised social skills. A man who is either unemployed, works varied menial jobs, or is some kind of weird tech-savant. It's unlikely that an average citizen would envision a Stanford University swimmer[10] a beloved television star,[11] or a hospital internist.[12] Also unlikely is that the average citizen is aware that perpetrators of sexual violence against women are usually known by their victims prior to the sexual violence and are often current or former intimate partners or acquaintances.[13]

An average citizen might describe the usual sexual assault as occurring in a private, secluded place, where the victim is alone, and vulnerable. People frequently have a hard time imagining that a sexual assault could occur in a residence while other people are home,[14] in close quarters with others,[15] or in a public place.[16]

When asked to describe the means of committing a sexual assault, most people would likely suggest a knife or gun. Few would think that threatening words, implicit threats, and intoxicants are widely used means of committing a sexual assault. An offender does not need to use physical force or a weapon when his victim is physically incapacitated by alcohol or drugs. He does not need to wield an actual weapon when his tone of voice and motions are violent and when he threatens to kill the victim, her children, or others she cares about.

These preconceived notions about sexual assault frequently influence the outcome of sexual assault cases in the criminal justice system. These

---

10   Michael James, "Brock Turner, Ex-Stanford University Swimmer Convicted of Sexual Assault, denied new trial," *USA Today*, August 10, 2018, https://www.usatoday.com/story/news/2018/08/08/stanford-university-swimmer-convicted-assault-denied-new-trial/943186002/.

11   Manuel Roig-Franzia, "Bill Cosby Convicted on Three Counts of Sexual Assault," *The Washington Post*, April 26, 2018, https://www.washingtonpost.com/lifestyle/style/bill-cosby-convicted-on-three-counts-of-sexual-assault/2018/04/26/d740ef22-4885-11e8-827e-190efafifiee_story.html.

12   Kristine Phillips, "Former Texas Doctor Convicted of Raping a Patient at a Hospital—Sentenced to Probation," *Tyler Morning Telegraph*, August 19, 2018, https://tylerpaper.com/news/texas/former-texas-doctor-convicted-of-raping-a-patient-at-a-hospital---sentenced-to/article_e58e8f34-a3f8-11e8-abce-8b9df41a0f71.html.

13   Smith, et al., *NISVS: 2010–2012 State Report*, 23.

14   State v. Kozlov, 276 P.3d 1207, 1212–1213 (Utah App. 2012).

15   Bree Burkitt, "Police Report: Behavior of Hacienda Nurse Accused of Raping Patient Changed in Months Before Birth," *Azcentral.com*, June 13, 2019, https://www.azcentral.com/story/news/local/arizona-health/2019/06/13/behavior-hacienda-nurse-nathan-sutherland-accused-rape-changed-months-before-birth/1447790001/.

16   Bruce Schreiner, "Woman in McDonald's Strip-Search Hoax Awarded $6.1 Million," *Chron*, October 6, 2007, https://www.chron.com/news/nation-world/article/Woman-in-McDonald-s-strip-search-hoax-awarded-1644501.php.

ill-informed ideas can be held by jurors, police officers, judges, lawyers, and others in the justice system. These notions can lead their holders to do inadequate investigation of cases, jump to conclusions about the veracity of the victim and the perpetrator, and even blame victims for being victimized. Knowledge that jurors likely hold these preconceived notions can cause even the most informed, well-intentioned prosecutors to make charging, plea, and trial-related decisions that seem less than just because of the realistic possibility of acquittal at a jury trial.

In criminal trials decided by juries, the problems caused by these preconceived notions are especially pronounced. The United States Constitution guarantees criminal defendants a jury of peers. This means jurors are not required to have any specialized training or legal experience. In practice, it often means that people with specialized training or legal experience are excluded from jury service. Jurors are selected for service for a particular trial through a process called *voir dire*. During that process, attorneys for the prosecution and the defense are usually permitted the opportunity to exercise peremptory strikes to exclude jurors from the jury on any ground not constitutionally protected. For example, a party may not remove a juror because of the juror's race or sex, but a juror may be removed because they have had certain life experiences, because they hold certain opinions, or because they have certain knowledge. In sexual assault cases, the most effective criminal defense attorneys use the *voir dire* process to ferret out those potential jurors who have knowledge, education, or experience about the realities of sexual assault and then exercise their peremptory challenges to remove those jurors. In any case that does not follow the rare patterns of the preconceived notions described above—that is, in most sexual assault cases—a criminal defendant is best served by juries who hold those misperceptions. When juries hear the evidence that does not match their preconceived notions, they can be quick to acquit, especially in the absence of DNA or video evidence. Even in cases where there is video or DNA evidence, jurors who hold the preconceived notions described above are more likely to believe even an ill-conceived consent defense; a claim that the victim made up the sexual assault allegations for attention, revenge, or to cover up her cheating; or suggestions that the victim might have done something to cause the assault.

These preconceived notions about sexual assault cases frequently lead to victim blaming in cases that don't mirror those circumstances. Jurors frequently develop negative attitudes towards victims, and victims in sexual assault cases often face harsher judgment than witnesses in other cases. Victim blaming creates challenges in the prosecution of every sexual assault case and decreases the likelihood of a conviction at trial. Improved community safety can only occur when the criminal justice system allows for offenders to be held accountable for their actions, and that occurs far too infrequently in sexual assault cases.

While our jury trial system is one that offers many important constitutional protections to the accused in a criminal case, it is one that works most effectively and best provides for public safety when jurors are unbiased; yet these preconceived notions prevent even the most well-intentioned jurors from being unbiased. Most jurors intend to serve fairly and decide in the way they think the evidence compels them to, but they might not recognize how their preconceived notions about sexual assault, their masked tendencies to blame victims by increasing the scrutiny on them and raising the burden of proof in sexual assault cases, and their desires to believe anything besides the ugly truth of sexual assault prevent them from doing justice in individual cases.

In every criminal trial, the prosecution must prove beyond a reasonable doubt that the defendant committed the offense of which they are accused. For sexual assaults, the elements that must be proven are that the sexual activity occurred and that it was not consensual. A lack of consent exists if the offender used threats or physical force to accomplish the sexual assault or if the victim was legally incapable of consent. While state statutes and definitions vary as to the capacity to consent, typically a person is incapable of consent if she is physically unable to communicate that consent, such as while she is unconscious, or if the victim has a mental illness or intellectual disability that would prevent her from forming the mental capacity to consent. While the age of consent can also vary between states, children under a certain age are also incapable of consent. Beyond a reasonable doubt is a high standard of proof, as it should be when a criminal defendant is facing potential imprisonment. However, it can become an impossible standard if a victim's credibility if unfairly assessed. The testimony of the victim is typically a significant part of any criminal trial, and the jurors are solely responsible for judging the credibility of witnesses.

Sexual assault trials often involve a consent defense, in which a defendant disputes the victim's report and the physical evidence by suggesting that the sexual activity was consensual. While there may be physical evidence to prove that the sexual activity occurred, such as DNA or biological fluids, the lack of consent is often only proven through the testimony of a victim. Many jurors expect physical evidence of the lack of consent, such as injuries to the victim. Many sexual assaults don't result in physical injuries to the victim. In most jury trials, a forensic nurse examiner or medical professional will provide testimony to explain that a lack of injury does not rule out forcible sexual activity. However, the lack of injury is frequently a defining factor in jury decisions. In cases involving child victims, jurors often acquit if the victim's hymen is intact, despite expert testimony that popular opinions about intact hymens as a sign of virginity are false, that many sexual assaults do not result in visible damage to the hymen, and that even when hymenal injury is present, it heals swiftly. Absent any evidence of physical injury, a conviction in sexual assault cases can occur only when jurors can accept victim testimony as credible.

Victim blaming sometimes makes it impossible to accept victim testimony as credible. It can occur because of moral judgments of the victim's character, behavior, or activities. It can also occur because basic human psychology sometimes makes it difficult for a person to accept that horrible things can happen to a person, sometimes entirely at random. Melvin Lerner explains the Just World Theory, or Belief in a Just World, as such: that in order for an individual to feel secure and to function comfortably in the world, that individual must believe that bad things will not happen to them unless they do something to bring about the negative events.[17] Studies show that people want to believe that a person must be at least partly responsible for any harm that comes to them. Such beliefs create an undeniable challenge in sexual assault trials, in which a defense attorney is specifically asking the jury to focus not on the acts of the offender but on the acts of the victim.

It is important to note that in a criminal trial, the defendant is not required to testify, and he maintains his right to remain silent. If he does not testify, he is never subject to cross examination and the jury never gets to evaluate his credibility as a witness. Instead, they judge him based upon his cleaned-up appearance and his calm and proper demeanor in the courtroom. However, it is rarely possible to conduct a sexual assault jury trial without the testimony of the victim, and the defendant has a constitutional right to confront and cross examine witnesses against him. If a defendant has issues that might affect his credibility, such as a prior felony conviction, he can generally avoid the disclosure of this type of information by electing not to testify. The victim has no such right.

In many sexual assaults, the victim is targeted because she is vulnerable in some way—she has been drinking or is under the influence; she misjudges the risk of a situation and allows herself to be alone with someone that she doesn't know well; or she is living in circumstances that require her to take risks in order to survive, such as not having stable housing. Like any criminal, sex offenders frequently look for circumstances that will make it easier for

---

17   Melvin J. Lerner and Dale T. Miller, "Just World Research and the Attribution Process: Looking Back and Ahead," *Psychological Bulletin* 85, no. 5 (1978): 1030–1031.

them to commit the offense and escape detection. This is not to suggest that the victim is in any way responsible for what happens to her, because no matter the circumstances, someone only becomes the victim of a sexual assault if they encounter a sex offender. However, these vulnerabilities are the types of circumstances that allow jurors to comfortably separate themselves from the reality that a sexual assault can happen to anyone and allow them to blame the victim in order to avoid acceptance of such a frightening reality. Good defense attorneys are particularly adept at capitalizing on these vulnerabilities and a jury's predisposition to want to blame the victim for what happened to her.

During a criminal trial, neither prosecutors nor defense attorneys can have any direct contact with jurors. However, the parties may speak with jurors after the completion of the trial. Prosecutors frequently do so in order to better understand the way in which jurors assess evidence, whether the trial ends in a conviction or an acquittal. The opinions that jurors express frequently confirm that victim blaming plays a role in their deliberations.

Following a jury trial in 2016, jurors were asked about their impressions of the evidence. The defendant was charged with felony assault, unlawful imprisonment, and sexual abuse. The defendant lived in an apartment building near the victim, and they knew each other. The victim went to his apartment one evening because the defendant had previously borrowed $17.00 from her and she wanted to ask for the money he owed her. The defendant held the victim in his apartment against her will, assaulted her, strangled her, and touched her vagina and licked her breast. He used duct tape and a torn sheet to bind her wrists and ankles. After she escaped by smashing out a window, he heard her screaming for help, and he ran after her and cut her several times with a knife. He fled when a neighbor heard her screams and turned on a porch light. The victim had extensive injuries from the knife, and she also had injuries that corroborated the assault and strangulation. When officers and medics arrived, she still had duct tape on her and torn strips of sheets on her ankles.

The victim gave a detailed report to officers and detectives. Upon a search of the defendant's apartment, they found some of the victim's clothing, as well as duct tape and torn sheets. During the trial, jurors heard testimony from the victim about the attack. They also heard from first responders, who described her as clearly traumatized. Jurors were able to view numerous photos of the victim's injuries, as well as photos of the crime scene. Detectives and officers testified about their investigation, which corroborated essentially every aspect of her report. Medical experts testified about the nature of her injuries, which were consistent with her report about how the assault occurred. One of her surgeons testified that her demeanor in the hospital was hyper-vigilant, which is consistent with someone who has been the victim of a violent trauma. During the forensic exam that was performed on the victim, they were able to locate saliva on the victim's breast, and a lab analyst testified that the DNA from that saliva matched the defendant. There was no foreign DNA found in her vaginal swabs, but the lab analyst testified that it is unlikely that DNA would be detected from the act of touching her vagina with his hand.

At the trial, the defense argued that the sexual activity was consensual. The defense suggested that the victim was smoking crack cocaine and because of that, she began behaving erratically and tied herself up in his bedroom. They further claimed that the knife wounds were from the glass that broke when she fled through the window. The medical experts testified that the nature and locations of the wounds were not consistent with being caused by climbing through a broken window. The treating doctors testified that lab tests did not show the presence of cocaine or other drugs or alcohol in her blood when she was tested upon arrival at the hospital.

The jury convicted the defendant for every act except the sexual abuse count for touching her vagina. In speaking with the jurors after the trial, they expressed that because the victim had a history of drug use and had a conviction for a drug offense, they were unwilling to convict based solely on her testimony. Several of them flatly stated that they were unwilling to accept her word as proof. Essentially every other fact that she reported to police officers was corroborated by the investigation, and the jury heard all this evidence. There was no evidence of any specific motive that the victim might have had to fabricate any of her testimony, and the defense was not able to present any direct evidence that she was being untruthful. And yet they still refused to accept her word as to one fact that could not be corroborated, even though there was a scientific explanation for why you would not expect DNA evidence from the act. While prosecutors certainly expect jurors to be discerning, and to require proof beyond a reasonable doubt, it is hard to imagine how that standard would ever be met with such impossibly high expectations from jurors.

Testifying can be a traumatic experience for victims. They are required to tell intimate details about the most humiliating, horrifying, and hurtful experience. They are required to recount the event, often multiple times, in front of a courtroom full of strangers, whose job is to judge whether they are being truthful. The person who did those horrible things to them is present, dressed well, presumed innocent, and protected by the law from having to say anything at all. Meanwhile, victims are asked to describe specific details about parts of their body and the perpetrator's body that few people ever talk about even in the privacy of their own doctor's office. Victims are subjected to cross-examination designed to confuse them, to blame them, or to convince the jury they are liars. They may even be asked to identify photographs of their naked bodies or the perpetrator's genitalia. And the photographs might be enlarged on a screen in front of everyone! When jurors' preconceived notions and interests in believing in a just world prevent them from listening with an open mind and instead send them immediately looking for a way to believe the charged crime did not occur, the presumption of innocence becomes an irrefutable conclusion of innocence. Justice is not served, reporting of sexual assault is not encouraged, and commission of sexual assault is not deterred.

In another case, a 15-year-old homeless girl was taken in by a nearly 50-year-old man. He essentially demanded sex with her in order for her to have a continued home. She relented. He impregnated her. He was charged with statutory rape—meaning there was no requirement that the sexual acts were committed by force, only that they were committed against a child who was less than 16 years old. At trial, the evidence included DNA testing that established that the man was the father of the girl's child, the girl's own testimony, and evidence that the defendant knew or had reason to know the girl's age. Though she was more than 16 by the time of trial, the girl still looked quite young and a photograph of her at the time of the sexual abuse was admitted into evidence. She appeared to be a youthful teenager in the photograph. The jury acquitted the man. They said the girl's behavior gave the man reason to believe she was at least 21. She drank alcohol and smoked with him. She essentially had sex with him to have a place to live. For these jurors, that was enough to blame her, even though he was more than three times her age.

Her case is not an outlier. If anything could be more difficult to hear about or imagine occurring than sexual assault between adults, it is child sexual abuse. Finding fault with and blaming the victim is much easier than believing that a grown adult would engage in sex acts with a child. As in the previous case example, that sometimes looks like blaming the victim of acting older and appearing to engage in sex consensually. Other times, it looks like accusing the victim of lying and being vengeful. In one case, a jury acquitted despite a straight-A student's detailed testimony about her stepfather's sexual abuse of her because they preferred to believe that she made it all up because she was mad that he did not buy her the prom dress she wanted. In another case, the jury believed the victim was scared because she was caught kissing a boy.

In cases involving younger children, the jury rarely blames the child in the same way. They can be quick to believe that a conniving mother coached a child to get custody in a bitter divorce. They can be eager to accept innocent explanations. A common one offered by perpetrators accused of fondling a child is that they were wrestling with the child and the child misunderstood what was happening. They can be quick to dismiss sexual abuse claims where the physical evidence does not match up with their inaccurate preconceived notions about intact hymens, physical injuries, or DNA evidence. As in sexual assault cases involving adults, in child sexual abuse cases, many well-intentioned jurors are compelled to believe anything besides that the abuse occurred. Doing otherwise disrupts any just world view.

Extreme level of judgment about victim credibility seems to exist more in sexual assault cases than in other criminal cases. In other types of criminal cases, the jurors rarely describe such doubts about victim testimony. In most criminal trials, the jurors assess all of the evidence as a whole and will assess a witness as credible if the physical evidence supports their testimony. In sexual assault cases, jurors frequently question the motives of the witness more so than in other cases—perhaps because accepting the victim's account often means acknowledging the type of cruelty and vileness that most people are more comfortable living their lives without knowing about. For this reason, as well, consent defenses and "rough sex" defenses can be appealing to jurors in cases where there is DNA or other physical, video, or photographic evidence. Accepting these defenses allows the jury to accept the scientific or recorded evidence while rejecting the horror that sexual assault is. They allow the jury to find the victim at least as culpable as the defendant for what occurred. While public awareness has softened the language used and the way in which we describe jurors' reactions, the reality still exists that victim-blaming undermines the effectiveness of the criminal justice system in holding sex offenders accountable for their actions.

During a trial in 2015, jurors heard from a victim of an attempted rape. The offender was someone that she had dated in high school, but the victim had not been involved with him for approximately ten years other than occasional contact on social media or when with mutual acquaintances. The victim described to the jury how the offender showed up at her apartment late one night and was extremely drunk, and he asked her if he could come in and get sober before going home to his wife and children. She did not think she had any reason to be fearful, and she allowed him to come inside. Once inside, he physically forced her into the bedroom, held her down on the bed and tore her clothing. She struggled and managed to get free, and when she told him that she was calling the police, he fled the apartment. The defendant did not testify, but the defense attorney told the jury that while he clearly wasn't much of a gentleman while he was drinking, the defendant should not be convicted of a crime. The result was a hung jury.

After the trial, jurors expressed concern about the strict penalties that could be imposed on sex offenders and did not believe that the victim was so traumatized that the case deserved such an outcome. The jurors also assumed that because they had dated in high school, they probably had engaged in sexual activity then, and therefore it was not as serious as if they had been strangers. One juror stated that "boys will be boys." One juror commented that his behavior was not uncommon when a man had been drinking and was spending time with a pretty girl. The victim had no criminal record, was employed, and had no motive to lie. However, the jurors minimized her experience to such an extent that they couldn't bring themselves to hold the offender criminally liable. The jurors chalked it up to bad behavior, rather than criminal behavior, despite the use of actual physical force.

Juror nullification is more common in sexual assault cases than in other violent crimes, in part because jurors weigh the potential penalties against what they believe to be the level of suffering that the victim endured. While jurors take an oath to render a verdict based on the evidence presented at trial and whether the elements of the charged offense are proven beyond a reasonable doubt, they admittedly consider factors such as the potential sentences and other consequences that are imposed upon convicted sex offenders. These other consequences often include lengthy sex offender registries with residency restrictions, public notifications, and employment hardships. Sexual assault rarely leaves significant, lasting physical injuries, and victims are rarely permitted to testify in much detail about the psychological and emotional impact rape has had on them when a jury is determining the guilt of the accused. Therefore, jurors can appease themselves that even if the act occurred as described, it lasted for a relatively brief, limited time, and the victim was left functioning—even so much so that she was able to go on with her life, get a job, raise her children, testify at trial, etc. For many jurors, their perceived harm of the sexual assault pales in comparison to consequences like lifetime sex offender registration or a lengthy prison sentence.

When sexual assault occurs in intimate partner relationships, the tendencies increase to blame the victim and to believe any other explanation than sexual assault. Nearly one-fifth of the approximately 43.6 million women in the United States who have experienced intimate partner violence in their lifetimes have experienced contact sexual violence.[18] Yet, there are still people who think that sex between two people who are in an intimate relationship cannot be rape. A 2018 survey of nearly 4,000 people across Great Britain, for example, found that almost one quarter of people think that sex without consent in a long-term relationship usually is not rape.[19] Eleven percent of

---

18   Smith, et al., *NISVS: 2015 Data Brief-Updated Release*, 8.
19   "YouGov/End Violence Against Women Coalition Survey Results," End Violence Against Women, September 19, 2018, https://www.endviolenceagainstwomen.org.uk/campaign/research-public-dont-understand-sexual-violence/.

respondents thought that a woman who was married to a person who sexually assaulted her would suffer less harm than any other woman.[20]

Homes are sacred, and fortunately, sexual violence is absent in most homes. As discussed previously, in criminal trials, jurors who have experience with or specialized knowledge about sexual violence or intimate partner violence will often be removed from juries. This leaves people on the jury who end up comparing the dysfunctional, violent relationship they hear evidence about with their own functional relationships. Unwittingly, they can be prone to rationalize, minimize, and even excuse intimate partner violence by saying things like, "we all get mad at our partner sometimes." They think of that one time their partner made them so angry they wanted to smack/slap/hit them or maybe even did. They then compare the perpetrator to themselves and think how sorry he must have been and how he does not deserve to go to jail or prison for that one-time shortcoming. In sexual assault cases, they might wonder about that one time their partner was not particularly enthusiastic about sex, though willing, or that time their partner woke them, and they groggily, though willingly engaged in sex and suspect that the victim is exaggerating one of these instances and turning it into a claim of sexual assault because of some grudge. Sexual assault, especially committed against someone the perpetrator supposedly loves, is so repugnant that jurors often look for other explanations or are, at least, quick to bite on another explanation dangled by an aggressive defense attorney.

People generally fail to recognize that intimate partner violence is not occasional anger, the rare expression of frustration, or a one-off drunken fight. Most often intimate partner violence is about control and dominance. In the 1980s, Domestic Abuse Intervention Programs, in Duluth, Minnesota, created the widely used power and control wheel to help with visualization of "the pattern of actions that an individual uses to intentionally control or dominate his intimate partner."[21] The wheel shows that the overriding motivation for intimate partner abuse is power and control, and that while the most visible means of achieving this is through physical and sexual violence, power and control is also gained through techniques like isolation; minimizing, denying, and blaming; coercion and threats; emotional abuse; economic abuse; and intimidation.[22] Unfortunately, juries do not often hear about all the other instances

20 End Violence Against Women, "YouGov/End Violence Against Women Coalition Survey Results."

21 "Facts About the Wheel," Domestic Abuse Intervention Programs, accessed August 27, 2020, https://www.theduluthmodel.org/wheels/faqs-about-the-wheels/.

22 "Wheels," Domestic Abuse Intervention Programs, accessed August 27, 2020, https://www.theduluthmodel.org/wheels/.

of physical or sexual abuse or the other behaviors designed to control and overpower victims. Sometimes the victim never describes the non-physical behaviors to police or prosecutors, so they are unaware of it at trial. This can happen because the victim does not see these behaviors as part of the abuse, because she knows that they are not criminal acts and does not think they are important to share, because she is ashamed that she let someone treat her that way, or because it was such a way of life for her that she is unable to conceptualize that there could be anything different. Sadly, sometimes the abuse itself has conditioned her to believe its truth—i.e., that she is stupid, that she deserves to be treated this way, etc. Sometimes, even when police and prosecutors are aware of the uncharged abusive and controlling acts, the rules of court do not allow evidence to be admitted at trial. Sometimes the rules allow it, but judges do not. And sometimes, even when the evidence is permitted, an effective defense attorney preys again on juror stereotypes. For example, if the prior abuse involved physical violence but the victim never reported to police, defense attorneys portray the account as unbelievable and attribute improper motive to the victim's current report. If the prior abuse involves financial abuse like preventing the victim from working and excessively restricting her spending or isolation by preventing the victim from seeing friends and family, a savvy defense attorney paints the victim as a conniving woman who wants more of the defendant's money or is mad at him because he did not like her friends. Unfortunately, these theories of defense can be effective with jurors who are uninformed about intimate partner violence and its denial is more consistent with their world view.

Existing myths about how victims respond to interpersonal violence also create unrealistic expectations among jurors. A person's response to any psychological trauma can be influenced by a myriad of factors. No two individuals cope with trauma in exactly the same manner, and their responses can be affected by past life experiences, current circumstances, and the existence or lack of a support network. For victims of intimate partner violence, their reactions are often colored by those other controlling behaviors that characterize the violence they have experienced. For instance, consistent emotional abuse, blaming, isolation, and threats to harm the children if a victim leaves can make a victim of sexual violence in an intimate partner relationship feel as if she deserves the abuse she has endured or that she is so untrustworthy, unattractive, and unintelligent that no one will ever believe her when she says that she did not want to have sex. It can leave her without friends, colleagues, or family members in whom she can confide. It can leave her fearing the consequences if she reports the abuse, tries to leave, or shows up to testify in court. And when a jury that does not understand intimate partner violence acquits an offender, it perpetuates the abuse because it affirms exactly what the offender promised the victim—that no one would believe her, that she deserved what happened, and that no one else cared for her besides the offender.

It is not uncommon for jurors or others to think that a woman in an abusive relationship should just leave the abusive relationship and that if she does not do so the continuing abuse is as much her fault as it is the abuser's. This victim-blaming approach is harmful because it fails to lay blame for abusive behavior on the perpetrator of the abuse and fails to account for the complicated situations in which many victims of intimate partner violence find themselves. In her book, *No Visible Bruises*, Rachel Louise Snyder explains that victims of intimate partner violence stay in abusive relationships "because they know that any sudden move will provoke the bear" and "because they have developed tools" like "pleading, begging, cajoling, promising, and public displays of solidarity" as a means of survival against the violent partner who is coming for them.[23] Victims often stay in relationships and sometimes even recant reports of violence to police or in front of juries to stay alive and to keep their children alive.[24] This can be incredibly difficult for jurors to understand. It can be nearly impossible for a prosecutor to explain when the victim—who is the only source of the evidence about the nature of the criminal physical or sexual abuse and the other tactics used to control, overpower, and manipulate the victim—is uncooperative because it is the only way she knows how to stay alive.

Delayed reporting is one of the most challenging aspects of a sexual assault prosecution. Many jurors express a reluctance to believe victims when they do not immediately report the offense. This can also be due to jurors preconceived notions about sexual violence or the tendency to compare realities. For example, when one thinks sexual violence is defined by stranger abductions and significant physical injuries, it is easy to believe that reporting sexual assault would be the natural, only response. In reality, many victims do not report immediately, for the same reasons that some victims never report at all—fear, shame, disbelief, the responses of others to prior victimizations, the need to continue to function despite the terrible trauma endured.

Substantial delays in disclosure of sexual assault also make prosecution difficult due to jurors' tendencies to weigh the minimal harm they perceive the victim suffered with the hefty sentences and collateral consequences for sex offenders. Particularly in cases where years or decades have passed before the disclosure, there is a tendency to think that the victim and perpetrator

23   Rachel L. Snyder, *No Visible Bruises: What We Don't Know About Domestic Violence Can Kill Us* (New York: Bloomsbury Publishing, 2019), 53.
24   Snyder, *No Visible Bruises*, 53.

have moved on and that there was no real, lasting harm. There is a tendency to blame the victim for trying to now ruin someone's life—especially if that someone has gone on to do remarkable things in life. What jurors cannot see is the lifetime of self-esteem problems, mental health issues, relationship dysfunction, and general health problems that many victims experience. These things are not often deemed legally relevant to whether the perpetrator is guilty of the charged offense, and in cases where they are admitted, they are used by skilled defense attorneys to give jurors another version of events that is more palatable than sexual assault—namely, that the victim is "crazy," "attention-seeking," or is vengeful because the perpetrator has gone on to be more successful than the victim.

Jurors frequently have unreasonable expectations of how a victim should demonstrate an "appropriate level" of trauma. A juror once commented that since the victim had gotten married after the sexual assault, it seemed that she had gotten over what happened to her. Again, the jurors often seem to weigh the suffering of the victim in reaching their decision about the evidence in a case. However, this can also impact a juror's assessment of a witness' credibility. If a victim does not behave in a certain way following the sexual assault, jurors are reluctant to believe the allegations. Despite that every individual responds to trauma in a different way and shock can lead to very unpredictable behavior, jurors discount any behaviors that do not clearly demonstrate sadness and fear. Jurors are generally less accepting of an angry response or of an unemotional response that may well be the result of disassociation. Particularly in cases involving intimate partner violence but also generally in cases involving female victims, an assertive, confident, or professionally successful woman or a woman who is knowledgeable about abuse can draw a jury's skepticism. Surely, they think, someone who is that assertive, that confident, that knowledgeable, that successful could not be a victim. But just because a woman can conduct a board meeting effortlessly or is articulate and less than timid in presentation does not make a perpetrator of abuse any less capable of sexual assault. In some cases, these very qualities may even be the draw for a perpetrator.

People can display a wide variety of responses after any trauma. Whether someone is involved in a horrific car accident, receives a serious medical diagnosis, loses a loved one, or is the victim of a violent crime, they can demonstrate varied reactions. However, jurors expect victims to behave in certain ways after an attack, and counterintuitive behaviors raise questions about their credibility. A lack of emotion or tears may be nothing more than a common symptom of shock, but jurors struggle with accepting that response to trauma. Some victims respond with fear and hyper-vigilance, while some respond with extreme risk-taking behaviors. Some victims suffer from noticeable depression and retreat into an isolated existence, while some become overachievers. Some victims never discuss their attack with others, while some become public speakers in order to advocate for crime victims. When jurors assess the "appropriateness" of a victim's response to trauma, they frequently ignore the reality of differing human experiences.

The criminal justice system is not known for swift and adequate response to sexual assault. It is not known for the precise way it holds perpetrators of sexual assault accountable to their victims and society. The system's failings are due, in large part, to preconceived notions about what sexual assault looks like and what the appropriate responses to sexual assault are, as well as basic desires to believe that bad things cannot happen to good, undeserving people. Because of the manner in which jury trials are conducted, it is likely that people who hold these beliefs will be on juries in sexual assault cases. The result is that in all but the most documented, scientifically provable cases—and sometimes even in those—juries tend to blame victims and find offenders less than deserving of the dire consequences of a sexual assault conviction. Knowledge of this looming outcome impacts the way sexual assault cases are handled from their initiation. For example, police and prosecutors may opt not to pursue charges where the only evidence is the victim's testimony—not because they do not believe the victim, but because they know how traumatic testifying can be for a victim, that the chances of a jury believing the victim are almost non-existent, and that an unjust acquittal might make a perpetrator feel affirmed, vindicated, or even emboldened. In recent years, there have been significant improvements in the training and education available to law enforcement agencies and increased knowledge about how trauma affects a victim's ability to communicate the details of her attack. Investigators are now being trained in the best investigative and interview techniques, and the mental health and medical communities have developed protocols to better address the specific needs of victims of sexual violence. However, a true culture shift must occur before the criminal justice system can provide an adequate response in these types of cases. Education about the real nature of sexual assault can help, but to be effective, it must be large scale. It must reach a sufficient number of learners that when a jury is selected, it is impossible to exclude from service in a sexual assault trial every juror who has any balanced, realistic idea what sexual assault is. When juries become more willing to listen to and accept the realities of sexual assault, prosecutors, police, and judges have better tools to hold offenders accountable and deter future sexual violence.

Bibliography

Burkitt, Bree. "Police Report: Behavior of Hacienda Nurse Accused of Raping Patient Changed in Months Before Birth." *Azcentral.com*, June 13, 2019. https://www.azcentral.com/story/news/local/arizona-health/2019/06/13/behavior-hacienda-nurse-nathan-sutherland-accused-rape-changed-months-before-birth/1447790001/.

Domestic Abuse Intervention Programs. "Facts About the Wheel." Accessed August 27, 2020. https://www.theduluthmodel.org/wheels/faqs-about-the-wheels/.

Domestic Abuse Intervention Programs. "Wheels." Accessed August 27, 2020. https://www.theduluthmodel.org/wheels/.

End Violence Against Women. "YouGov/End Violence Against Women Coalition Survey Results." September 19, 2018. https://www.endviolenceagainstwomen.org.uk/campaign/research-public-dont-understand-sexual-violence/.

James, Michael. "Brock Turner, Ex-Stanford University Swimmer Convicted of Sexual Assault, denied new trial." *USA Today*, August 10, 2018. https://www.usatoday.com/story/news/2018/08/08/stanford-university-swimmer-convicted-assault-denied-new-trial/943186002/.

Lerner, Melvin J. and Miller, Dale, T. "Just World Research and the Attribution Process: Looking Back and Ahead," *Psychological Bulletin* 85, no. 5 (1978): 1030–1051.

Morgan, Rachel E., Oudekerk and Barbara A. *Criminal Victimization, 2018*. Washington, D.C.: U.S. Department of Justice, Bureau of Justice Statistics, September 2019. https://www.bjs.gov/content/pub/pdf/cv18.pdf.

Peterson, Cora, DeGue Sarah, Florence, Curtis, and Lokey, Colby N. "Lifetime Economic Burden of Rape Among U.S. Adults." *American Journal of Preventive Medicine* 52, no. 6 (June 1, 2017): 691–701. https://doi.org/10.1016/j.amepre.2016.11.014.

Phillips, Kristine. "Former Texas Doctor Convicted of Raping a Patient at a Hospital—Sentenced to Probation." *Tyler Morning Telegraph*, August 19, 2018. https://tylerpaper.com/news/texas/former-texas-doctor-convicted-of-raping-a-patient-at-a-hospital---sentenced-to/article_e58e8f34-a3f8-11e8-abce-8b9df41a0f71.html.

RAINN. "The Criminal Justice System: Statistics." Accessed August 26, 2020. https://www.rainn.org/statistics/criminal-justice-system.

Roig-Franzia, Manuel. "Bill Cosby Convicted on Three Counts of Sexual Assault." *The Washington Post*, April 26, 2018. https://www.washingtonpost.com/lifestyle/style/bill-cosby-convicted-on-three-counts-of-sexual-assault/2018/04/26/d740ef22-4885-11e8-827e-190efafifiee_story.html.

Schreiner, Bruce. "Woman in McDonald's Strip-Search Hoax Awarded $6.1 Million." *Chron*, October 6, 2007. https://www.chron.com/news/nation-world/article/Woman-in-McDonald-s-strip-search-hoax-awarded-1644501.php.

Smith, Sharon G., Xinjian Zhang, Basile, Kathleen C., Merrick, Melissa T., Wang, Jing, Kresnow, Marcie-jo, and Chen, Jieru. *The National Intimate Partner and Sexual Violence Survey (NISVS): 2015 Data Brief-Updated Release.* Atlanta, GA: National Center for Injury Prevention and Control, Centers for Disease Control and Prevention, 2018.

Smith, Sharon G., Chen, Jieru, Basile, Kathleen C., Gilbert, Leah K., Merrick, Melissa T., Patel, Nimesh, Walling, Margie, and Jain, Anurag. *The National Intimate Partner and Sexual Violence Survey (NISVS): 2010–2012 State Report.* Atlanta, GA: National Center for Injury Prevention and Control, Centers for Disease Control and Prevention, 2017.

Snyder, Rachel L. *No Visible Bruises: What We Don't Know About Domestic Violence Can Kill Us.* New York: Bloomsbury Publishing, 2019.

State v. Kozlov, 276 P.3d 1207 (Utah App. 2012).

CHAPTER 2

Intentionally Inclusive Pedagogy

Pedagogical Practice as an Act of Social Justice

Tammy Hatfield, Portia Allie-Turco, Sarah E. Johansson and Melissa Brennan

1   Positionality

The practice of teaching is contextualized by the institutions, social structures, and social positions of instructors. Teaching and learning cannot be separated from the context in which they are produced and enacted. All participants in a classroom or other learning environment have personal identities and social locations that shape their social realities and bring unique perspectives to the learning space. Recognizing that individuals cannot separate social locations from ways of viewing the world, the authors of this chapter wish to share our positionality.

I, Tammy Hatfield, am a female professor who is a cisgender, heterosexual, White, educated, middle class, Appalachian, person of size who was also a first-generation college student. I currently teach graduate level courses in counseling and psychology at a Historically White Institution. I am married to a first-generation African immigrant and have a stepdaughter who is a US resident and is enrolled in undergraduate education as an English language learner. In addition to professional experiences teaching in face-to-face, blended, and online formats, the lived experience of partnering with an immigrant who, in the United States, is socially located as Black and parenting a daughter whose social locations include Black and English language learner has shaped and informed my approach to pedagogy.

I, Portia Allie-Turco, am a doctoral student, a counseling clinic director, a program coordinator and lecturer in a graduate program in counselor education. I identify as a naturalized immigrant Black Xhosa woman, born and raised during apartheid South Africa and now married to a White Italian man and raising two biracial girls. The legacies of apartheid ensured that discrimination was pervasive across all contexts of my experience as a young girl and impacted access to education, the quality of education and promoted a colonized version that was destructive to the esteem of Black students. As an educator and doctoral student in the United States I am passionate about racial healing and believe that one of the most meaningful ways to challenge oppression is to redesign curricula that shares a broad view of historical events and celebrates the achievements of all cultures.

I, Sarah E. Johansson, am a doctoral student, teaching assistant, professional school counselor and associate professional counselor. I identify as cisgender, White, heterosexual, educated, non-religious, able-bodied, and middle class. I am married to a first-generation Swedish immigrant who works in academia and we are childless. As a professional school counselor, I have the lived experience of working with students of varying racial and ethnic backgrounds both similar and different to my own. I have seen injustice in every community in which I have lived and worked. This led to my continuing advocacy efforts and formation of my pedagogical approach.

I, Melissa Brennan, am a doctoral student and teaching assistant, professional school counselor and licensed professional counselor. I identify as a cisgender and heterosexual female from a Caucasian, middle-class, non-religious background. My husband is of Hispanic and Caucasian decent. My experiences as an educator in San Antonio, Texas have ignited and fueled my desire to advocate for racial, gender, and sexual orientation equality, shaping my pedagogical approach to include an emphasis on social justice.

Sharing information about our identities and social locations in this chapter is an act that mirrors our approach to teaching and is rooted in inclusive pedagogies. By sharing aspects of who we are in the classroom with students, we lead with the notions that teaching and learning are value-laden, rather than neutral, value-free activities, there are multiple ways of knowing, narratives are contextualized, power is disrupted, and the door is opened for all to bring their perspectives and lived experiences into the learning space.

2   Pedagogy and Student Experiences

Each of us have a conceptual or theoretical lens through which we view the world and through which we approach teaching and learning. This guiding conception or theoretical lens may both implicitly and explicitly impact the lives of the students we teach. Both instructors and students enter the classroom with their own lived experience and their own ways of viewing the world and the world of education. Professors and students have their own beliefs about how students best learn. Pedagogy is defined as the "art, science, or profession of teaching."[1] Pedagogical approaches are based on theoretical perspectives. Therefore, pedagogy could also be considered our theoretical conception of teaching and the practice of teaching.

When I (Tammy) began my undergraduate education at a large public university with a Carnegie classification as a Research 1 institution, I had little understanding of how things work at large institutions. I came to the university as a first-generation, cisgender, fat, female college student from a small, rural, Appalachian town. I had never met anyone with a doctoral degree (other than our local family physician). I attended a public high school and there were four teachers who left me thirsty for knowledge. With my White female math (algebra, geometry, etc.) teacher, I felt challenged and pushed to excel. She was able to explain what I thought were difficult concepts in a way that made them seem simple. She also made the class experiential and engaging. She had the expectation that everyone would participate, and I felt engaged in the experience. My history teacher was what I will describe as a charismatic White male who jumped up on desktops and carried a stick with him as he shared details about historical events with us. While there wasn't a lot of sharing and interaction in his class, his style of teaching maintained my interest and kept me engaged. The other two teachers who had the biggest influence on my desire to pursue higher education were sisters. I was fascinated by these two White women. They were world travelers, spoke languages other than English, and had perspectives that were not shared by other teachers. One of the sisters taught a foreign language course in the high school, and through her efforts, I became excited about learning how language provides information about culture. The other sister amended the high school curriculum by adding a course that focused on global current events. Instead of the typical textbooks, we used popular magazines and news sources to stimulate our conversations about world issues. This was my first experience connecting politics and world events to daily life. I found that course to be the most fascinating one offered at my high school. I viewed (and still view) these teachers as strong, independent women who stimulated my desire to learn more about the world in which we live, and the way things work.

Looking back, each of these teachers and their approach to teaching were quite distinct. Yet, all of them had a positive influence on my desire to learn. One common theme I can pull out across those teachers was that I had a positive relationship with them, and they left me with the sense that I was valued

---

1   Merriam-Webster, "Pedagogy," accessed August 1, 2020, https://www.merriam-webster.com/dictionary/pedagogy.

and that my perspectives were valued. Positive relationships with teachers, in high school, have been shown to promote student engagement in the classroom.[2] In fact, research shows that the more positive relationships students have with teachers, the more engaged they are in school.[3] Each of these teachers used different strategies to promote engagement in the course material and process, but I felt connected to all of them and believed that they expected me to succeed. As I type this, I am mindfully aware that it is likely that other students who were from poor and racial minority backgrounds had vastly different experiences than I did. Scholarly literature informs us that "Black female students regularly experience microaggressions which communicate messages of inferiority, criminal status, abnormal cultural values, and rigid stereotypes."[4] The experiences of Black girls and women, while seeking education, demonstrate how interlocking systems of oppression (at the intersection of race and gender in this case) work to create experiences of marginalization in the classroom. I acknowledge that even though my gender and size were areas of disadvantage and oppression, being socially located as White and middle class offered me great privilege in the classroom.

I arrived at the large public institution with little awareness of how systems work to maintain and support the current iteration of the system. At that point, I didn't have words for what a system was and certainly did not understand how it was shaping and influencing me (and everyone else). In other words, I didn't know much about 'how things work.' In my small town of origin, I knew that personal relationships paved the pathway for success. While at the time, I didn't realize this 'knowing people and being known' system was also connected to systems of oppression. I brought with me the knowledge that I needed to build relationships with people in power to be successful. I found, however, that engaging in such a large system and developing those relationships was not an easy task. Because I was a first-generation college student and because I never had a conversation with anyone about how to navigate the university environment, I felt lost in such a big space and system. I found myself observing power dynamics in the institution and learning how to connect with

2   Andrew J. Martin and Rebecca J. Collie, "Teacher–Student Relationships and Students' Engagement in High School: Does the Number of Negative and Positive Relationships with Teachers Matter?" *Journal of Educational Psychology* 111, no. 5 (2019): 861, https://doi.org/10.1037/edu0000317.

3   Martin and Collie, "Teacher-Student Relationships," 861.

4   Crystal R. Chambers, *Black Female Undergraduates on Campus: Successes and Challenges: Diversity in Higher Education* (Bingley: Emerald Group Publishing Limited, 2012), 75–76, http://search.ebscohost.com/login.aspx?direct=true&AuthType=shib&db=e000xna&AN=432671&site=eds-live.

people who had power over me. Which, at that time, was most directly, my professors. While I, at that time, did not have words to explain this power-based system nor really know how to navigate it, building relationships was an intuitive practice for me. So, I leaned on my skill set with little awareness of how my whiteness and class was paving the pathway for me. Over the next few years, I learned much about myself and about what needed to happen with the professor and in the classroom to support my success.

I found that I was best motivated when instructors opened the door for engagement and participation, shared information about their own connection to the content, helped me find a way to connect to the content and, most importantly, demonstrated that they cared about my learning and valued my perspectives. Consistent with my personal experience, scholarly literature related to student engagement suggests that students are most engaged when professors can build a strong personal relationship with students, demonstrate their own connection to content and help students build real life connections to the content, and show passion and enthusiasm about the content they are teaching.[5] I discovered that if I could build relationships with professors, I felt more comfortable in the classroom. Interestingly, I found that this could happen in large lecture halls or in small classrooms. While most of my courses in large lecture halls, with several hundred people, did nothing to stimulate my interest or engagement, I discovered that some professors found a way to reach me even in the large group setting. One White female psychology professor, in particular, required that we write two papers per week connecting our personal experience to the content in the classroom. She provided timely feedback that made it clear she was reading what I wrote. Her suggestions, some of which were personal, indicated from my perspective, that she cared about me and my learning. Again, I felt affirmed and valued. Her approach, in the large lecture hall, suggested that one's approach to teaching was more important than whether there were ten people or three-hundred people in the classroom. There was something about her pedagogy that resonated with me and pulled me in. I will add that this professor was highly popular among students on campus and, during conversations with other students who took her courses, it was clear that others also felt engaged by the way she approached teaching. In contrast, I took an advanced seminar during my senior year of college with a total of eight students. In this classroom, I felt disconnected and disengaged and did not believe that my voice was wanted nor welcome. Although I did

---

5   Tanya Lubicz-Nawrocka and Kieran Bunting, "Student Perceptions of Teaching Excellence: An Analysis of Student-Led Teaching Award Nomination Data," *Teaching in Higher Education* 24, no. 1 (2019): 69–73, https://doi.org/10.1080/13562517.2018.1461620.

not have the words for it at the time, I now believe that what happened in this classroom was a display of White male power that, at the time, left me silenced and feeling incompetent. I would now surmise that although it may not have been the intention of this White male professor to silence the voices of women in the classroom, that is, in pedagogical practice, what happened.

The positive experiences I had with some teachers and professors that left me feeling valued is consistent with the findings in a recent study that focused on the experiences of transgender and gender non-conforming (TGNC) gradu-ate students.[6] This study surveyed ninety-one TGNC university students about their experiences in higher education and found that the misgendering of TGNC students is a common stressor in the classroom that can leave TGNC students feeling "othered" and "devastated."[7] Nonbinary students were found to be at increased risk, when compared to students with binary genders, for misgendering.[8] In addition to misgendering, transgender students experience interpersonal and institutional discrimination and this increases their vulner-ability to minority stress.[9] When nonbinary students, in particular, do not feel a sense of belonging on campus, they are more likely, compared with other sexual and gender minority students, to be negatively impacted by minority stress.[10] When students are concerned about their physical and emotional safety in the classroom, engagement in course material can become more dif-ficult. When the TGNC students in this study made efforts to address misgen-dering by their professors, it often led to "unpleasant" consequences and left them feeling disempowered.[11] Interpersonally, faculty members are viewed as demonstrating lack of knowledge and sensitivity to TGNC students while cisnormative practices live systemically.[12] When TGNC students encounter

---

6   Abbie E. Goldberg, Katherine Kuvalanka, and Lore Dickey, "Transgender Graduate Students' Experiences in Higher Education: A Mixed-Methods Exploratory Study," *Journal of Diversity in Higher Education* 12, no. 1 (2019): 48, https://doi.org/10.1037/dhe0000074 .

7   Goldberg, Kuvalanka, and Dickey, "Transgender Graduate Students," 38.

8   Goldberg, Kuvalanka, and Dickey, "Transgender Graduate Students," 46.

9   Abbie E. Goldberg, JuliAnna Z. Smith, and Genny Beemyn, "Trans Activism and Advocacy Among Transgender Students in Higher Education: A Mixed Methods Study," *Journal of Diversity in Higher Education* 13, no. 1 (2020): 66, https://doi.org/10.1037/dhe0000125 .

10 Stephanie L. Budge, Sergio Domínguez Jr., and Abbie E. Goldberg, "Minority Stress in Nonbinary Students in Higher Education: The Role of Campus Climate and Belongingness," *Psychology of Sexual Orientation and Gender Diversity* 7, no. 2 (2020): 222, https://doi.org/ 10.1037/sgd0000360 .

11 Goldberg, Kuvalanka, and Dickey, "Transgender Graduate Students," 46.

12 Goldberg, Kuvalanka, and Dickey, "Transgender Graduate Students," 48–49.

affirmative and validating professors, the opportunity is created for students to feel a sense of belonging and engagement.[13]

3   Power and Pedagogy

Traditional approaches to pedagogy are power-based and view the instructor as an expert who imparts knowledge to those who do not know. Traditional approaches are also hierarchical, and patriarchal and stem from Eurocentric and androcentric perspectives that perpetuate colonized ways of being and doing in higher education. These traditional approaches are seen as normative, and while contextualized in whiteness, tout their objectivity and fairness by suggesting that all students are treated equally without regard for social location and factors that may have served as barriers to participation and success in higher education. Traditional approaches to pedagogy instill the notion among instructors that there is one correct way of doing something that is accessible to all learners and dissuade professors from being self-involving and valuing the lived experiences, as co-learners, of their students. I (Tammy) find it interesting that traditional pedagogy is called "pedagogy" while more inclusive approaches are named as specific types of pedagogies. It reminds me of our American history of calling male sports teams the name of their teams (e.g. Cardinals) while only adding gender to a team when it is a girls or women's team (e.g. Lady Cardinals). Gender, race, class, and other social identities are added only when they are deviations from what is considered the standard (i.e. male, White, heterosexual, middle to upper class). This process of "othering" centers the perspectives of the dominant group and marginalizes others.

4   Critical Consciousness

Critical consciousness refers to "an individual's capacity to critically reflect and act upon their environment" and is viewed as a "prerequisite for liberation from oppression."[14] Three components of critical consciousness include

---

13   Goldberg, Kuvalanka, and Dickey, "Transgender Graduate Students," 48.

14   Isaac Prilleltensky and Ora Prilleltensky, "Synergies for Wellness and Liberation in Counseling Psychology," *The Counseling Psychologist* 31, no. 3 (2003): 273–281, https://doi.org/10.1177/0011000003252957. Matthew A. Diemer, Aimee Kauffman, Nathan Koenig, Emily Trahan, and Chueh-An Hsieh, "Challenging Racism, Sexism, and Social Injustice: Support for Urban Adolescents' Critical Consciousness Development," *Cultural*

critical reflection, political efficacy, and critical action.[15] The process of critical reflection involves thoughtfully and intentionally examining social interactions and situations through a historical and structural/systemic lens to determine where inequity exists, and to reject the inequity and view it as a form of oppression. Becoming increasingly competent at critical reflection can lead to political efficacy. This is the ability to find a way to engage within the political arena to ultimately produce socially just change. The development of critical consciousness results in taking action against social injustices, reducing and eliminating oppression, and creating equity and inclusion.[16] To disrupt power and promote social justice advocacy, pedagogical approaches must aim to help students develop critical consciousness.

5 Critical Theories

Critical thinking serves as the foundation for critical theories. Critical theories challenge societal norms, seek to bring awareness and understanding to marginalization and oppression, and provide direction for social change.[17] Critical theories developed as a way of critically reflecting on the way things work in systems, providing a lens through which power and interlocking systems of oppression can be examined.[18]

5.1 *Queer Theory*
Queer theory seeks to examine and deconstruct the sex/gender system in which sex, gender, and sexuality are intertwined, one determining the other.[19] The notion of interconnection between sex and gender lead to the oppression of non-normative sexualities and gender identities. Within Queer theory, it is

---

Diversity and Ethnic Minority Psychology 12, no. 3 (2006): 444–460, https://doi.org/10.1037/1099-9809.12.3.444.

15 Roderick Watts, Matthew Diemer, and Adam Voight, "Critical Consciousness: Current Status and Future Directions," *New Directions for Child and Adolescent Development*, no. 134 (2011): 43–57, https://doi.org/10.1002/cd.310.

16 Watts, Diemer, and Voight, "Critical Consciousness," 43–57.

17 Stephen D. Brookfield, *The Power of Critical Theory: Liberating Adult Learning and Teaching*, (San Francisco: Jossey-Bass, 2005), 25.

18 Victor C.X. Wang and Geraldine Torrisi-Steele, "Online Teaching, Change, and Critical Theory," *New Horizons in Adult Education & Human Resource Development* 27, no.3 (2015): 20.

19 Gayle Rubin, "The Traffic in Women: Notes on the Political Economy of Sex," *Toward an Anthropology of Women*, (1975): 157–210.

these assumptions that lead to the perceived inferiority of women and members of the LGBTQ+ community.

Words and labels are important within the Queer framework. While there has always been diversity in gender and sexual identity, some terms describing sexual orientation have been used as a derogatory label and a way to group people as different and deviant.[20] Queer theory purports that language matters. Word choices can include or exclude people. Words like gay, lesbian and transgender are rarely found in schools, unless they are being used as insults.[21] As a way to deconstruct the disparaging meaning the word, "queer" was adopted during the gay rights movement.[22] Society views the normative way to live as cisgender, binary, and heterosexual, and Queer Theory rejects the categorical perspective on identities. Instead, it notes the intersection of identities, and how the relationship between identities involves power and authority. "Queer" brings attention, identity, and value back to some individuals who have been erased by heteronormative structures.[23]

Queer pedagogy addresses the typical educational model in which people are often alienated and excluded due to non-heteronormative and cisgender identities. Queer pedagogy does not offer a single path or 'right' way to approach education. Instead, it proposes we question our practices and notions of equality and acceptance.[24]

5.2   *Critical Race Theory*

Developed in the 1970's, Critical Race Theory (CRT) questions the societal ideas of equality, legal reasoning, and constitutional law.[25] The foundation of CRT comes from legal studies and radical feminism. Beginning in law, Critical Race theory is now prevalent in many domains, including education. Legal indeterminacy, the idea that legal cases often lack one definite outcome, helped shaped Critical Race Theory. It was observed that most legal cases could go either way, and that those with power and authority often win, putting those with less power at a disadvantage.[26] CRT rejects the notion of universal truths

20   Michael Foucault, *The History of Sexuality: An Introduction* (New York: Pantheon Books, 1978).

21   Joao Nemi Neto, "Queer Pedagogy: Approaches to Inclusive Teaching," *Policy Futures in Education* 16, no. 5 (2018): 590.

22   Nemi Neto, "Queer Pedagogy", 590.

23   Nemi Neto, "Queer Pedagogy," 590.

24   Nemi Neto, "Queer Pedagogy," 591.

25   Richard Delgado and Jean Stefancic, *Critical Race Theory: An Introduction* (New York: University Press, 2017), 4.

26   Delgado and Stefancic, *Critical Race Theory*, 5.

determining the way we live, and assumes race exists solely for reasons of social stratification.[27] Within this framework, racism is seen as socially constructed and omnipresent, and also unacknowledged. CRT promotes change by identifying racism and oppression, bringing it to the forefront, and presenting it for examination.

Critical Race Theory posits that racism intersects with other marginalized identities such as sex, class, and national origin.[28] Being socially located in multiple systems of oppression, with regard to race, gender, and class, among others, is shown to lead to feelings of alienation throughout one's educational experience.[29] However, in Critical Race Pedagogical Theory, students work *with* the instructor. The role of the instructor is reframed into one of collective participant. This is an influential step in inviting the voices of students of color into class discussions. Providing a space where students have an opportunity to share and where members of oppressed groups have access to the same space with their classmates and instructor provides a powerful opportunity to create change.

Learning is a traditionally passive process where students simply receive information presented by the instructor. Critical Race Theory draws attention to the need for students to actively engage and learn with, not from, their instructor. I (Sarah) was a student in Dr. Hatfield's Multicultural Counseling and Supervision course. It felt like we were sailing the ship together. Dr. Hatfield embedded diversity in her teaching. Effective diversity teaching means an examination of social structures, institutions, and ways of being.[30] It is clear that Critical Race Theory impacted the structure and instruction of the class. We worked together in learning about diversity, diving into our own experiences, learning from others, and collaborating to evaluate existing social structures to determine areas where change is needed.

5.3   Black Girls in School

It has been over 65 years since schools were legally desegregated by the Supreme Court decision of *Brown v. Board of Education*, which overturned *Plessy v. Ferguson*, stating that separation of educational facilities is unequal, yet the United States school system still struggles with issues relating to fair

---

27   Larry Ortiz and Jani Jayshree, "Critical Race Theory: A Transformational Model For Teaching Diversity," *Journal of Social Work Education* 46, no. 2 (2010): 189.

28   Kimberlé Williams Crenshaw, "Mapping the Margins: Intersectionality, Identity Politics, and Violence Against Women of Color," *Stanford Law Review* 43, (1991): 1241–1299.

29   Delgado and Stefancic, *Critical Race Theory*, 5.

30   Ortiz and Jani, "Critical Race Theory," 189.

education of racial minority children. Critical Race theory recognizes that for racial minority girls, schools can be toxic to their developing identities.[31] In school, they receive mixed messages about who and what is valued. Literature on the experiences of Black girls in public and private schools suggest that the social construction of gender and femininity intersecting with race shape their educational outcomes negatively.[32] This is because societal gender norms delineating femininity are aligned with White, middle-class values.[33] My (Portia) early experiences in school mirror those of many Black girls, starting with my experience in what was called the South African 'Bantu education' system. The policy of Bantu (Black African) education was aimed to direct Black or non-white youth to the unskilled labor market, by shaping the curricula to teach that higher education was beyond the scope of Black intellect. Furthermore, schools were significantly under resourced and teacher training was limited. Similarly, in the United States, educational curricula have been criticized as reinforcing racist and sexist pedagogy. Scholars argue that the mainstream curriculum in the schools is part of a legacy of colonization that continues to marginalize and racialize students.[34] This is because the content promotes messages that reinforce White achievement over other races. This contributes to internalized racism, and damages the self-concept of non-white students.

Furthermore, research on school discipline indicates that throughout the United States, girls of color, particularly Black girls, are disproportionately disciplined compared to their peers.[35] Scholars argue that this discipline stems from colonial views that criminalized the behavior of minorities and is implicated in the zero tolerance policies which are accused of feeding the school

31   Monique Morris, *Pushout: The Criminalization of Black Girls in Schools* (New York: New Press, 2015).

32   Jamilia Blake, Bettie Ray Butler, and Danielle Smith. "The Cause of Black Females' Disproportionate Suspension Rates," *Closing the School Discipline Gap: Equitable Remedies for Excessive Exclusion,* ed. Daniel J. Losen (New York: Teachers College Press, 2015).

33   Subini Ancy Annamma, "Innocence, Ability and Whiteness as Property: Teacher Education and the School-to-Prison Pipeline," *Urban Review* 47, no. 2 (2015): 293–316, https://doi:10.1007/s11256-014-0293-6. Gloria Ladson-Billings, *The Dreamkeepers: Successful Teachers of African American Children* (San Francisco: Jossey-Bass, 1994).

34   Marie Battiste, *Decolonizing Education: Nourishing the Learning Spirit* (Saskatoon: Purich, 2014). Tara J. Yosso, Laurence Parker, Daniel G. Solorzano and Marvin Lynn, "From Jim Crow to Affirmative Action and Back Again: A Critical Race Discussion of Racialized Rationales and Access to Higher Education," *Review of Research in Education,* 28 (2004) 1–27.

35   M. Raffaelle Mendez, Linda. and Howard M. Knoff, "Who Gets Suspended from School and Why: A Demographic Analysis of Schools and Disciplinary Infractions in a Large School District, *Education and Treatment of Children* 26, (2013): 30–51. Morris, *Pushout,* 2015.

to prison pipeline. Colonial views of women of color are most apparent in the criticism of Black girls' behavior at school. Literature on the discipline of Black girls in the classroom indicates that they are often seen as too outspoken and assertive. Black feminists believe that this has been influenced by White patriarchal middle-class values of "submissive and ladylike" views of femininity. Collins describes this as the lasting racist view of the aggressive and dominant Black female matriarch.[36] Other scholars view this as signifying *misogynoir* a term used to describe the oppression against Black women's experience due to the intersection of being deemed inferior in both race and gender.[37]

6   Intersectional Black Feminist Pedagogy

Intersectionality was originally conceptualized within Critical Race theory by Black feminist, legal scholar Kimberlé Crenshaw and, soon thereafter by Black feminist, sociologist, and social theorist Patricia Hill Collins.[38] Crenshaw used the term intersectionality to refer to the experiences of Black women at the intersection of racism and sexism.[39] Her work highlights the notion that being socially located as Black does not fully explain one's experience as a Black woman and being socially located as a woman does not fully explain one's experience being a Black woman. Crenshaw pointed out that understanding the lived experience of Black women means recognizing the implications of how these two interlocking systems of power intersect and create oppression. For, it is at the intersection of our social locations that creates unique lived experiences. Collins considers what it means to situate intersectionality as a critical social theory and positions it as a social theory that searches for both truth and social meaning, or scientific and narrative traditions.[40]

Naming this type of pedagogy becomes complicated because calling it intersectional pedagogy does not fully honor the *herstorical* foundations rooted in Black feminist scholarship, calling it Black feminist pedagogy might detract from the intersectional focus, and referring to this type of pedagogy as feminist

---

36   Patricia Hill Collins, *Black Feminist Thought: Knowledge, Consciousness, and the Politics of Empowerment* (New York: Routledge, 2000).

37   Moya Bailey and Trudy, "On Misogynoir: Citation, Erasure, and Plagiarism," *Feminist Media Studies* 18, (2018): 762–768.

38   Collins, *Black Feminist Thought*, 2000. Kimberlé Crenshaw, "Demarginalizing the Intersection of Race and Sex: A Black Feminist Critique of Antidiscrimination Doctrine, Feminist Theory, and Antiracist Politics," *University of Chicago Legal Forum* (1989): 139–167.

39   Crenshaw, "Demarginalizing the Intersection." 139–167.

40   Patricia Hill Collins, *Intersectionality as Critical Social Theory*, 2019.

pedagogy may increase the risk of the extraction of the work of Black feminists in service of the credit for White feminists. Naming, citing authors, and giving proper credit are important strategies within Intersectional Black Feminist pedagogy. For the purposes of this written work, and for the reasons stated herein, we will refer to this type of pedagogy as Intersectional Black Feminist pedagogy (IBFP). Others may argue that calling this approach Black Feminist pedagogy sufficiently includes intersectionality. I will consider that, perhaps, it is because I (Tammy) am White that I find it necessary to include "intersectional" in the title. Black feminist work is known to be intersectional, while centering race. Readers will want to consider that other works may use the terms Intersectional pedagogy, Black Feminist pedagogy, and Feminist pedagogy to describe Intersectional Black Feminist pedagogy. And, while feminist pedagogies have some common principles that they share, feminist pedagogies are not monolithic and represent a diverse group of perspectives and strategies in the practice of teaching.

Common themes found across feminist pedagogies, that differentiate them from other approaches to teaching, include knowledge co-creation, community building, centering the experiences and voices of those who have historically been left out of curriculum, and critical self-reflection.[41] These themes, along with social justice action, are foundational for IBFP.

Intersectional Black feminist pedagogical strategies support critical thought about selection and presentation of course content while also examining the institutions, structures, and social positions that contextualize lectures, discussions, and activities, valuing the lived experience of students, co-creating knowledge, building a sense of community and connection in the classroom, and inclusion of readings, voices, and perspectives that have been historically left out of curriculum. Taking an IBFP stance positions both the instructor and the student as knowledge co-creators. Both instructors and students bring their unique lived experiences at the intersections of their social locations. The co-creation of knowledge is an act of inclusivity and valuing of diverse perspectives. It allows for, or rather calls for, dialogue and self-involvement in the curriculum. It centers the perspectives of the diverse learner, while highlighting gaps in the literature and whose voices have been left out. In this way, IBFP approaches also serve to decolonize education and the replication of White supremacy in the education arena. IBFP places value in community building.

---

41   Lindsay Onufer and Lizette Munos Rojas, "Teaching at PITT: Introduction to Feminist Pedagogy," *University Times*, (2019): https://www.utimes.pitt.edu/news/teaching-pitt-8.

Building an engaged community of learners who feel valued, heard, and supported is another foundational piece of IBFP.

Using intersectionality as a guiding conception assists instructors in considering the complexity of examining "both privileged and oppressed social identities that simultaneously interact to create systemic inequalities, and therefore, alter lived experiences of prejudice and discrimination, privilege and opportunities, and perspectives from particular social locations."[42] Intersectional approaches to teaching and learning are important because they provide a framework for understanding the diversity of lived experience and the social structures and processes that create, influence, and maintain oppression, marginalization, and inequality. More specifically, the valuing of personal lived experiences of diverse individuals serves as an intentional socio-political action, or point of advocacy, and results in the development of strategies to include the perspectives of those who are marginalized in the classroom. Inclusion of these diverse points of view provides insight into the structural influences in our lives and questions colonized ways of developing and implementing coursework.

7   Pedagogy in Practice: Techniques and Strategies in the Classroom

While theory serves as a guiding conception in our educational practice, technique is the application of various strategies. It is our theoretical understanding that guides us in choosing strategies or techniques that are congruent with the key concepts of our pedagogical approach. While we may use a variety of strategies in the classroom, our understanding of why and how they are implemented is informed by our pedagogical stance. The strategies presented in this section are informed by intersectional, Black feminist, feminist, culturally responsive, culturally sustaining, and indigenous approaches to the practice of teaching.

7.1   *Including Diverse Perspectives*
While having specific educational aims, schools also provide students an education about their value in the world around them. Because of the mainstream colonized curricula, students from minoritized backgrounds, whose language and culture do not resemble the dominant culture of the school, may become

---

42   Kim A. Case, "Toward an Intersectional Pedagogy Model," *Intersectional Pedagogy: Complicating Identity and Social Justice*, ed. Kim A. Case (New York: Routledge, 2017), 9.

alienated and disadvantaged in the learning process. This colonial agenda
could pressure students from minority cultures to acculturate and rid themselves of their cultural beliefs and norms in order to assimilate into the majority culture. This is detrimental to the socioemotional well-being of minority
students and impacts their learning and success in school. Studies have found
that a strong racial-ethnic identity is linked to higher self-esteem and a positive
outlook on academic achievement in racial minorities.[43]

Culturally responsive teaching approaches recognize that diverse students
bring varied knowledge, experience, and perceptions that are enriching to the
learning experience. The role of the educator is to build a trusting and affirming
classroom environment that promotes inclusive and meaningful teaching.[44]

7.2   Affirming Students' Cultures and Identities

We encourage educators to critically reflect on their instruction, ensuring
that diversity is reflected in the study materials, textbooks and visual images.
Explore whether all students can find relatable content throughout the process of learning. Review and ensure that class content does not perpetuate
bias and stereotypes or silence diverse communities. Be intentional about your
choice of materials and activities in class. Allowing students to bring their own
examples from their real-life experience into the classroom is another way to
provide an affirming space.

Educators who pay attention to culture recognize that individuals from different cultures may learn differently and that their expectations for the learning environment may be different. For example, students from collectivistic
cultures may prefer to learn in cooperation with others, and students from
individualistic cultures may prefer to work autonomously. To maximize learning opportunities, teachers should gain knowledge of the cultures represented
in their classrooms and adapt lessons so that they reflect ways of communicat-
ing and learning that are familiar to the students. Intentional effort, on the part
of the instructor, to use a variety of learning strategies, that are culturally relevant to the students in their classroom, helps students relate to classroom content and feel affirmed in the learning environment. Giving choice in a diverse

---

43   Jean S. Phinney, Cindy Lou Cantu, and Dawn A. Kurtz, "Ethnic and American Identity
      as Predictors of Self-Esteem Among African American, Latino, and White Adolescents,"
      Journal of Youth and Adolescence 26, no. 2 (1997): 165–185.

44   Gloria Ladson-Billings, "Culturally   Relevant   Pedagogy   2.0:   a.k.a.   The   Remix,"
      Harvard   Educational   Review   84,   no.1   (2014):   74–84.   https://doi.org/10.17763/
      haer.84.1.p2rj131485484751.

group of students is a way to allow individuals the opportunity to determine their own path.

7.3   *Exploring the Use of Language*

Diverse students have communication styles that are influences by their culture. Second language English speakers are disadvantaged by the deficit model that singularly focuses on acquiring proficiency in English instead of celebrating their mastery of other languages. Language and culture also impact the style of interaction and communication which may influence the formality in the use of the English language. Learn about the language skills students bring to the classroom. Code switching is a common language phenomenon observed in African American students when they switch between the mainstream standard American English dialect (considered professional language) and African American dialects. The ability to navigate between different languages and to switch at a moment's notice is an unrecognized cognitive ability of diverse students.

Family collaboration is a crucial aspect of culturally responsive teaching. The notion of autonomy can impede the successful integration of family in the educational life of diverse students, therefore inclusive pedagogy incorporates family outreach and explores barriers that may limit the involvement of families.

7.4   *Naming*

In her 2019 book about intersectional pedagogy, researcher in gender and peace studies, Gal Harmat, discusses the relevance and importance of name story sharing and name analysis. This is "an educational practice in which participants and students of a course, workshop or dialogue, share their name stories and are able to question, challenge, and explore identity, language, heritage, privileges, and (power) relations right from the beginning."[45] Names are contextualized within a family and culture and may contain values, hopes, and beliefs of families across aspects of identity. Since this type of self-reflection may bring up many thoughts, feelings, and questions, it is important that students be allowed to engage in this reflective action without input from others unless it is requested.[46] Instructors may ask specific questions and have students consider the origins of the name, why it was chosen for them, what it means and how it has impacted them in their own sociocultural context.

---

45   Gal Harmat, *Intersectional Pedagogy: Creative Education Practices for Gender and Peace Work* (New York: Routledge, 2020), 2.

46   Harmat, *Intersectional Pedagogy*, 18–19.

7.5   *Building Community*

Culturally responsive educational strategies to support racial minority girls emphasize the connection between teaching and caregiving, as this has been identified as an essential component when educating students of color, and serves as a buffer against the racialized and gendered experiences they encounter at school.[47] Other-mothering is a teaching philosophy that has been applied to Black female educators who nurture students' educational opportunities by attending to their social-emotional lives and educational needs.[48] These female educator behaviors are often compared to kinship behavior due to the emphasis on nurturing, advocating, advising and reprimanding associated with family caregivers.[49]

Other scholars term this student focused engaged teaching role as that of a "warm demander."[50] Kleinfeld coined the phrase warm demander to describe the type of teacher who was effective in teaching Native American and Inuit students.[51] These educators have high expectations for students and are firm and warm in their instructional methods.[52] Garza also found that caring relationships with teachers is crucial for educational engagement among Latina students.[53] Latina students showed strong preference for educators who build an affectionate and trusting relationship and made an effort to engage them outside the requirements of the school schedule and accommodated the demands of their lives outside of school.[54]

---

47 Ladson-Billings, *The Dreamkeepers,* 1994. Monique W. Morris, "Protecting Black girls," *Educational Leadership* 74, no. 3 (2016): 49–53.

48 Collins, *Black Feminist Thought,* 2000.

49 Alonzo M. Flowers, Jameel A. Scott, Jamie R. Riley, and Robert T. Palmer, "Beyond the Call of Duty: Building on Othermothering for Improving Outcomes at Historically Black Colleges and Universities," *Journal of African American Males in Education* 6, no. 1 (2015): 59–73.

50 Blaire Cholewa, Ellen Amatea, Cirecie A. West-Olatunji, and Ashley Wright, "Examining the Relational Processes of a Highly Successful Teacher of African American Children," *Urban Education* 47, no.1 (2011): 250–279.

51 Judith Kleinfeld, "Effective Teachers of Eskimo and Indian Students," *School Review* 83, (1975): 301–344.

52 Amy Carpenter Ford and Kelly Sassi, "Authority in Cross-Racial Teaching and Learning (Re)considering the Transferability of Warm Demander Approaches," *Urban Education* 49 (2014): 39–74.

53 · Ruben Garza, "Latino and White High School Students' Perception of Caring Behaviors," *Urban Education* 44, (2009): 297–321.

54 Debra L. Roorda, Helma M. Koomen, Jantine L. Spilt and Frans J. Oort, "The Influence of Affective Teacher–Student Relationships on Students' School Engagement and Achievement: A Meta-Analytic Approach," *Review of Educational Research* 81 (2011): 493–529, https://doi:10.3102/0034654311421793 .

7.6   *Emphasizing Social Change*

In liberatory, critical, and feminist classrooms, an aim is to promote advocacy, activism, and social justice efforts that result in social change. Instructors can create a brave classroom space wherein they work with students to promote inclusivity and to challenge all forms of marginalization and oppression.

Collaboration between students and instructors allows them to work together for social change. Inclusivity is crucial for students who may feel alienated. Instructors can engage students in identifying and challenging gender and sexuality norms in text.[55] Educational systems are historically heteronormative, meaning one's educational experience is as well. Schools exist almost entirely as binary systems, therefore engaging students in curricula that challenges heteronormative systems is essential in supporting marginalized students.

7.7   *Valuing Lived Experience*

Inclusive pedagogical practices promote the development of a sense of community in the classroom. Students from diverse backgrounds can be brought together through authentic and open conversations that draw from students' lived experiences and social locations. Course content is also more likely to engage and empower students when it is culturally and socially relevant to them personally.[56]

Inclusive pedagogies reject the notion that students either have or have not succeeded with no consideration to the learning process or the student as an individual. Viewing teaching and learning as "sink-or-swim" concepts can create barriers, especially for marginalized students, throughout the learning process. To develop a truly inclusive classroom environment an instructor must be open to, and respectful of, varied perspectives.[57]

7.8   *Disrupting Power through Qualitative Research Strategies*

Autoethnography is a strategy that has been implemented by indigenous groups to offer their own personal stories as members of their community. This practice serves to disrupt power in research, dismantle colonization, and

---

55   Mollie V. Blackburn and Jill M. Smith, "Moving Beyond the Inclusion of LGBTQ-themed Literature in English Language Arts Classrooms: Interrogating Heteronormativity and Exploring Intersectionality," *Journal of Adolescent & Adult Literacy* 53, no.8 (2010): 625–634.
56   Ladson-Billings, "Culturally Relevant Pedagogy 2.0," 2014.
57   Julie Vaudrin-Charette, "Melting the Cultural Iceberg in Indigenizing Higher Education: Shifts to Accountability in Times of Reconciliation," *New Directions for Teaching and Learning* 157 (2019): 105–118, https://doi.org/10.1002/tl.20333n.

provides a way for group members to share their own narratives instead of being viewed from the position of an outsider (as has been historically typical in ethnographic research).[58] Autoethnographic methods make the values and experiences of the researcher explicit rather than viewing the researcher as neutral and unbiased. Autoethnography is "one of the approaches that acknowledges, and accommodates subjectivity, emotionality, and the researcher's influence on research, rather than hiding from these matters or assuming they don't exist."[59]

To write an autoethnography, one must be a member of the group one is studying. It is a form of qualitative research inquiry that focuses on self-reflection of personal experience and connects this personal experience to larger social, political, and cultural meanings. This strategy can be used in research and it can also be used in the classroom. Having students write a mini-autoethnography provides a way for them to examine their lived experience while simultaneously connecting those experiences to the systems of oppression that influence them. This process makes power structures and inequalities visible. While I (Tammy) implement this strategy with doctoral students, it can be used at any level of higher education. For example, one professor chose to develop an assignment that he called "Gender Autobiography" for a course that was cross-listed in psychology and women's studies.[60] His assignment description asked students to "connect academic scholarship on the psychology of gender to everyday life experiences of gender socialization, gender identity development, and social inequalities (including privilege and oppression across multiple dimensions of differences, including but not limited to gender, sexuality, race, and class)."[61] Because this assignment required students to systematically analyze their own experiences, related to gender, and use relevant research literature to highlight how these experiences represent systemic and structural issues, this assignment can be considered a mini-autoethnography. Additionally, this assignment honors the complexity of holding multiple social identities while centering gender.

I (Tammy) developed an assignment for a doctoral level course in Counselor Education that I call "Intersectional Cultural Autobiography". This assignment

58   Carolyn Ellis, Tony Adams, and Arthur Bochner, "Autoethnography: An Overview," *Forum: Qualitative Social Research* 11, no. 1 (2011): para. 16, https://www.qualitative-research.net/index.php/fqs/article/view/1589/3095.

59   Ellis, Adams, and Bochner, "Autoethnography," para. 3.

60   Patrick Grzanka, "Undoing the Psychology of Gender," *Intersectional Pedagogy: Complicating Identity and Social Justice,* ed. Kim Case, (New York: Routledge, 2017), 75–76.

61   Grzanka, "Undoing Gender," 75.

requests that students use both autoethnography and the qualitative strategy of photovoice to reflect on their lived experience across identities and social locations and how those experiences intersect with structural power. Here's an excerpt from my assignment description.

> This assignment provides an opportunity for reflection on your lived experience across multiple social locations while connecting those lived experiences to the broader social world. Your task is to utilize intersectional theory as a framework to explore your personal social locations (you will include both marginalized and privileged social locations) and then discuss how your lived experiences, across the various social locations, intersect with structural power to create systemic issues. Ultimately, the critical focus will be on systemic issues (the way things work) in the larger sociocultural context. There are two parts to the assignment: a photovoice project and a written analysis (paper).[62]

Using the qualitative research strategy of photovoice provides a space for and assigns value to different ways of knowing. For this part of the assignment, students creatively display images (photos of people or things and drawings) that represent the various aspects of their identities. Since I teach this course online, students typically format the images into a PowerPoint slideshow or create a digital video file. The student is encouraged to be creative in their format and display. The second part of the assignment is the autoethnography. I set the expectation that intersectionality will be used as a guiding theory and ask students to examine identities that are socially located in oppression and those that are socially located in privilege. I want them to be able to grasp the notion that most of us have one or more locations of oppression and also some locations of privilege. I have found, through my experience teaching, that many students come to the classroom, centering one of their oppressed social identities and may not have given as much thought to the oppression located in their other identities or the privilege afforded to them by other aspects of where they are socially located. Without grasping the significance of interlocking systems of oppression, social change may be less likely.

I (Melissa) participated in the Intersectional Cultural Autobiography assignment from the student perspective. The experience of examining my own social locations and their interaction with systems of power felt intimidating

---

62   Tammy Hatfield, "Multicultural Issues in Counseling and Education," (Syllabus, University of the Cumberlands, Kentucky, Spring 2020).

at first. The assignment lead to a better understanding of my own positionality (personally and professionally), forcing me to confront and acknowledge my own implicit biases that I had developed throughout my life experiences. This form of self-examination and self-expression was cathartic, as it created an opportunity to consider how my beliefs and actions can impact social change. This experience was especially engaging and impactful due to the incorporation of relevant personal experiences.

I (Sarah) also participated in the Intersectional Autobiography assignment as a student. The project made me question the idea of authentic identities. While I became more aware of my social locations, I also began re-evaluating some of the boxes I, and society, use to categorize people. Much of how we define ourselves exists due to social construction. The Intersectional Autobiography assignment helped me understand my power and privilege. I enjoyed the choice and creativity allowed in the assignment. My classmates and I were encouraged to truly be ourselves and delve deeply into our identity formation, beliefs, and values. This assignment was unlike any other I'd completed up to that point.

I (Portia) also engaged in the Intersectional Autobiography assignment as a student. This project allowed me to explore the intersection of my other identities. As a Black female, my experience has been that this identity is the one that has shaped my experience of marginalization the most and therefore has defined my interactions with the world. I appreciated the assignment for allowing other parts of my identity to be explored and brought to the forefront. Additionally, issues of safety, and vulnerability are part of this exploratory process. For most marginalized individuals there is increased need for the environment to be able to hear and validate these experiences without explaining, blaming or defending. As a group we were able to move to this non-defensive level which made this a healing experience.

8   Accountability and Action

8.1   *Engaging in Self-work*
Being socialized into whiteness (as a White person, this occurs, at least initially, mostly outside of awareness), struggling with unpacking and discovering my own implicit biases, sitting with the cacophony of teaching and administrative voices at a Historically White Institution, while trying to find ways to deconstruct and dismantle all forms of White supremacy in higher education in an effort to support the liberation of Black and Indigenous People of Color (BIPOC), can feel overwhelming and result in immobilization. To engage in

socially just and anti-racist practice as educators, I (Tammy) must take action and develop a pathway for accountability and action.

Because I am socially located as White, race is an area of privilege in my life, and I am left with much self-work to do in understanding how whiteness impacts my daily life and experiences. I understand that whiteness gives me unearned power, privilege and advantage when compared to persons who are BIPOC. Taking an intersectional perspective, that power is offset a bit by my gender and size. While my social locations move with me through space and time, and are determined by the observer, I have found that my most salient identities, across time and space, have been gender and body size. I notice that I have not had to work as hard to uncover the impact of lack of access and oppression that comes at the intersection of sexism and sizeism. I can recount many experiences, throughout my lifetime, that have experienced power used to undermine my value based on being female and large-bodied.

8.2 Practicing De-colonization in Higher Education

As educators who strive to practice through an Intersectional Black Feminist lens that is both culturally responsive and sustaining to promote social justice, we have found that it is easy to feel isolated in the context of higher education where many institutions sustain oppressive policy and practices that developed through colonization. There is often a failure to acknowledge and respond to the violently oppressive context in which higher education was developed in the United States.

Most modern-day institutions of higher education are historically white (HWIs) or predominately white institutions (PWIs). Whiteness is also structured into these institutions as we, often without explicit awareness, practice White ways of viewing and being in the world. Traditional pedagogy honors and sustains these practices and we believe that without the development of critical consciousness and intentional action to promote inclusive educational spaces, we will continue to harm marginalized and oppressed groups of people. We, the chapter authors, believe that practicing de-colonization efforts in the educational setting is necessary to create more inclusive classroom spaces.

8.3 Creating Accountability Partnerships

All educators will encounter situations where they demonstrate bias in the classroom. Sometimes this occurs within our explicit awareness and we are able to repair the damage and repair the relationships and, other times, our bias is implicit. Developing accountability partnerships creates a process for addressing both implicit and explicit biases and allows for additional perspective to be taken into consideration. This can foster ongoing critical examination of one's practice and can result in the development of more inclusive practices. In the practice of accountability, educators consult with their colleagues regarding course design and implementation, ensuring they are creating inclusive course content and structure. Educators may also use accountability partnerships to develop a space where they can process interactions that occurred in their classrooms with students and examine, with their accountability colleague, any bias that may have been displayed.

Accountability partnerships may take form as a mentorship, cohort peer group, or simply an agreement between two colleagues. I (Melissa) have experienced working in isolation and on teams throughout my career. I have found that working within a team of like professionals, while challenging in some aspects, has significantly contributed to my growth as a counselor and educator. Being exposed to multiple perspectives and teaching styles on a regular basis has afforded me the opportunity to reflect on my own pedagogical practices and identify areas to improve.

9   Discussion and Conclusion

As the writing of this chapter ends, I (Tammy) want to share my excitement and hopefulness that we can continue to build and enact social justice efforts in higher education settings. One of the things about sharing this chapter that is most exciting to me is the possibility that readers will become passionate about building inclusive spaces and will leave with some strategies they can use to engage in social justice action in higher education settings. I am also hopeful that the feelings of loneliness and isolation that are sometimes experienced when we are not connected with others who are actively working to change systems, will be somewhat assuaged. When I first discovered that many conceptual, theoretical, and practical strategies for building inclusive classrooms already exist, I was thrilled and relieved. Women and nonbinary people have been doing this work for a long time and we have a responsibility to continue building and expanding theories, be more inclusive in teaching and research practices, and engage in the critical self-examination required to sustain this work.

Bibliography

Annamma, Subini Ancy. "Innocence, Ability and Whiteness as Property: Teacher Education and the School-to-Prison Pipeline." *Urban Review* 47, no. 2 (2015): 293–316. https://doi:10.1007/s11256-014-0293-6.

Bailey, Moya and Trudy. "On misogynoir: Citation, erasure, and plagiarism" *Feminist Media Studies* 18, (2018): 762–768.

Battiste, Marie. Decolonizing Education: Nourishing the Learning Spirit. Saskatoon: Purich, 2014.

Blackburn, Mollie V. and Jill M. Smith. "Moving Beyond the Inclusion of LGBTQ Themed Literature in English Language Arts Classrooms: Interrogating Heteronormativity and Exploring Intersectionality." *Journal of Adolescent and Adult Literacy* 53, (2010): 625–634.

Blake, Jamilia, Bettie Ray Butler, and Danielle Smith. "The Cause of Black Females' Disproportionate Suspension Rates." Edited by Daniel J. Losen. *Closing the School Discipline Gap: Equitable Remedies for Excessive Exclusion.* New York: Teachers College Press, 2015.

Brookfield, Stephen D. *The Power of Critical Theory: Liberating Adult Learning and Teaching.* San Francisco: Jossey-Bass, 2005.

Budge, Stephanie L., Sergio Domínguez Jr., and Abbie E. Goldberg. "Minority Stress in Nonbinary Students in Higher Education: The Role of Campus Climate and Belongingness." *Psychology of Sexual Orientation and Gender Diversity* 7, no. 2 (2020): 222–229. https://doi.org/10.1037/sgd0000360.

Case, Kim A. "Toward an Intersectional Pedagogy Model." *Intersectional Pedagogy: Complicating Identity and Social Justice.* Edited by Kim A. Case. New York: Routledge, 2017.

Chambers, Crystal R. *Black Female Undergraduates on Campus: Successes and Challenges (Diversity in Higher Education).* Edited by Crystal R. Chamers and Rhonda V. Sharpe. Bingley: Emerald Group Publishing Limited, 2012.

Cholewa, Blaire, Ellen Amatea, Cirecie A. West-Olatunji, and Ashley Wright. "Examining the Relational Processes of a Highly Successful Teacher of African American Children." *Urban Education* 47, no.1 (2011): 250–279.

Cokley, Kevin O. *The Myth of Black Anti-intellectualism: A True Psychology of African American Students.* Santa Barbara: Praeger, 2015.

Collins, Patricia Hill. *Black Feminist Thought: Knowledge, Consciousness, and the Politics of Empowerment.* New York: Routledge, 2000.

Crenshaw, Kimberle Williams. "Mapping the Margins: Intersectionality, Identity Politics, and Violence Against Women of Color." *Stanford Law Review* 43, (1991): 1241–1299.

Crenshaw, Kimberle. "Demarginalizing the Intersection of Race and Sex: A Black Feminist Critique of Antidiscrimination Doctrine, Feminist Theory, and Antiracist Politics." *University of Chicago Legal Forum* (1989): 139–167.

Delgado, Richard and Jean Stefancic. *Critical Race Theory: An Introduction.* New York: University Press, 2017.

Diemer, Matthew A., Aimee Kauffman, Nathan Koenig, Emily Trahan, and Chueh-An Hsieh. "Challenging Racism, Sexism, and Social Injustice: Support for Urban

Adolescents' Critical Consciousness Development." *Cultural Diversity and Ethnic Minority Psychology* 12, no. 3 (2006): 444–460. https://doi.org/10.1037/1099-9809.12.3.444.

Ellis, Carolyn, Tony Adams, and Arthur Bochner. "Autoethnography: An Overview." *Forum: Qualitative Social Research* 11, no. 1 (2011). http://dx.doi.org/10.17169/fqs-12.1.1589.

Flowers, Alonzo M., Jameel A. Scott, Jamie R. Riley, and Robert T. Palmer. "Beyond the Call of Duty: Building on Othermothering for Improving Outcomes at Historically Black Colleges and Universities." *Journal of African American Males in Education* 6, no. 1 (2015): 59–73.

Ford, Amy Carpenter and Kelly Sassi. "Authority in Cross-Racial Teaching and Learning (Re)considering the Transferability of Warm Demander Approaches." *Urban Education* 49 (2014): 39–74.

Foucault, Michael. *The History of Sexuality: An Introduction.* New York: Pantheon Books, 1978.

Garza, Ruben, "Latino and White High School Students' Perception of Caring Behaviors." *Urban Education* 44, (2009): 297–321.

Goldberg, Abbie E., JuliAnna Z. Smith, and Genny Beemyn. "Trans Activism and Advocacy among Transgender Students in Higher Education: A Mixed Methods Study." *Journal of Diversity in Higher Education* 13, no. 1 (2020): 66–84. https://doi.org/10.1037/dhe0000125.

Goldberg, Abbie E., Katherine Kuvalanka, and Lore Dickey. "Transgender Graduate Students' Experiences in Higher Education: A Mixed-Methods Exploratory Study." *Journal of Diversity in Higher Education* 12, no. 1 (2019): 38–51. https://doi.org/10.1037/dhe0000074.

Grzanka, Patrick. "Undoing the Psychology of Gender." *Intersectional Pedagogy: Complicating Identity and Social Justice.* Edited by Kim Case. New York: Routledge, 2017.

Harmat, Gal. *Intersectional Pedagogy: Creative Education Practices for Gender and Peace Work.* New York: Routledge, 2020.

Hatfield, Tammy. "Multicultural Issues in Counseling and Education." Syllabus, University of the Cumberlands, Kentucky, Spring 2020.

Kleinfeld, Judith. "Effective Teachers of Eskimo and Indian Students". *School Review* 83, (1975): 301–344.

Ladson-Billings, Gloria. *The Dreamkeepers: Successful Teachers of African American Children.* San Francisco: Jossey-Bass, 1994.

Ladson-Billings, Gloria. "Culturally Relevant Pedagogy 2.0: a.k.a. The Remix." *Harvard Educational Review* 84, no.1 (2014): 74–84. https://doi.org/10.17763/haer.84.1.p2rj1314854847451.

Lubicz-Nawrocka, Tanya and Kieran Bunting. "Student Perceptions of Teaching Excellence: An Analysis of Student-Led Teaching Award Nomination Data." *Teaching in Higher Education* 24, no. 1 (2019): 63–80. https://doi.org/10.1080/13562517.2018.1461620.

Martin, Andrew J. and Rebecca J. Collie. "Teacher–Student Relationships and Students' Engagement in High School: Does the Number of Negative and Positive Relationships with Teachers Matter?" *Journal of Educational Psychology* 111, no. 5 (2019): 861–76. https://doi.org/10.1037/edu0000317.

Mendez, Linda. M. Raffaelle and Howard M. Knoff. "Who Gets Suspended from School and Why: A Demographic Analysis of Schools and Disciplinary Infractions in a Large School District." *Education and Treatment of Children* 26, (2013): 30–51.

Merriam-Webster. "Pedagogy." Accessed August 1, 2020. https://www.merriam-webster.com/dictionary/pedagogy.

Morris, Monique. *Pushout: The Criminalization of Black Girls in Schools.* New York: New Press, 2015.

Morris, Monique W. "Protecting Black girls." *Educational Leadership* 74, no. 3 (2016): 49–53.

Nemi Neto, Joao. "Queer Pedagogy: Approaches to Inclusive Teaching." *Policy Futures in Education* 16, no. 5 (2018): 589–604.

Onufer, Lindsay and Lizette Munos Rojas. "Teaching at PITT: Introduction to Feminist Pedagogy." *University Times,* (2019). https://www.utimes.pitt.edu/news/teaching-pitt-8.

Ortiz, Larry and Ani Jayshree. "Critical Race Theory: A Transformational Model for Teaching Diversity." *Journal of Social Work Education* 46, no. 2 (2010): 175–193.

Phinney, Jean S., Cindy Lou Cantu, and Dawn A. Kurtz. "Ethnic and American Identity as Predictors of Self-Esteem Among African American, Latino, and White adolescents." *Journal of Youth and Adolescence* 26, no. 2 (1997): 165–185.

Prilleltensky, Isaac and Ora Prilleltensky. "Synergies for Wellness and Liberation in Counseling Psychology." *The Counseling Psychologist* 31, no. 3 (2003): 273–281. https://doi.org/10.1177/0011000003252957.

Roorda, Debra L., Helma M. Koomen, Jantine L. Spilt and Frans J. Oort. "The Influence of Affective Teacher–Student Relationships on Students' School Engagement and Achievement: A Meta-Analytic Approach". *Review of Educational Research* 81 (2011): 493–529. https://doi:10.3102/0034654311421793.

Rubin, Gayle. "The Traffic in Women: Notes on the Political Economy of Sex." *Toward an Anthropology of Women,* (1975): 157–210.

Vaudrin-Charette, Julie. "Melting the Cultural Iceberg in Indigenizing Higher Education: Shifts to Accountability in Times of Reconciliation." *New Directions for Teaching and Learning* 157 (2019): 105–118. https://doi.org/10.1002/tl.20333n.

Wang, Victor C.X. and Geraldine Torrisi-Steele. "Online Teaching, Change, and Critical Theory." *New Horizons in Adult Education & Human Resource Development* 27, no.3 (2015): 18–26.

Watts, Roderick, Matthew Diemer, and Adam Voight. "Critical Consciousness: Current Status and Future Directions." *New Directions for Child and Adolescent Development,* no. 134 (2011): 43–57. https://doi.org/10.1002/cd.310.

Yosso, Tara J., Laurence Parker, Daniel G. Solorzano and Marvin Lynn. "From Jim Crow to Affirmative Action and Back Again: A Critical Race Discussion of Racialized Rationales and Access to Higher Education." *Review of Research in Education* 28, (2004): 1–27.

CHAPTER 3

The Dangers of "You Are Not Your Own"

How Purity Culture Props Up Rape Culture

Tara M. Tuttle

Purity culture is the cornerstone of rape culture. Though its proponents believe it promotes protection and high regard for women, it results in objectification, fragmentation, victim-blaming, hostile and benevolent sexism, and rape apologism. Purity culture also encourages submissiveness and discourages agency among women and girls. The promotion of purity culture by Christians makes their faith communities not merely complicit in rape culture but responsible for one of its pillars. This chapter will discuss how the damaging messages circulated in purity culture serve to prop up rape culture not only by encouraging sexualization, objectification, and fragmentation, but also by fostering silence and shame surrounding both consensual sexual activity and nonconsensual sexual violence. This culture of silence and shame often discourages survivors from reporting assaults and misconduct, prevents survivors from accessing resources and support they need, and leads to the complicity of relatives, community members, and even church officials in ensuring perpetrators are shielded from responsibility for their crimes.

1 What Is Purity Culture?

The term "purity culture" may refer broadly to any set of cultural beliefs that construe sexual activity as contaminating or impure; more specifically, in this chapter it refers to a Christian social movement following and reacting to the sexual liberation movement of the 1970s and the AIDS crisis of the 1980s. This movement was solidified by the development and dissemination of Christian sexual education curricula emphasizing abstinence from sexual activity and sexual thoughts. Such curricula also fail to include accurate information about contraceptives, sexually transmitted infections, LGBTQ sexualities, and abortion. The True Love Waits program founded in 1993 by Richard Ross and a team at Lifeway Christian Resources became the most prominent of these, and its messages were circulated via pledge cards, posters, t-shirts, books, Christian popular music albums, rings marking one's commitment to remain a virgin until marriage, and other paraphernalia in addition to the curricula adopted by numerous congregations.[1]

Initially adopted by Southern Baptist churches, its scope expanded denominationally and internationally within a year as the program was embraced by other Christian groups including the Assemblies of God and the Roman Catholic Church. By the late 1990s, reports from the True Love Waits staff at Lifeway were distributed to the U.S. Surgeon General, the U.S. Senate and House of Representatives, and other officials and were used to influence decisions about government-funded abstinence-only sexual education campaigns.[2] By 2004, BBC News reported that over 2.5 million American teens had taken a virginity pledge.[3] Teens of various genders comprised these pledgers, but for girls, purity culture sometimes also included father-daughter dances called purity balls, during which they would verbalize a pledge that cast their fathers as the guardians of their chastity until their marriages to male spouses.

At no point in my research did I discover evidence of similar events involving mothers and sons as part of this purity movement. This discrepancy illustrates the way in which purity culture tilts toward the control of the bodies of women and girls. Boys and men have not been free from its messages and damaging effects, but its emphasis has been upon the repression of female sexuality. This reaffirms the male control inherent in patriarchy in positing fathers as protectors over daughters but not mothers over sons and illuminates how boys are seen as agents whereas girls are reduced to their bodies as objects. It also exemplifies how the sexuality of boys is less a source of shame and that the virginity of boys is less of a concern in purity culture; boys are subject to fewer rituals that reinforce the notion that their holiness is tied to their abstinence.

Purity culture then as I refer to it in this chapter includes the social scripts about sexual practices that targeted American teenagers in the 1990s and 2000s linking Christian belief and identity to abstinence, social scripts disseminated in abstinence-only sexual education programs, individual congregations, movements like True Love Waits with its abundance of merchandise such as purity rings and t-shirts, book and pamphlet publications, conferences, and church materials such as pledge cards and curricula, and the megaphones of the loose network of political and religious organizations called the religious

---

1 Lifeway Christian Resources, "True Love Waits History," *True Love Waits* (2020), https://s7d9.scene7.com/is/content/LifeWayChristianResources/True_Love_Waits_Historypdf.pdf (accessed June 23, 2020).

2 Ibid.

3 BBC News, How effective are abstinence pledges?, *BBC News* (June 29, 2004). http://news.bbc.co.uk/2/hi/uk_news/magazine/3846687.stm (Accessed 6 23, 2020).

right, which includes Focus on the Family, the Council for Biblical Manhood and Womanhood, and the Southern Baptist Convention. Purity culture extends beyond what I have named here and is not confined to practitioners of Christianity or to American contexts, but this describes what I consider the epicenter of purity culture in the United States.

2   What Is Rape Culture?

The term "rape culture" was used in the 1974 book *Rape: The First Sourcebook for Women* by the New York Radical Feminists[4] to describe an environment in which sexual assault is rampant and in which this violence is normalized, minimized, trivialized, or otherwise tacitly accepted. It is perpetuated through the objectification of bodies, typically the bodies of women and girls, largely through media representations of sexualization and violence; through indifference to this violence on the part of law enforcement, political officials, administrators of institutions exhibited by victim-blaming procedures and policies that are not trauma-informed, along with barriers to holding perpetrators responsible for their crimes; through language about sex, violence, intimacy, and bodies that is dehumanizing and the widespread acceptance of myths about how rape happens and to whom; and through the impact of members of society knowing that consequences of sexual assault are so rare for perpetrators and so high for victims that women and girls modify their behavior in daily life to address the threat of sexual violence. In a rape culture, the burden of the responsibility for sexual violence is placed on the victim; vulnerable populations are expected to modify their behaviors to avoid getting raped. Consequently, many women and girls, both cisgender and transgender, and members of LGBQ+ populations are likely to live according to a "rape schedule," a term coined by Dianne Herman[5] in 1984 to name the way women and girls are likely to make choices intended to reduce the threat of sexual violence including but not limited to when they go out, which paths they take, how they dress, whether they travel alone or in groups, in which activities they engage and with whom, whether or not they consume alcohol or drugs, and

---

4 New York Radical Feminists, *Rape: The First Sourcebook* (New York: New American Library, 1974).

5 Dianne F. Herman, "The Rape Culture," in *Women: A Feminist Perspective*, by Ed. Jo Freeman (Mountain View, Co: Mayfield, 1984). http://homepage.smc.edu/delpiccolo_guido/soc1/soc1readings/rape%20culture_final.pdf.

other decisions, both conscious and unconscious, affecting their activities and interactions of daily life.

3   Male Domination, Female Submission, Anti-autonomy

Women and girls inhabiting a rape culture often become accustomed to commonplace restrictions that hinder them from equal access to opportunities and experiences. While not all men are perpetrators of sexual violence, and while men and boys are also victims of sexual violence, men and boys as a group benefit from the ways in which the threat of violence restricts the full participation of women and girls in the culture. Purity culture, too, restricts what is considered acceptable from girls and women and reinforces traditional ideas about gender norms that maintain a gender binary and reinforce separate spheres of activity for men and women. Together, rape culture and purity culture reinforce the male dominance of patriarchy and women's subsequent subjugation.

Sexist interpretations of Christian beliefs are significant pillars of patriarchy, purity culture, and rape culture. Consider the following commentary from the *Men's Devotional Bible*: "*Little boys are the hope of the next generation*. Little girls, too, will benefit because they'll grow up with a clear vision of the kind of men who will make godly husbands."[6] Why are little girls not also the hope of the next generation? They are assumed to be absent from the group of those who would contribute to the improvement of the community, at least in the public realm. They are assumed to be mere supporters of those young boys who will become the change agents in the culture rather than change agents themselves. This reaffirms the ways in which both purity culture and rape culture reduce women to vulnerable bodies valuable only when deemed chaste, i.e., uncontaminated by sexual activity and sexual violence.

This quoted passage reminds me of a conversation I had in 2008 with young female students attending Liberty University as undergraduates. These young women explained to me the current dress code at Liberty University actually offered more flexibility for young women, in their opinion, because they were permitted to wear hooded sweatshirts while young men were not. "Why not?" I asked, unprepared for the justification. "Because the boys will be entering the workforce," one young woman explained. "They have to wear business casual every day to get ready for their jobs," another chimed in. These young women

---

6   *Men's Devotional Bible*, NIV (Zondervan, 1993, p. 651).

did not need to become accustomed to work dress codes because the assumption was that they would not enter the workforce like their male counterparts. They were expected to dress modestly but not professionally. I was familiar with Liberty University's conservative positions on gender and sexuality, but the conversation was still stunning to me for the acceptance with which these bright young women pursuing their educations dismissed such obvious sexism and segregation of opportunity based on gender. They did not fail to see it; they laughed at my raised eyebrows and widened eyes. One young woman said, "I know, right?," but they tacitly accepted the premise that they were future homemakers. The problem here is coercion, not the life path itself. We must be mindful of how poor women and women of color, groups which often overlap due to systemic racism, have been denied opportunities to be stay-at-home mothers when they might have welcomed such a privilege, but the discouragement of young women from entering the workforce means discouraging them from economic self-sufficiency and from finding meaning and purpose in professions and vocations beyond the home and church. This further establishes male domination in their communities, in their churches, and in their relationships. This inhibits their autonomy.

This is the legacy of what historian Barbara Welter calls the "Cult of True Womanhood" which promoted piety, purity, domesticity, and submissiveness as virtues for women and girls.[7] Male domination and female submission are reinforced explicitly within purity culture. Purity culture teaches girls literally that their bodies are not their own. This phrasing comes from 1 Corinthians 6:19–20, which reads, "Or do you not know that your body is a temple of the Holy Spirit within you, whom you have from God? You are not your own, for you were bought with a price. So glorify God in your body." Though this verse does not explicitly address a message about gender, this verse was re-emphasized in the Council on Biblical Manhood and Womanhood's 2017 "Nashville Statement,"[8] an update and reaffirmation of the 1987 "Danvers Statement"[9] articulating the council's beliefs about what the Bible instructs about gender and sexuality. Called "the Nashville Statement" because it was drafted in the August 2017 Nashville gathering of the Southern Baptist Convention by their

---

7   Barbara Welter, "The Cult of True Womanhood: 1820–1860." *American Quarterly* 18, no. 2 (1966): 151–74. Accessed October 4, 2020. doi:10.2307/2711179.

8   Council of Biblical Manhood and Womanhood, "Nashville Statement" (2017), CBMW, https://cbmw.org/nashville-statement/ (Accessed June 29, 2020).

9   Council of Biblical Manhood and Womanhood, "Danvers Statement" (1988), CBMW, https://cbmw.org/about/danvers-statement/ (Accessed June 29, 2020).

Ethics and Religious Liberty Commission,[10] it states: "We are not our own. Our true identity, as male and female persons, is given by God. It is not only foolish, but hopeless, to try to make ourselves what God did not create us to be." This statement, which opposed marriage equality, LGBQ sexualities, transgender identities, polyamory, and extramarital sexual activity, currently has over 24,000 signers, which include council members, seminary presidents, pastors, theologians, editors, and lay persons from a variety of evangelical communities and institutions.

This statement speaks of both male and female persons, but it reinforces a complementarian, binary, essentialist, transphobic, and ultimately hierarchical view of gender that not only coerces individuals into adherence to traditional expressions of gender and sexuality but also coerces women into sexual activity. Upon entering marriage (heterosexual, of course, according to the Southern Baptist Convention and other denominations that oppose marriage equality), women still are not entitled to full ownership of their bodies under purity culture at any point. Married women who decline sex with their spouses are "selfish" according to Mark and Grace Driscoll in their book, *Real Marriage.*[11] Mark Driscoll is an American evangelical author and former pastor of Mars Hill Church, a multi-site megachurch he co-founded. In this and other passages, the rhetoric he and his wife use reveals an understanding of women's bodies as belonging to their male spouses and not themselves and a prioritization of male desire over female consent.

Women's bodies are not only described as *for* men, women themselves are deemed incomplete without men in the Christian evangelical strain of purity culture. In *Captivating: Unveiling the Mystery of a Woman's Soul,* John and Stasi Eldredge write, "Mary had Joseph. Esther had Mordecai. Ruth had Boaz. We will not become the women God intends us to be without the guidance, counsel, wisdom, strength, and love of good men in our lives."[12] The insistence that women need heterosexual male partners is part of compulsory heterosexuality, a term used by Adrienne Rich to describe how heterosexuality and

---

10   Holly Meyer, "What is the Nashville Statement and Why Are People Talking About It?" (August 30, 2017), *The Tennessean,* https://www.tennessean.com/story/news/religion/2017/08/30/what-nashville-statement-and-why-people-talking-it/616064001/ (Accessed June 30, 2020).

11   Grace Driscoll and Mark Driscoll, *Real Marriage: The Truth About Sex, Friendship, and Life Together* (Nashville, TN: Thomas Nelson, 2012), 156.

12   Stasi and John Eldredge, *Captivating Revised and Updated: Unveiling the Mystery Of A Woman's Soul* (Nashville: Nelson Books, 2010), 223.

male domination are enforced within patriarchy.[13] Wanda Swan, Director
and Founder of The Swan Center for Advocacy & Research, explains, "Young
girls and women are not seen as whole people deserving of holistic agency,
but rather these bringers of the gift of virginity and upholders of strict heteronormative relationship dynamics."[14] One might assume this burden is placed
equally on both men and women, but in practice differences abound. "Young
boys and men don't face the same amount of scrutiny as women and girls,
but there they also lack general education around consent and non-heteronormative bodily autonomy. They are taught to value some people, women,
over others, and that this value must always cater to those who have a closer
proximity to the set standards of sexual purity," Swan clarifies.[15] Not only are
the bodies of women and girls deemed not their own because their bodies
belong to God, but their bodies are even further removed from self-possession
in that they belong to fathers and then spouses. In purity culture, the specter
of the future male spouse looms so large that girls are coerced into abstinence
and modesty in order to retain their value for a man they may not have even
yet met.

4   Objectification and Fragmentation

This thinking casts their bodies, particularly the sexualized portions of their
bodies, as objects. Purity culture is a form of objectification that reduces and
assesses the value of women and girls to what they do with or what is done to
the sexualized portions of bodies. My students have shared with me examples
of metaphors of chewed gum, rubbed peaches, tape that has lost its stickiness
and other "used," ostensibly undesirable objects to deter girls and women from
engaging in sexual activity as regular parts of their religious sexual educations. This thinking promotes a fragmented and sexualized understanding of
female bodies, and it deprives women and girls of autonomy in that it assigns
ownership of their bodies to entities other than themselves (fathers, future
spouses, and God). Laora Mastari, Bram Spruyt, and Jessy Siongers found in
their research of 755 parent-child dyads that among those promoting traditional beliefs about gender "women are continuously being subordinated and

---

13   Adrienne Rich, "Compulsory Heterosexuality and Lesbian Existence," *Signs: Journal of
      Women in Culture and Society* 5 no. 4 (1981): 631–660.
14   Interview with Wanda Swan, Director of The Swan Center for Advocacy & Research (June
      28, 2020).
15   Ibid.

gender equality is discouraged by persuading women that protection and love will be granted to them (by men) if they comply with these traditional and sexist beliefs. If not, men will have to react with hostile sexist attitudes in order to preserve the status quo."[16] Girls and women who do not comply with traditional gender role expectations and purity culture face the threats of rejection and violence.

However, men are not the only ones who strive to preserve patriarchy and the rape culture and purity culture that prop it up. Men are more likely to hold positions of authority that amplify their voices, but women, too, have participated in the dehumanizing messaging of purity culture. Describing the instruction of purity messaging from adult women in the church, Pastor Nadia Bolz-Weber writes, "The women who taught them were perpetuating a pernicious system of female submission and male domination. And yet, if all we girls had was this one form of currency, perhaps it was also generous and protective for older women to help us know how to make the most of it."[17] Older women perpetuate purity culture in damaging ways, as Bolz-Weber notes, but their motivations for doing so may be that they wish to help younger women and girls retain their value in a culture that already devalues them.

This means girls in purity culture are taught they are responsible for keeping their value by keeping themselves "pure," not only by remaining untouched in sexual ways but also by maintaining the appearance of purity through modesty. Popular Christian authors Hayley DiMarco and Justin Lookadoo write in *Dateable: Are You? Are They?* "A guy will have a tendency to treat you like you are dressed. If you are dressed like a flesh buffet, don't be surprised when he treats you like a piece of meat."[18] DiMarco's influence is wide in evangelical circles. She is also a co-founder of Hungry Planet, a company which creates spiritual content for teens. When she tells young women "don't be surprised when he treats you like a piece of meat,"[19] she is alleviating the hypothetical male date from responsibility for sexualizing and objectifying the young woman in question. DiMarco is also suggesting that showing skin is objectifying oneself, making oneself into a "flesh buffet," a metaphor of consumption

---

16   Laura Mastari, Bram Spruyt, and Jessy Siongers, "Benevolent and Hostile Sexism in Social Spheres: The Impact of Parents, School and Romance on Belgian Adolescents' Sexist Attitudes," *Frontiers in Sociology: Gender, Sex, & Sexualities* 4 (2019): Article 47, p. 4, doi:https://doi.org/10.3389/fsoc.2019.00047 (accessed June 27, 2020).
17   Nadia Bolz-Weber, *Shameless: A Sexual Reformation* (New York: Convergent Books, 2019), 36.
18   Hayley DiMarco and Justin Lookadoo, *Dateable: Are You? Are They?* (Grand Rapids, MI: Revell, 2003) 118.
19   Ibid.

that reinforces the idea of purity culture that young women's bodies, like their virginity, are objects to be presented and taken and that their value as young women is primarily tied to a state of not-having-been-sexually-active. This reinforces the idea that sexual activity is transactional, contaminating, and depleting rather than an act of shared intimacy, mutual desire, and pleasure that can foster partnership. Sex is not food to be consumed, yet it is telling that this metaphor is deployed in a way that focuses on the consumption rather than the nourishment of relationship that is possible though shared physical intimacy. The bodies of women and girls are not "leftovers" for another lover after an encounter with an initial sexual partner, but purity culture teaches this lesson. These understandings of sex reinforce the ways in which purity culture assesses value for women and girls based on what they have refrained from doing and kept others from doing to them rather than assessing them based upon other deeds and demonstrations of virtue, service, generosity, and compassion.

This objectification is not simply used as a deterrent for teenage sexuality. It is not merely a tool used to promote abstinence; it permeates messages about marital sexuality, too. Pastor Mark Driscoll offered the following commentary on a verse of Song of Solomon, telling women in the audience at Edinburgh Scotland, "your breasts are the petting zoo" for their male spouses.[20] The metaphor of a petting zoo, with its literal understanding of incarcerated animals visited by guests who pay their owners for the privilege of petting the captive creatures, is quite literally dehumanizing. Such a message both objectifies and fragments the bodies of married women and ascribes to married men an entitlement to the bodies of their wives. Not surprising, then, is what follows among men in the circles in which these messages circulate. Brandon Ambrosino reports for *Politico* that "Longtime Liberty officials close to [Jerry] Falwell [Jr.] told me the university president has shown or texted his male confidants— including at least one employee who worked for him at Liberty—photos of his wife in provocative and sexual poses."[21] Nonconsensual circulation of sexual or nude photographs is increasingly understood as a form of violence, but purity culture messaging has suggested even images of his wife's body are his to share in this way. She is not her own but his.

---

20   Mark Driscoll, "Sex, a Study of the Good Bits from Song of Solomon," Edinburgh, November 18, 2007, https://peterlumpkins.typepad.com/files/driscoll-scotland-sermon-copypdf.pdf (Accessed June 23, 2020).

21   Brandon Ambrosino, " 'Someone's Gotta Tell the Freakin' Truth': Jerry Falwell's Aides Break Their Silence," *Politico*, September 9, 2019, https://www.politico.com/magazine/story/2019/09/09/jerry-falwell-liberty-university-loans-227914 (Accessed May 21, 2020).

In this way, purity culture constitutes hostile sexism, the more overt sexism that makes apparent the investment in hierarchically arranged gender norms. Mastari, Spruyt, and Siongers explain, "Hostile sexism aims to preserve men's dominance over women by underlining men's power. It is expressed in a blatant and resentful way toward women who violate traditional roles. Women who don't comply with these traditional (gender) roles are perceived as a threat to men's dominant position. Hostile sexism overtly keeps women in a subordinate position and is even a precursor for sexual harassment and violence toward women."[22] Moreover, this hostile sexism is so pervasive it is written into sermons. Former president of both the Southern Baptist Convention and Southwestern Baptist Theological Seminary Paige Patterson included this "joke" in one of his messages at an Awaken Conference—a conference for young adults—in Las Vegas in 2014. Patterson relayed,

> About that time, a very attractive young co-ed walked by. And she wasn't more than about 16, but mmmmmm. Let me just say, she was nice. As she walked by, they didn't think that momma was paying any attention to them, and one young man turned to the other one and he said, "Man, is she built." In the middle of the synod, she stopped, wheeled around, slapped a hand over his mouth, loosened his teeth, said, "Young man, don't you ever say anything like that again. If you do, I'll mop up the face of the earth with you!" I saw my opportunity. I said, "Ma'am, leave him alone. He is just being biblical. That's exactly what the Bible said. Lord God brought her, he built her, and brought her unto the man!"[23]

Despite the sexism, pedophilia, and objectification in this story, Patterson would not be fired from his post at Southwestern Baptist Theological Seminary until 2018, four years after making these remarks. Over 3,300 women signed a letter calling for his resignation after Benjamin S. Cole began posting video of Patterson's sexism under the username "baptistblogger" on YouTube.

This incident was not, of course, an isolated occurrence of sexism. In addition to the objectification of teenage girls, Patterson also counseled victims of domestic violence to stay with their abusive husbands.[24] While the letter

---

22   Mastari, Spruyt, and Siongers, 2.

23   "Paige Patterson Objectifies a 16 Year Old Girl," YouTube. Posted by Benjamin S. Cole, edited by BaptistBlogger, May 6, 2018, https://www.youtube.com/watch?v=gDRUVmcaQ3k (Accessed September 13, 2020).

24   Letter to SWBTS Board of Trustees, May 6, 2018. https://swbtsletter.com (Accessed September 13, 2020).

writers' call for Patterson's resignation was both just and ultimately successful, the authors of this letter invoked a defense of purity culture in their argument to the SWBTS Board. They wrote that Patterson's "pattern of discourse ... fails in the call to protect the helpless, the call of Christ to love our neighbor as ourselves, and the biblical standard of sexual purity."[25] They found Patterson's objectification of the teenager too explicit and crude to abide but did not examine their own promotion of purity culture's inherent objectification that directs their leaders into believing it grants them permission to speak about women and girls in this degrading way.

Purity culture is rape culture because purity culture entails the ultimate form of objectification in its reduction of people, usually girls and women, to their bodies. This is the opposite of what adherents of purity messaging believe about the values they express; they argue that advocating "purity" is protective, is upholding the value of women and girls and even sexuality. However, its emphasis on the body has long-term damaging effects for those exposed to its ideas and contributes to a culture of violence. Purity culture manifests as both hostile and benevolent sexism. Benevolent sexism is biased behaviors or ideas rooted in ideas about gender that may seem positive to those expressing them, as many of the ideas expressed in purity culture seem positive to those who spread them. Mastari, Spruyt, and Siongers explain, "This form of sexism is instigated through paternal and traditional beliefs that perceive women as beautiful and pure, yet delicate and precious, and therefore in need of protection provided by men."[26] The "purity" of girls and women is ostensibly protected by fathers and churches whose teachings about chastity are intended to protect women from the devaluation believed to transpire through engagement of sexual activity. This perception of the inherent purity of women, however, has not historically been extended to Black women and other women and girls of color. This means purity culture also contributes to the discrimination and stereotyping these women and girls face. It can result in even stricter expectations of hyper-respectability by parents of young women or even the young women themselves in efforts to counteract racist beliefs about the supposed hypersexuality of Black women and girls and other women and girls of color. The gender hierarchy is not the only hierarchy purity culture reinforces.

---

25   Ibid.
26   Mastari, Spruyt, and Siongers, 2.

5   Purity Culture and White Supremacy

Purity culture is tangled up in the violence of white supremacy. Several blog-
gers of color have addressed the ways in which purity culture messaging casts
women of color, queer, and trans women as "starting from a deficit of purity."[27]
Tamara Winfrey Harris, former blogger, former senior editor of *Racialicious*
and author of *The Sisters Are Alright: Changing the Broken Narrative of Black
Women in America,* writes, "For us, gender-biased concepts of female sexuality
intersect with racist ones, leaving Black women fighting the stereotype that we
are innately hypersexual, and thus, particularly valueless."[28] Their work shares
testimony of the damage done by purity culture, but it differs in its analysis of
the ways in which white female bodies are assumed to be pure until acted upon,
but female bodies of color are deemed impure from the start and are subject
to suspicion in white supremacist cultures. Harris points out that sexual activity deemed impure when engaged in by a woman of color doesn't just sully
her reputation: "Our alleged irresponsible fornicating is blamed for everything
from the welfare state to urban violence and poverty. To fail at sexual purity
is not just to let down God (as if that isn't enough), but to let down 39 million
African Americans, while confirming racial stereotypes."[29] Calling this out and
offering analyses of Christian sexual ethics from a hermeneutic of pleasure,
these writers strive to dismantle purity culture and its role in white supremacy.
A hermeneutic is a theory or method of interpretation. These authors employ
a hermeneutic of pleasure to affirm the positive aspects of pleasure. For Crunk
Feminist Collective, Brittney Cooper, under the pen name of Crunktastic,
wrote, "Sex is a form of creative power. And it is in the literal fact of its creative aspects that we feel alive, fully human, and connected. I think God wants
nothing less than this for us, and that requires regular, intimate connections
of bodies, or at the very least a very regular, intentional and unapologetic intimate connection with our own body."[30]

These insights are shared by researchers and violence prevention advocates.
Wanda Swan, Director of The Swan Center for Research and Advocacy, explains,

---

27   Tamara Winfrey Harris, "Sunday Kind of Love: Sex and Spirituality in the Black Church,"
      Bitch Media, October 4, 2018, https://www.bitchmedia.org/article/sex-and-spirituality-in-
      the-black-church (accessed March 5, 2020).
28   Ibid.
29   Ibid.
30   Brittney Cooper, "Single, Saved, and Sexin: The Redux." Crunk Feminist Collective., March
      14, 2013 http://www.crunkfeministcollective.com/2013/03/14/single-saved-and-sex-in
      -the-redux/ (accessed March 5, 2020).

"Because Black women and girls' sexuality is so highly politicized by both the church and a host of other institutions, the presence of Black female-identified folks in these conversations almost always situates us at the intersection of weaponized religion, sexism and racism. There is a type of emotional whiplash that happens for us when we are subjected to layering the practice of purity culture on top of these other harms, because purity culture and religion's over-all shtick to the Black community are organically at odds."[31] The burden then of purity culture upon Black women and girls is even heavier than for white women and girls. Swan explains, "The outcome of purity culture, though not ideal for White women and girls, is starkly contradictory due to deeply-rooted sexual stereotypes of the 'unrapable' Black woman and the sexualized Black girl because of the lack of humanity that lies in the white supremacist gaze and governance of Black bodies. This also reverberates through our communities in the same way as others: with a strict hetero-normative lens, lack of com-munication around consent and pleasure, and a value being placed on those folks with close proximity to purity."[32] The results of this layering of oppressive ideologies are even more dire when sexual violence occurs.

6   Undermining Sexual Violence Prevention and Response

Purity culture is also rape culture in the ways it undermines sexual violence prevention and response measures. Because many forms of Christianity uphold patriarchy, many Christian communities fail victims of sexual vio-lence by enforcing a culture of silence through the shaming of survivors of sexual assault as less valuable following the assault, as responsible for the violence, and as less important than the perpetrator. Pastor Nadia Bolz-Weber asserts, "The issue behind most sexual harassment and misconduct is one of male domination, the kind that religion often tells us is 'God's will.' "[33] If male domination is believed to be the will of God, women and girls live in pre-carity, vulnerable to any men who would abuse such authority to perpetrate harassment, stalking, assault, and other forms of violence. Male domination as a religious ideology ensures men assume leadership positions, and the sta-tus and stature of these male leaders is often protected when allegations of

---

31   Interview with Wanda Swan, Director of The Swan Center for Advocacy & Research (June 28, 2020).

32   Ibid.

33   Nadia Bolz-Weber, *Shameless: A Sexual Reformation* (New York: Convergent Books, 2019), 44.

misconduct surface within congregations. Yet purity culture messages ensure harsh consequences for disclosure in the ways it objectifies women based upon constructions of "chastity." Rather than the perpetrator whose violence caused what is considered a loss of "purity," the victim is more commonly led to feel ashamed. A victim of sexual assault has little incentive to report the violence against them if revealing the assault results in public devaluation of their body and subsequently their self. Author of *Pure: Inside the Evangelical Movement that Shamed a Generation and How I Broke Free,* Linda Kay Klein writes, "the purity movement classifies sexual violence by systematically silencing and hiding it, and that if and when it is exposed, the purity movement then *mis*classifies sexual violence as 'sex' rather than 'violence.' "[34] This led the parents of one survivor Klein interviewed to consider their daughter not "solely a survivor, but also a sinner, and [they] were more focused on their daughter's sins and how they led to the loss of her 'purity' than on the violence that was perpetrated against her."[35] Purity culture is rape culture because it teaches the harmful myth that the raped body is worth less than the un-raped body. It teaches that any sexual contact, both consensual sex and nonconsensual violence, outside of heterosexual marriage devalues the touched body. It also shifts blame from the perpetrator of violence onto the victim of that violence.

What is especially appalling is that in purity culture's sexist applications, the body of the perpetrator is likely exempted from devaluation. Overwhelmingly, perpetrators of sexual violence are men,[36] and men's bodies are less regulated by purity culture. The bodies of men and boys are understood to be less contaminated (or not contaminated at all) by sexual activity. This is the inevitable consequence of the gender hierarchy of patriarchy. In *Purity and Danger* Mary Douglas writes, "It is not difficult to see how pollution beliefs can be used in a dialogue of claims and counter-claims to status. [...] patterns of sexual danger can be seen to express symmetry or hierarchy."[37] Even when victims of sexual violence are male, sexual violence reinforces the gender hierarchy inherent in patriarchy as victims of violence are understood as "feminized" through their

---

34   Linda Kay Klein, *Pure: Inside the Evangelical Movement That Shamed a Generation of Young Women and How I Broke Free* (New York: Atria Books, 2019), 91.

35   Ibid.

36   Centers for Disease Control, The National Intimate Partner and Sexual Violence Survey 2010 Summary Report. November 2011, https://www.cdc.gov/violenceprevention/pdf/nisvs_report2010-a.pdf (accessed September 13, 2020).

37   Mary Douglas, *Purity and Danger*, (New York, NY: Routledge Classics, 2004; Originally published 1966) 4.

disempowerment regardless of gender in a culture that understands power as more clearly affiliated with traditional understandings of masculinity and men.

Consider again the accusation that girls and women who dress in a way that does not conceal their skin are creating a "flesh buffet."[38] Linda Kay Klein explains how such understandings of girls' and women's bodies can have devastating effects. She writes, "At first glance, the modesty doctrine may appear harmless—perhaps even healthy—but the logic of victim-blaming that we too often see in rape cases begins here. When we demand that an individual dress in just the right way so as not to inspire sexual feelings in others, we set a precedent of blaming individuals for the thoughts feelings, and actions of other people that can play out in dangerous ways in rape and abuse cases."[39] This shifting of blame runs counter to the message of Matthew 5:29 in which Jesus instructs listeners to gouge out their own eyes if they lead them into sin, a message of personal responsibility for guarding one's own behavior.

Violence prevention advocates routinely see the damage done by purity culture upon the survivors they serve. Survivors who have grown up hearing purity culture messaging may have a harder time navigating the aftermath of an assault because the way purity culture ideology assesses value further traumatizes them. Cara Tuttle Bell, Director of the Project Safe Center for Sexual Misconduct Prevention and Response at Vanderbilt University, asserts, "Purity culture reinforces discomfort and fear in confronting issues related to sexuality and sexual harm. The inability to confront and explore sexual health and, indeed, sexual pleasure is a primary obstacle in educating or re-educating young adults to view sexual activity as a collaborative form of communication involving verbal and nonverbal practices that are sometimes fraught with risk."[40] Fellow violence prevention and response advocate Wanda Swan explains "Purity culture absolutely hinders anti-violence work in three major ways: (1) it refuses to address consent; (2) it reinforces gendered stereotypes that supports patriarchy, inequity, and the male gaze; and (3) it victim blames survivors of violence by equating their experience with failing God. [...] Purity culture is dangerous in how it stifles, silences, and sustains rape culture in the name of God for the preservation of the traditional family unit recognized by the church. Its negative impact is one that many of us in this field, as both educators and advocates, work to unravel within our specific communities."[41]

38   DiMarco and Lookadoo, 118.
39   Klein, 92.
40   Interview with Cara Tuttle Bell, Director of the Project Safe Center for Sexual Misconduct Prevention and Response at Vanderbilt University (June 27, 2020).
41   Interview with Wanda Swan, Director of The Swan Center for Advocacy & Research (June 28, 2020).

Purity culture's demands make it hard for victims of sexual violence to report their assaults and get the assistance they need, including medical attention, psychological services, family support, and legal recourse. Purity culture is rape culture for these explicit reasons and the ways in which it suggests harmed individuals are somehow responsible for and devalued by their own rapes. The devastating effects of this on survivors is obvious, but activists of faith also point out how the way purity culture functions as rape culture also harms religious communities. Too many survivors have turned to their churches for support and found their leaders complicit in promoting shame and silence. Author, attorney, and survivor Rachael Denhollander writes of institutional betrayals, "This damages God's children. It damages the gospel. And it should matter. Even, and especially, when it hurts and costs. Not because we want the church, or the gospel damaged, but because we want it seen in all its true beauty, and this mars it horribly."[42] When she led the group of hundreds of gymnasts who came forward against perpetrator Larry Nassar, Denhollander did not find her own church supportive. Denhollander wrote for *The New York Times*, "I lost my church. [...] Fear of jeopardizing some overarching political, religious, financial or other ideology—or even just losing friends or status—leads to willful ignorance of what is right in front of our own eyes."[43] When church leaders shield perpetrators from consequences, they are complicit in rape culture. Church leaders who perpetrate harassment and violence and those who shield perpetrators create an environment that fosters further violence in the way they tacitly sanction such conduct. Furthermore, their own silence on the issue of sexual violence as sin is another way that churches prop up rape culture. Linda Kay Klein writes a statement in *Pure* that I could have written myself: "I've never seen a sermon crafted for people who suffered from sexual trauma."[44] In refusing to name sexual violence as a significant social problem or sin to be avoided, churches bear responsibility for helping to create the rape culture in which we live.

Fortunately, some congregations and their pastors do address the issue of sexual violence. Pastor Nadia Bolz-Weber writes, "Being bearers of God's image allows us to insist on the self-determination of our bodies and our pleasure

---

42   Rachael Denhollander, Facebook Post, May 1, 2018, https://www.facebook.com/notes/
       rachael-denhollander/when-its-in-our-own-community-evangelicals/1807296366017342/
       (accessed September 13, 2020).

43   Rachael Denhollander, "The Price I Paid for Taking On Larry Nassar," *The New York Times*,
       January 26, 2018, https://www.nytimes.com/2018/01/26/opinion/sunday/larry-nassar
       -rachael-denhollander.html?smid=tw-share (accessed September 13, 2020).

44   Klein, 94.

and our hearts. [...] It allows us to call out and reject harassment, assault, the sexualization of children, and every other thing that compromises the inherent dignity of human bodies."[45] In order to combat rape culture's relationship to Christianity, more clergy should follow the model of Bolz-Weber's direct and scripture-backed approach to discussing a Christian sexual ethics without endorsing a culture of shame.

7   Anti-pleasure, Anti-desire

The consequences of the shame taught by purity culture can be devastating. Not only do those consequences deter reporting of sexual violence among victims, but they also prevent those unharmed by sexual violence from engaging in healthy, pleasurable sex as consenting adults. Tina Schermer Sellers, director of the Medical Family Therapy Program at Seattle Pacific University writes, "One of the things I started noticing about ten years ago was that I was seeing more and more amounts of sexual shame, of religious sexual shame [...] horrendous amounts. The self-loathing that people were feeling and describing about themselves really paralleled the kind of self-loathing that you often see with somebody who's experienced childhood sexual assault."[46] This is not sexual health. Purity culture is rape culture in that it impedes sexual health even among many adults who have adhered to its regulations.

The World Health Organization's definition of sexual health asserts "Sexual health requires a positive and respectful approach to sexuality and sexual relationships, as well as the possibility of having pleasurable and safe sexual experiences, free of coercion, discrimination and violence."[47] Individuals in purity cultures are subject to an emphasis upon contaminating understandings of sexuality that do not simply evaporate overnight upon entering into marriage. Both Bolz-Weber and Klein observed in their interviews with adults who had grown up hearing purity culture messages the problem of shame interfering with sexual pleasure even within adult, consensual, marital sexual relationships. They often still experience shame surrounding sex acts and sometimes

---

45   Bolz-Weber, 45.

46   Tina Schermer Sellers, "Sexuality and Spirituality," *The Sexuality and Spirituality Forum.* Seattle: The Seattle School of Theology and Psychology, 2012, https://digitalcommons.spu .edu/av_events/95/ (accessed June 27, 2020).

47   World Health Organization, "Defining Sexual Health," *WHO* (2020) https://www.who .int/reproductivehealth/topics/sexual_health/sh_definitions/en/ (accessed September 13, 2020).

ignorance of the mechanics of pleasure and sexual response. In "Naked and Ashamed: Women and Evangelical Purity Culture," Amanda Barbee writes, "Growing up within the purity movement, I was never taught about my own sexual response and sexual desire; I was only taught how to control the sexual response of the men around me."[48] Given the aforementioned messages to married couples about male entitlement to female bodies and the prioritization of male desire, women raised in purity cultures are often left without crucial models or knowledge that would facilitate their own embrace of a healthy sexuality that includes the pursuit of pleasure. Bolz-Weber refers to this as "sexual flourishing." "Sexual flourishing is for every type of body, every type of gender, every type of sex drive, every type of human," she insists.[49] "What does sexual flourishing look like? It looks like: Incarnation, Gratitude and generosity, Everyone, without exception, Accompaniment, Forgiveness, Connection, Holiness, Poetry, Shamelessness," she explains.[50] This is not an argument for sexual lawlessness and abandon but for an approach to sexuality that prioritizes consent, knowledge, and agency, not in spite of but because of faith. She writes, "These principles, which the faith provides us, can be our guide. They can lead us through our sexual reformation, through redefining the stale and oppressive sexual ethic the church has taught for so long. They can lead us to become good stewards of our bodies and of others' bodies. They can provide insight into what we teach our children about sex and their bodies, and what we teach ourselves about sex and our bodies. They were there all along."[51]

Desire can emerge from care and love instead of from objectification, but purity culture teaches that desire is lust and that lust is exploitative, contaminating, and degrading to the worth of those who engage in sex. Those exposed to purity messaging learn that they have to suppress desire to establish love and to establish love before engaging in sexual activity to that the sex will "mean something." But it never meant that women and girls were not still objectified. It meant that they were objectified and loved at the same time, that love makes the objectification acceptable or that love reduces the possibility of objectification. This is obviously not always the case. Consider what some evangelical leaders have instructed husbands and wives about marital sexuality and what

---

48   Amanda Barbee, "Naked and Ashamed: Women and Evangelical Purity Culture," *The Other Journal: An Intersection of Theology and Culture*, March 3, 2014, https://theotherjournal .com/2014/03/03/naked-and-ashamed-women-and-evangelical-purity-culture/ (accessed June 23, 2020).

49   Bolz-Weber, 192.

50   Bolz-Weber, 198.

51   Ibid.

prominent leaders have said and done to their own wives. Their remarks reveal the objectification is part of how they understand even marital sexuality.

8   Conclusion

Many of the writers and activists I have quoted in this chapter are grappling with the purity culture messaging of their religious communities and specifically the interpretations of scripture on which purity culture depends. This is of course a feminist hermeneutic, but one that specifically depends upon a premise of a right to pleasure while specifically engaging the politics of pleasure through a sacred lens. Their reconsiderations of the damage of purity culture messaging ask us to consider a reinterpretation of God as a creator who affirms pleasure, who bestowed pleasure, specifically sexual pleasure, upon humans. Concurrently, they resist and reject interpretations of scripture that preach a gospel of shame and contamination central to purity culture. They vehemently reject the way purity culture depends upon the objectification of women, the absolute reduction of their worth to what has and has not happened to their bodies.

Sellers writes, "When we continue to shroud sexuality in silence and an abstinence only discourse, we continue to burden faith filled children, adolescents, young adults and adults with a deep shame that interrupts their ability to fully know God's love and grace. Shame modulates distance in intimacy and sexual expression in the monogamous relationships that are foundational to community living and a significant expression of God's active love."[52] The instruction of shame is, in the view of many, counter-biblical. As Bolz-Weber interprets the creation stories in the first three chapters of the book of Genesis, she says, "The very first blessing was sex."[53] Moreover, she adds, "Let us grieve that we were not taught to love and respect the inherent dignity of our own human bodies. Grieve the decades we avoided sex when we could have been enjoying sex."[54] This understanding reflects an appreciation for a creator God who designed bodies for pleasure, not domination, and a rejection of rape culture and the purity culture on which it depends.

---

52   Tina Schermer Sellers, "Christians Caught Between the Sheets—How 'abstinence only' Ideology Hurts Us," *The Other Journal: An Intersection of Theology & Culture* 7 (Gender & Sexuality Issue 2006), https://theotherjournal.com/2006/04/02/christians-caught -between-the-sheets-how-abstinence-only-ideology-hurts-us/ (accessed June 27, 2020).

53   Bolz-Weber, 30.

54   Bolz-Weber, 158.

Old Testament scholar Katherine Sakenfeld asserts, "Christian feminists who intend and hope, like the biblical prophets, to work within their religious heritage must address themselves to the authority of the Bible in the life of their community of faith. They must seek faithful ways of recovering, reinterpreting, and discerning God's way in the tradition handed on in the Bible."[55] The hermeneutic of pleasure deployed by Bolz-Weber, Klein, Cooper, and other contemporary Christian feminists challenging purity culture reinterprets the bible's messages about human sexuality in ways that refuse the reduction of sexuality to procreation, that reject the idea that non-procreative sex is shameful and contaminating, that negates an understanding of pleasure as inherently threatening, and which demands agency, consent, and accurate information as crucial to engaging in sexual activity in accordance with a Christian ethic of dignity and sacredness of human life. "Purity is not the same as holiness. [...] Purity most often leads to pride or to despair, not to holiness. Because holiness is about union *with*, and purity is about separation *from*," Bolz-Weber clarifies.[56] The embrace of purity culture currently separates many Christian communities from possibly playing a role in undermining rape culture because purity culture perpetuates it. Propping up rape culture must be understood, in any theology that affirms the dignity of each human life, to hinder the pursuit of holiness by these communities. May these communities hear the calls of Bolz-Weber, Klein, Cooper, Denhollander, Harris, Tuttle Bell, Swan, Barbee, Sellers, this author, and others to divest from purity culture, to stand in solidarity with survivors of sexual violence, and to affirm the sexual flourishing of their members, regardless of gender identity and sexual orientation. This requires abandoning the conservative interpretation of "you are not your own" promoted by purity culture proponents that dehumanizes and objectifies girls and women and advocating instead for the instruction of sexual ethic that asserts a right to safety, pleasure, affirmative consent, and accurate knowledge about bodies, sexualities, and sexual practices for all.

Bibliography

Ambrosino, Brandon. "'Someone's Gotta Tell the Freakin' Truth': Jerry Falwell's Aides Break Their Silence." *Politico.* September 9, 2019. Accessed 5 21, 2020. https://www.politico.com/magazine/story/2019/09/09/jerry-falwell-liberty-university-loans-227914.

55   Katherine Sakenfeld, "Feminist Uses of Biblical Materials," *Feminist Interpretation of the Bible,* edited by Letty M. Russell (Philadelphia: The Westminster Press, 1985) 55.
56   Bolz-Weber, 22, 26.

Anonymous. *Men's Devotional Bible,* NIV, Grand Rapids, MI: Zondervan Publishing House, 1993.

Barbee, Amanda. "Naked and Ashamed: Women and Evangelical Purity Culture." *The Other Journal: An Intersection of Theology and Culture.* March 3, 2014. Accessed June 23, 2020. https://theotherjournal.com/2014/03/03/naked-and-ashamed-women -and-evangelical-purity-culture/.

BBC News. How effective are abstinence pledges? *BBC News.* June 29, 2004. Accessed June 23, 2020. http://news.bbc.co.uk/2/hi/uk_news/magazine/3846687.stm.

Bell, Cara Tuttle, interview by Tara Tuttle. Director of the Project Safe Center for Sexual Misconduct Prevention and Response at Vanderbilt University (June 27, 2020).

Bolz-Weber, Nadia. *Shameless: A Sexual Reformation.* New York: Convergent Books.

Centers for Disease Control, 2019. The National Intimate Partner and Sexual Violence Survey 2010 Summary Report. November 2011. Accessed September 13, 2020. https:// www.cdc.gov/violenceprevention/pdf/nisvs_report2010-a.pdf.

Cole, Benjamin S. "Paige Patterson Objectifies a 16 Year Old Girl". YouTube. Edited by Baptist Blogger. May 6, 2018. Accessed September 13, 2020. https://www.youtube .com/watch?v=gDRUVmcaQ3k.

Cooper, Brittney. "Single, Saved, and Sexin: The Redux." *Crunk Feminist Collective.* March 14, 2013. Accessed March 5, 2020. http://www.crunkfeministcollective.com/ 2013/03/14/single-saved-and-sexin-the-redux/.

Council of Biblical Manhood and Womanhood. "Danvers Statement." *CBMW,* 1988. Accessed June 29, 2020. https://cbmw.org/about/danvers-statement/.

Council of Biblical Manhood and Womanhood. "Nashville Statement." *CBMW,* 2017. Accessed June 29, 2020. https://cbmw.org/nashville-statement/.

Denhollander, Rachael. Facebook Post. May 1, 2018. Accessed September 13, 2020. https://www.facebook.com/notes/rachael-denhollander/when-its-in-our-own -community-evangelicals/1807296366017342/.

Denhollander, Rachael. The Price I Paid for Taking On Larry Nassar. *The New York Times.* January 26, 2018. Accessed September 13, 2020. https://www.nytimes.com/2018/01/ 26/opinion/sunday/larry-nassar-rachael-denhollander.html?smid=tw-share.

DiMarco, Hayley and Justin Lookadoo. *Dateable: Are You? Are They?* Grand Rapids, MI: Revell, 2003.

Douglas, Mary. *Purity and Danger.* New York, NY: Routledge Classics. 2004 (Originally published 1966).

Driscoll, Grace Driscoll and Mark. *Real Marriage: The Truth About Sex, Friendship, and Life Together.* Nashville, TN: Thomas Nelson, 2012.

Driscoll, Mark. "Sex, a Study of the Good Bits from Song of Solomon." Edinburgh, November 18, 2007. Accessed June 23, 2020. https://peterlumpkins.typepad.com/ files/driscoll-scotland-sermon-copypdf.pdf.

Eldredge, Stasi and John. *Captivating Revised and Updated: Unveiling The Mystery Of A Woman's Soul.* Nashville: Nelson Books, 2010.

Harris, Tamara Winfrey. "Sunday Kind of Love: Sex and Spirituality in the Black Church." *Bitch Media.* October 4, 2018. Accessed March 5, 2020. https://www.bitchmedia.org/article/sex-and-spirituality-in-the-black-church.

Herman, Dianne F. "The Rape Culture." In *Women: A Feminist Perspective*, by Ed. Jo Freeman, n.p. Mountain View, Co: Mayfield, 1984. http://homepage.smc.edu/delpiccolo_guido/soc1/soc1readings/rape%20culture_final.pdf.

Klein, Linda Kay. *Pure: Inside the Evangelical Movement That Shamed a Generation of Young Women and How I Broke Free.* New York: Atria Books, 2019.

Lifeway Christian Resources. "True Love Waits History." *True Love Waits*, 2020. Accessed 6 23, 2020. https://s7d9.scene7.com/is/content/LifeWayChristianResources/True_Love_Waits_Historypdf.pdf.

Mastari, Laora, Bram Spruyt, and Jessy Siongers. "Benevolent and Hostile Sexism in Social Spheres: The Impact of Parents, School and Romance on Belgian Adolescents' Sexist Attitudes." *Frontiers in Sociology: Gender, Sex, & Sexualities* 4: Article 47, 2019. Accessed June 27, 2020. doi:https://doi.org/10.3389/fsoc.2019.00047.

Meyer, Holly. "What is the Nashville Statement and Why Are People Talking About It?" *The Tennessean.* August 30, 2017. Accessed June 30, 2020. https://www.tennessean.com/story/news/religion/2017/08/30/what-nashville-statement-and-why-people-talking-it/616064001/.

New York Radical Feminists. *Rape: The First Sourcebook.* New York: New American Library, 1974.

Rich, Adrienne. "Compulsory Heterosexuality and Lesbian Existence." *Signs: Journal of Women in Culture and Society* (The University of Chicago Press, 1981) 5 (4): 631–660.

Sakenfeld, Katharine Doob. "Feminist Uses of Biblical Materials." *Feminist Interpretation of the Bible.* Letty M. Russell, ed. Philadelphia: The Westminster Press, 1985. 55–64.

Sellers, Tina Schermer. "Sexuality and Spirituality." *The Sexuality and Spirituality Forum.* Seattle: The Seattle School of Theology and Psychology, 2012. np. Accessed June 27, 2020. https://digitalcommons.spu.edu/av_events/95/.

Sellers, Tina Schermer. "Christians Caught Between the Sheets—How 'abstinence only' Ideology Hurts Us." *The Other Journal: An Intersection of Theology & Culture* 7, 2006 (Gender & Sexuality Issue): np. Accessed June 27, 2020. https://theotherjournal.com/2006/04/02/christians-caught-between-the-sheets-how-abstinence-only-ideology-hurts-us/.

Swan, Wanda, interview by Tara Tuttle. Director of The Swan Center for Advocacy & Research (June 28, 2020).

Welter, Barbara. "The Cult of True Womanhood 1820–1860." *American Quarterly* 18 (2): 151–174 (1966). Accessed October 4, 2020. www.jstor.org/stable/2711179.

World Health Organization. Defining Sexual Health, 2020. Accessed September 13, 2020. https://www.who.int/reproductivehealth/topics/sexual_health/sh_definitions/en/.

CHAPTER 4

Objectification and Sexualization of Girls

A Case Study

Debra Meyers

Twenty-first century scholars recognize the negative impact degrading females to mere objects or possessions has had on our entire society.[1] And female objectification has led to a significant increase in the sexualization of girls at younger ages. However, this phenomenon is not a recent development linked primarily to the media's representation of sexualized and objectified females as has been argued elsewhere.[2] We can see clearly the objectification and sexualization of girls in the mid twentieth century. Our case study from the 1960s and 70s illustrates the clear and oppressive presence of female objectification and sexualization through the lens of divorce, birth control, domestic violence, and sexual abuse. Furthermore, the study illustrates Christianity's culpability for these developments and the devastating long-term effects on society's rape culture today. (Note: the names in the following case study have been removed to protect domestic abuse survivors.)

1   Objectification and Sexualization of Girls: A Case Study

After moving to Greece, New York in the early 1960s my father's appearances were few and far between. The situation lasted for several years until my mother shattered her relationship with the Roman Catholic priests who insisted that she hold the family together as her duty to God. Her current situation, they argued, was her just punishment from God for her own sinfulness. Priests unanimously said that a cheating husband who neglected his family

---

1 See for instance, Linda Hatch, "The American Psychological Association Task Force on the Sexualization of Girls: A Review, Update, and Commentary" in *The Journal of Treatment and Prevention* (Volume 18, 2011) and L. Monique Ward, "Media and Sexualization: State of Empirical Research, 1995–2015" in *The Journal of Sex Research* (Volume 53, 2016).
2 American Psychological Association, "Report of the APA Task Force on the Sexualization of Girls" Retrieved from the APA website on August 5, 2020 https://www.apa.org/pi/women/programs/girls/report.

was a sinful wife's punishment to endure. She must, according to their directive, repent for her sinful behaviors if God was ever to grant her a reprieve from her punishment. I carried the guilt of pushing my mother into this drastic action that forced the church to excommunicate her.[3]

I forced my mother into this drastic position after I found an earring in the front seat of the family car. While I was thrilled to have found such a treasure, my mother was horrified. My mother didn't own any jewelry outside of her wedding ring. The next time that my father appeared in the house after the jewelry's discovery, my mother picked up a pot of boiling water off the stove and threatened to pour it on him. He grabbed her arm in time to avoid this ghastly outcome—it was the first time I witnessed such violence aimed at my father. Normally she focused all of her aggression and hatred on us. I thanked God that I never provoked her to such an act since I wouldn't be able to defend myself like my father had.

After the boiling water incident, my mother threw my father's clothes out into the garage. She screamed and threw things at no one and everyone throughout the day. The depth of her anger frightened all of us.

Begging money from all of her relatives in order to purchase the necessary proof of gross negligence and infidelity, she hired a lawyer and private detective to lay the groundwork for a divorce.

Once my father had moved out, he began picking us up on Sunday afternoons for scheduled visits during the legal separation period. All of my siblings and I were thrilled with this new arrangement since we rarely ever saw my father and now we would have his attention once a week for a few hours. For the first few Sundays, he took us to the park just outside of the zoo. The old dilapidated playground didn't have much to offer a hoard of children between the ages of three and thirteen, but we were in my father's presence and his attention was on us. It felt great!

On the fourth Sunday of these separation visitations, it rained. My father dutifully picked us up at the agreed upon time and drove us around for three hours before dropping us back home. My father lost his temper multiple times with six children in a car for three hours. It wasn't the best Sunday, but it certainly felt good to be included in my father's world even if he was just trying to convince a judge that he cared for his kids. The visits soon became more sporadic when it became clear to my father that he was not going to win the court battle or the best dad award.

---

3   The Roman Catholic church reserves the rite of excommunication for the worst sins in which the excommunicated may no longer participate in the sacraments or services of the church.

On what would be our final Sunday visit with our father, he took us to his latest girlfriend's house. She seemed pleasant enough, but I could tell from her facial expressions that we were unwelcome guests in her home. She instructed us to sit quietly on the couch while the adults disappeared down a long hallway. Six children, however, couldn't remain quiet for very long. Minutes later, my angry father reappeared. He hustled us out of the house and into his car. We were all silent. He drove us home without saying a thing. He never picked us up for a Sunday visit again.

When my parent's marriage finally ended, my life changed dramatically. My mother began to leave us alone in the house more often as she searched for a new husband. Sometimes, she brought us with her to Parents Without Partners picnics or other single parent family events, but most times she left the house without us. My brother and I—thirteen and twelve respectively—were ill-equipped to care for our four siblings. Our three-year-old brother fell off the top of his bunk bed one of these evenings, and sliced his forehead opened with a gash that wouldn't stop bleeding. There was so much blood, I thought he might die. In desperation, I sought help from a neighbor who stopped the bleeding. I knew that I would be held responsible for my brother's gaping wound *and* my mother's embarrassment. I wasn't surprised. No more playing around when my mother was away, I vowed.

2   Objectification and Sexualization: Religious Dogma

The mother in our case study divorced her husband after eleven long years of having absolutely no control over her own body and her ability to limit her fertility. At the age of 19, she gave birth to her first child and additional children followed in regular intervals until she had amassed a brood of six children long before she reached her thirtieth birthday. Her religion told her that she must yield to her husband's demands for sex regardless of her own desires or the immense stress on her body each new pregnancy imposed upon her. She was an object, not a human being. If a middle-class woman wanted to end a pregnancy, she needed both a doctor and her husband to support a D and C procedure (dilation and curettage) for health reasons.

In addition to the physical abuse of successive pregnancies, the husband's emotional abuse as a serial adulterer took its toll on the young mother in our case study. She was powerless to stop her emotional abuser and she was powerless to provide for her expanding brood. She never had enough money to pay for clothes or food for her hungry family and working outside the home to supplement the family's income was not an option. White married women with children did not work outside the home. It was not socially acceptable, and it was not feasible given the large number of children who needed supervision. After having to depend on male relatives to secure a lawyer and private detective, the photo evidence of his flagrant infidelity did not guarantee a divorce. The battle was long, expensive, and difficult. Courts assumed a husband behaved badly in response to a wife's deficiencies based on the religious dogma perpetrated in every church.[4]

Televised religious programs in the 1960s addressed marriage problems at a time when many wives sought solutions for their abusive relationships that were often sanctified by religious authorities.[5] In the minds of male ministers, male infidelities and their physical and emotional abuse of wives were all justified intimate partner violence. Male clergy cited biblical text, such as Ephesians 5:22–33 (NIV): "Wives submit yourselves to your own husbands as you do to the Lord. For the husband is the head of the wife as Christ is the head of the church ... and let the wife see that she respects her husband." This immutable Christian mandate demanded that women be subservient to their husbands regardless of a husband's failure to provide for his family or his physical or emotional abuse. Indeed, male preachers also regularly pointed to a letter to the Colossians sometimes attributed to Paul demanding that "Wives be subordinate to your husbands, as is proper in the Lord" (Colossians 3:18).[6] Clearly, the word of God transcribed in the Christian Bible formed the very foundation of the objectification and sexualization of females even in the mid-twentieth century. In particular, the Roman Catholic church's prohibition against divorce only reified the grave injustice against women imprisoned in

---

4   Debra Meyers, "I Am Heartily Sorry: The Roman Catholic Church and Domestic Abuse," in Debra Meyers and Mary Sue Barnett, eds. *Crisis and Challenge in the Roman Catholic Church: Perspectives on Decline and Reformation.* Pittsburgh, PA: Rowman and Littlefield (2020) 223–244.

5   Many of Bishop Sheen's televised programs on marriage have been uploaded into YouTube by far-right Catholic groups in their efforts to reinvigorate efforts to subjugate women. See for instance, Sensus Fidelium, "Marriage & Incompatibility—Archbishop Fulton Sheen," (originally broadcast in 1964), YouTube video, December 29, 2012. Retrieved from https://www.youtube.com/watch?v=QtMKPaG7vVA.

6   Biblical scholars are deeply divided concerning the authorship of Colossians. Only seven of the thirteen letters attributed to Paul in the New Testament are widely judged to be Paul's writings; namely, Corinthians 1&2, Galatians, Philemon, Philippians, Romans, 1 Thessalonians. See for instance: James Dunn and John Rogerson, *Eerdmans Commentary on the Bible* (Eerdmans Publishing, 2003) and David Aune, *The Blackwell Companion to the New Testament* (Blackwell Publishing, 2010).

abusive marriages.[7] Religious dogma dominated our culture's objectification of women who existed only for the pleasure of men or for procreation.

Limiting an abused woman's access to divorce by placing the cost of a lawyer and private detective largely out of reach for most women provided another pathway for the patriarchy to control women. We can see this control in American history before the revolution when divorce was rare. For all intents and purposes, a woman's access to divorce rested on a woman's total dependence on a man for her economic survival after a husband's desertion. Under these circumstances, a divorce was a woman's pathway to subsistence in colonial America. Granting a divorce after desertion allowed a woman to remarry and thus, she and her children would pose less of a burden to her community.

Men, on the other hand, began to see divorce as their right to "liberty" on their road to their "pursuit of happiness" after the American Revolution. Men frequently left their wives to fend for themselves as they took all of the marital property—real estate, furniture, and other material goods—after a divorce. Some men had their wives committed to an insane asylum, but if they wanted to remarry, men had to file for a legal divorce. A man seeking divorce also legally owned the family's children. When a middle-class man sued for divorce, he typically only allowed his wife to leave the family home with her jewelry and her personal clothing. She had few options for financially supporting herself.

Women by the middle of the twentieth century had gained more opportunities to file for divorce and often had the ability to keep her children, but courts rarely granted divorce without solid proof of blatant infidelity as well as proof of a husband's failure to adequately provide food, clothing, and a suitable place to live for his family. Such obstacles proved insurmountable for most women who did not have access to bank loans, credit cards, or savings accounts. It wasn't until 1969 that a woman could file for a "no-fault" divorce in California on the basis of irreconcilable differences, but it took a long time for other states to grant women a way out of an abusive marriage without having to hire expensive private detectives.[8] Even then, a divorced woman faced social stigma and few economic pathways to support herself and her children unless she remarried.

Standardized tests revealed in the 1960s that scholastic achievement for girls declined by the time they reached high school as caregivers and teachers

---

7 Hayley Gleeson and Julia Baird, "'Their cross to bear': The Catholic women told to forgive domestic violence," *ABC News*, November 4, 2017, abc.net.au/news/2017-11-04.

8 See for instance, Stephanie Coontz, "The Origins of Modern Divorce" in *Family Process* (Volume 46, 2007).

inculcated their own low-level expectations on girls.[9] And yet even with low expectations for intellectual achievements, many women had to work to survive. These women were often paid much less than men. In response to this reality, the Equal Pay Act of 1963 required equal wages for men and women doing the same work. Further, the Civil Rights Act of 1964 prohibited discrimination based on sex for any companies that had more than 25 employees. But discrimination continued to exist long after these laws were adopted. In the 1970s women made approximately half of what their male counterparts earned, a trend that continues today.[10] Mid-twentieth century married women could not possess a credit card in their names, could not apply for a loan, and could not undergo elective surgery without their husband's permission. Divorced and single women found it nearly impossible to purchase a car or a house. And married women who did find work as teachers, nurses, librarians, clerks, retail saleswomen, and in the food service industry were summarily dismissed if they became pregnant. No one wanted to see a pregnant woman outside of her home. Society held women responsible and penalized them for their large bellies, but in actual fact women had very little choice in managing their fertility.

When methods of birth control were available, they remained largely under the control of men. After the first rubber condom infiltrated popular culture in the United States, male legislators adopted the 1873 Comstock Act prohibiting the sale of condoms via the US postal system. Male legislators also had the power to sterilize women who they deemed insane, diseased, or feeble-minded. These laws targeted women of color in particular and poor women in general. In 1914, Margaret Sanger used the term "birth control" to counter what many women believed to be forced motherhood and she began her campaign to educate women and provide clinics for women's healthcare. Women opened nearly 400 birth control clinics across the country by 1939 often providing diaphragms in order to give women real control over their fertility for the first time in history. The Food and Drug Administration approved the first oral hormone-based contraceptive in 1960, but a woman needed her husband's permission to gain access to the drug. Oral contraceptives for unmarried women would

---

9   Bart Golsteyn and Trudie Schils, "Gender Gaps in Primary School Achievement: A decomposition into endowments and returns to IQ and non-cognitive factors," in *Economics of Education Review* (Volume 41, August 2014) 176–187.

10   See for instance, Marlene Kim, "Women Paid Low Wages: Who They Are and Where They Work," in *Monthly Labor Review* (Issue 9, September 2000) 26–30 and Mahshid Jalilvand, "Married Women, Work, and Values" in *Monthly Labor Review* (Issue 8, August 2000) 26-31.

not be legalized until 1972.[11] The entire controversy over women's access to contraception and abortion always harkens back to the early Christian dogma placing females in subordinate positions objectified and sexualized until they become merely vessels for male sperm.

3   A Case Study Continued

Eventually, my mother found a suitable mate and they made plans to move us to his house in Webster, New York right after their nuptials. It seemed like a good plan to me at the time. This new man in my mother's life always greeted me with warmth and affection, something that I desperately wanted. He was tall, thin, balding, and had blond facial hair and soft hands. A stark contrast to my father's calloused hands, massive build, dark complexion, and clean-shaven face. My new stepfather always had a smile on his face. We didn't seem to annoy him—at least in the beginning.

His own daughter was exactly the same age as my youngest brother. She came to play several times at the house in Webster, but she was easily over-whelmed by our collective presence. And as quickly as she had entered our lives, she disappeared. No one explained her total absence from our new family, and we were not encouraged to talk about it. I had a terrible sense of foreboding. There was something that didn't feel quite right about the new situation. I just couldn't put my finger on it yet.

My stepfather's split-level house had a colossal fish tank near the front door with dozens of beautiful tropical fish, and a family room, and bathroom on the entry level. The second level contained the living room, dining room, and kitchen. Three bedrooms and another bathroom were on the third floor. My stepfather planned to build a fourth bedroom for his expanding family in the basement next to his workshop. It all seemed OK at first. Well, almost OK.

My mother had arrived home from a short honeymoon in Florida sporting a huge blackeye. She told everyone that she had fallen and that she was so glad that her new husband had been there to take care of her. But I knew that my new stepfather had established his dominance with this physical abuse. The message was quite clear for all of us. My mother was notably subservient in his presence after this first violent act. She waited on him with deference and kept his rules and daily schedule with marked precision from that day forward.

---

11   Linda Gordon, *The Moral Property of Women: A History of Birth Control Politics in America*, Chicago: University of Illinois Press, 2002.

I met this new power hierarchy with a good deal of ambivalence. What could be worse than the mental and physical abuse my mother had doled out for years, I wondered. I didn't have long to wait to find out.

After preparing her clothes, hair, and makeup for an hour, my mother would meet my stepfather at the door with a warm smile, a freshly made cocktail, and kiss on the cheek when he came home from work every night at 5:30. He would sit in his living room recliner and listen to classical music with his perfect Manhattan in hand until my mother had dinner on the table at precisely 6:30. He encouraged me to sit with him and listen to the music before dinner. Starved for positive parental attention, I eagerly complied. I enjoyed the music and I took great pleasure in his undivided attention as he explained the composers' work. I felt special and valued for the first time in my life. After dinner, I would clear the table, wash the dishes, put them away, and then put my younger siblings to bed. If there was time after my chores were done, I did my homework. I felt grateful for the stable environment in this new life. This routine felt very comfortable and we appreciated the new regular dinner arrangements that included meat, potatoes, and vegetables every night.

I easily pushed my trepidation to one side when my stepfather invited me to a restaurant to celebrate my fourteenth birthday. I never had a birthday party. Indeed, my mother did not celebrate birthdays at our house. Having been deprived of parental affection up until this point, my stepfather's level of interest in me helped to push my reservations to the back of my mind. He took me to the Aloha! restaurant. Decorated as I thought a restaurant in Hawaii might look like, dimmed lights, a waterfall, soft ukulele music, and a wall painting of volcanoes filled me with awe. While we waited for our dinners to arrive, he took me to the dance floor for a slow dance. I welcomed this new level of affection, attention, and intimacy. I felt loved. But this satisfying feeling of love would not last long.

"You stink," my mother said matter-of-factly one day when I arrived home from school. She presented me with a can of deodorant spray and told me that I needed to apply this liberally before sitting with my stepfather in the evening. I dutifully complied.

The next rule applied to all six of us. My siblings and I must only use the first-floor bathroom because we left the upstairs bathroom in a mess constantly. No problem. I would comply with that rule too.

And then I heard the noise. I sat down on the toilet and heard metal scraping metal. It wasn't a loud noise, but it was real. Strange, I thought to myself.

Another evening after I had cleaned the kitchen and put the youngest siblings to bed, I thought I'd take a shower. As I removed my clothes in the downstairs bathroom, I took the opportunity to stare at myself in the mirror. My body was changing.

And then I heard the now familiar metal scraping sound. Odd, I thought. The metal scraping sound occurred with some regularity now, but only in the evenings. It seemed to be coming from the heating vent located on the wall near the floor.

Curious, I went into the basement to investigate the heating vent after school one day. I opened the often-locked door to my stepfather's workshop and much to my horror I found a flange on the sheet metal that covered the heating vent for the main floor bathroom. The sheet metal could be moved back and forth to provide an unobstructed view into the first-floor bathroom. I vomited when I replayed in my mind the many times I heard the metal scraping noise while I was naked. Welcome to a new kind of hell, I thought.

I quickly cleaned up the vomit and placed everything back exactly as I had found it so that he wouldn't know I had discovered his secret. Should I say something to my mother? Should I tell my sisters? Even if someone believed me, what good would come of it? He might just retaliate in ways that I couldn't imagine. Best to keep quiet right now, I thought.

From then on, I only used the toilet and shower before he arrived home from work or after he went to bed. When my sisters used the bathroom when he was home, I would distract him with questions about classical music. Problem solved, I thought.

And then he implemented rule number three: no locks on the doors. My stepfather spent an entire Saturday taking the locks off of the bedroom and bathroom doors. He did not, however, take the locks off his bedroom, his bathroom, or his basement workshop. He never said why he was taking this peculiar action and my mother didn't seem to care one way or another. Everyone went about their day without even acknowledging my stepfather's predatory actions. This new development didn't bode well for me. I knew instinctively that he was coming for me.

I felt like my personal hell was spiraling downward at a faster pace. But why? What had I done to deserve this horrendous hell? My Catholic upbringing told me that I was being punished for my actions, my beliefs, or my thoughts. I needed to figure out what kind of sin I was committing before my punishments spiraled out of control.

God was punishing me for something terrible—I just wish I knew what it was. Was I so evil that I couldn't even identify my sin? Oh God. Perhaps that was it. But whatever action I thought I could take to avoid my stepfather's next step was too little, too late.

It was late, nearly midnight, when he quietly opened the door to the room I shared with my sisters. The moonlight streaming through the window lit up the room well enough for me to see who the intruder was. My stomach contents started creeping up into my throat. I held my breath in anticipation of his next move. Should I scream? Should I comply? Would my sisters wake up before he was done with me? Would he touch my sisters too? So many questions and absolutely no answers. My previous experiences didn't prepare me for what would happen next. I squeezed my eyes tightly closed. Silent obedience would be my default setting.

The assault ended quickly. He stood up and adjusted his clothes before opening the door. He left without saying a word. I could still feel his hot moist breath on my neck and the disgusting slime between my legs. I thanked God that he didn't touch my sisters.

I instinctively knew that my mother would blame me if I told her what happened. She witnessed and encouraged my nightly classical music liaisons with my stepfather. She would point to my daily practice of sitting on the arm of his recliner every evening before dinner. And wasn't I the one who carefully sprayed deodorant under my arms every evening before he arrived home? It was entirely my fault. I asked for his sexual assaults. There would be no reason to blame her husband and there was the real possibility that she was an accomplice in this.

Of course, I couldn't tell anyone else. First, there was no one else to tell. My father, who never actively participated in my life, had disappeared from our lives entirely. No loving extended family members ever materialized in my life to provide safety and security. I had no teacher or counselor take an interest in me at school. There was no one to tell and even if there was, they would just confront my mother and stepfather. I was mature enough to know that a confrontation would make my life worse.

And when all was said and done, I truly believed that I had asked for this situation. I had to take the blame for wanting someone to hold me, value me, love me. So, I kept our secret meeting to myself.

4   Objectification and Sexualization: Grooming Girls

Older men intent on exploiting young girls for sexual satisfaction often possess a keen eye for vulnerable girls desperate for adult attention.[12] Offenders

---

12   See Jennifer E. O'Brien and Wen Li, "The Role of the Internet in the Grooming, Exploitation, and Exit of United States Domestic Minor Sex Trafficking Victims," in *Journal of Children*

condition their victims in a process that is often referred to as grooming. After having selected a malleable target, the pedophile watches the victim carefully in order to identify specific needs of his victim. Once identified, the offender takes on the role of caretaker when he attends to the victim's needs—in this case, providing attention and affection. Once he has established trust as the victim's caretaker filling a social or psychological void, he can create intimate space in which to foster a strong connection with the victim to cement emotional dependence, such as the daily classical music liaisons in our case study. Once the perpetrator has created emotional dependence, he initiates sexual contact. This process ensures, to a certain degree, the predator's ability to maintain control over the victim. It is difficult for a child entangled in this sexualized relationship to call for an end to the relationship which would mean an end to the emotional and material needs that the perpetrator is providing. Children may often feel that the loss of this relationship and the consequences of exposing it may actually make the child feel more unwanted and unloved.[13] This prevents most women from coming forward even decades after they have been violated.

This grooming process proves to be efficacious as vulnerable girls seeking compassion and love, once violated, struggle with the emotional attachment the grooming process created alongside the knowledge that they were violated by an adult they trusted. These conflicting perceptions lead to guilt feelings that prevent victims from reaching out for help even years after the assaults. Indeed, they often feel that they have initiated the abuse by their own desire to feel valued and loved as we see in our case study.[14] Manipulating the victim into essentially a cooperative partner reduces the likelihood that the victim will ever disclose the violations to anyone of consequence. And in our case study scenario, our predator appears to have sought assistance in the grooming process from the victim's mother relying on her own low self-esteem and

and Media (Volume 14, issue 2, 2020) and Cindy Miller-Perrin and Sandy Wurtele, "Sex Trafficking and Commercial Sexual Exploitation of Children," in Women and Therapy (Volume 40, issue 2, 2017) 123–151.

13   Michael Welner, "Child Sexual Abuse: 6 Stages of Grooming" Retrieved from website on August 10, 2020 http://www.oprah.com/oprahshow/child-sexual-abuse-6-stages-of-grooming/all.

14   See for instance, "What is Grooming of Sexual Abuse Victims?" From the Doan Law Firm website accessed August 14, 2020. Retrieved from https://www.thedoanlawfirm.com/blog/2020/july/what-is-grooming-of-sexual-abuse-victims-/. See also "The Scope of Child Sexual Abuse Definition and Fact Sheet," Retrieved from Stop it Now! Website accessed August 14, 2020 at https://www.stopitnow.org/faq/the-scope-of-child-sexual-abuse-definition-and-fact-sheet.

his physical dominance over her to gain her cooperation.[15] All the while, both mother and daughter accepted the sexual and emotional abuse as righteous punishment for their sins as they had been directed to do after years of religious indoctrination.

5   A Case Study Continued

I didn't tell anyone what had happened. Instead, I continued to work on becoming a better Catholic as a means to a better and safer life. I cleansed myself of bad thoughts and deeds and prayed the Act of Contrition every day: "Oh my God, I am heartily sorry for having offended Thee, and I detest all my sins because of Thy just punishments, but most of all because they offend Thee, my God, Who art all-good and deserving of all my love. I firmly resolve, with the help of Thy grace, to sin no more and to avoid the near occasions of sin." And yet, my hellish punishments didn't subside regardless of how "heartily sorry" I was.[16]

I ran away from home (twice) thinking that I could escape my punishment from hell, but the police returned me home both times—even when I got as far away as South Carolina. True to form, my mother punished me for my lack of concern for others and the cost of my plane ticket home. I would do my regular chores after school and then spend my weekends in my room. No bathroom privileges, no food, no contact with others from sundown on Friday until Monday morning. I took this new hell in stride. I squirreled away crackers and containers of water in several different places in my room. I kept a pee pot and toilet paper under my bed, and I made sure that I had all the materials necessary for completing my homework before the end of the school day on Fridays. This hell was manageable. My stepfather's punishments, however, would not be.

Once a week while I was sequestered in my room for the weekend, my stepfather would take me into his basement workroom and lock the door. He

---

15   Martin Shawn Rutledge, "Biological Father/Daughter Sexual Abuse and Step-Father/Step-Daughter Sexual Abuse Compared" thesis for Master of Social Work at the University of Manitoba (1991).

16   The Act of Contrition is part of the Roman Catholic ritual of reconciliation in which the sinner repents for all of their sins and is then absolved by a priest. This is a necessary prerequisite to receiving the sacrament of the holy Eucharist (bread transformed through the process of transubstantiation into the body of Christ) symbolizing one's communion with the congregation and God as a visible sign of God's grace.

demanded that I remove all of my clothes and bend over for the paddling I so righteously deserved. This somehow felt more degrading, disgusting, and disabling than the sexual assaults that continued unabated. But it also reinforced the notion that I was the sinful accomplice. Indeed, the message clearly conveyed that I was responsible for *his* behavior.

And then there was rule number four. If you are not useful to the head of household, you are not welcome in his house. Few of my father's children made the cut and they were abruptly shipped off to other relatives to live. I didn't have a chance to say goodbye to my brothers and sisters. Once my stepfather determined that one of my siblings had no value, he or she was gone the next day. Of course, possible witnesses to his sexual assaults, such as my sisters, were the first to be sent away. I prayed that their lives would be better in their new homes. In the end, my new half-brother, still in diapers, my older brother, and I were the only children in the house.

Let me rephrase that. My two brothers were children, I never felt like a child. I felt more like an unwanted dog. Useful for a short time and then totally valueless—that was how I would characterize myself. Like an unwanted dog, I knew that I had to provide some valuable service in order to survive.

So, I cleaned, cooked, did the laundry and the ironing, babysat my youngest brother, and serviced the master of the house while my older brother mowed the lawn, shoveled the driveway, painted, took care of the garbage, and cleaned the garage. My older brother often had free time after completing his chores. He joined the school wrestling team and attended events with friends. My usefulness took up nearly all of my time. I hardly had time to complete homework and I definitely did not have time for friends.

I didn't really recognize my resentment toward my brother until his 16th birthday. My mother spent a day decorating the house. She had scrimped on the family's meager food budget for weeks in order to buy enough ground beef, hamburger buns, soda pop, and potato chips for the special occasion. And of course, there was cake. A beautiful vanilla cake with chocolate frosting—enough for two dozen teenagers.

I was responsible for inviting all of my brother's friends to his surprise party. With a blatant disregard for my most important survival strategies—silent obedience—I only invited one person, a neighbor that my brother disliked. My brother was deeply hurt. I had ruined his birthday. I had ruined his life.

My mother was furious. Absolutely furious. She worked so hard to make this 16th birthday party special and I had ruined everything. My inability to adequately assess the ramifications of my actions had been superseded by my need for revenge. Or was it an unconscious death wish?

My mother grew increasingly hostile after this event. In addition to my weekend incarcerations, she began to crash through my bedroom door in the middle of the night to yank me by my hair to redo a cleaning task that did not meet her approval. Scrubbing the kitchen floor at two o'clock in the morning became a fairly regular part of my daily routine.

If only my knight in shining armor knew my situation. All of the fairy tales I had ever heard assured me that he would come and save me. But he never came. I began to wonder if he ever really existed at all.

6   Objectification and Sexualization of Girls: The Media

Our case study survivor waited for her knight in shining armor to save her. Films, fairy tales, and television shows all shared that same message for young girls—a man will save you from the abuses you suffer.[17] But no one acknowledged our survivor's abuses. And certainly no one came to rescue her, or her mother, or her siblings.

The 2007 landmark American Psychological Association (APA) Task Force report on the sexualization of females highlighted the role the media plays in objectifying and sexualizing girls at a young age that in turn contributes to the abuse of women and girls in a rape culture society. Oversexualizing females in the media, according to the study, contributes to attitudes and assumptions in both males and females that promote sexism leading to significant mental health problems. Some of the most detrimental mental health issues, according to the study, that stem from hypersexualized media and marketing include feelings of shame, body appearance anxiety, low self-esteem, depression, eating disorders, and injurious ideas relating to sexual consent. The hyper sexualization of females in the media and marketing directly impact the objectification and dehumanization of females that can manifest in pervasive violence against females.[18] According to the National Statistics Domestic Violence, *one*

---

17   See for instance, Bell, Haas, et al., *From Mouse to Mermaid: The Politics of Film, Gender, and Culture,* Johnson Cheu, *Diversity in Disney Films: Critical Essays on Race, Ethnicity, Gender, Sexuality and Disability,* Holtzman and Sharpe, *Media Messages: What Film, Television, and Popular Music Teach Us About Race, Class, Gender, and Sexual Orientation,* and Benshoff and Griffin, *America on Film: Representing Race, Class, Gender, and Sexuality at the Movies.*

18   American Psychological Association, "Report of the APA Task Force on the Sexualization of Girls" Retrieved from the APA website on August 5, 2020 https://www.apa.org/pi/women/programs/girls/report.

out of every five women in the United States has been raped and these women suffer from much higher rates of depression and suicide than other females.[19]

Yet, the findings in the American Psychological Association Task Force report are not unique to the United States and they do not depend entirely on the media. Our case study survivor, for instance, had very little access to the media. She saw one movie during her childhood, the household did not have books, and they often had no working television. Moreover, many places throughout the world have little access to the media. And yet, the objectification and subsequent dehumanization of females forms the basis of rape culture that pervades the globe. According to UNICEF, "The objectification and sexualization of girls in the media is linked to violence against women and girls worldwide. Media normalizes the act of dominance and aggression against women by constantly showcasing them as objects of pleasure and associating them with commodity."[20] Patriarchy across the globe appears to be the foundation of this objectification and sexualization. And the patriarchy is supported and empowered by Christianity.

Christian dogmas for more than a thousand years have marginalized women as a means to solidify cultural patriarchy that forms the foundation of the major religious sects in the United States.[21] The central premise of women

---

19   NCADV, *National Statistics Domestic Violence Fact Sheet*. NCADV webpage retrieved August 19, 2020 from https://www.ncadv.org/statistics.

20   Jaimee Swift and Hannah Gould, "Not an Object: On Sexualization and Exploitation of Women and Girls" (January 2020) Retrieved from UNICEF USA's website on August 5, 2020 https://www.unicefusa.org/stories/not-object-sexualization-and-exploitation -women-and-girls/30366?webSyncID=7b2514a7-6d5d-6ec1-a073-b5571d0576a8& sessionGUID=65879593-3442-144b-6887-053827d3ec94&_ga=2.121551435.2132436888.15967 22461-858287951.1596722461.

21   See for instance, Carol Newsom and Sharon Ringe, eds. *Women's Bible Commentary*, Westminster John Knox Press (2012) and Loreen Maseno and Elia Shabani Mligo, *Women within Religions: Patriarchy, Feminism, and the Role of Women in Selected World Religions*, Wipf and Stock (2019). Karen Armstrong argues that it was the development of monotheistic religions, with their all-powerful male Gods (such as Judaism, Christianity and Islam) that directly led to the patriarchal and sexist core or religious dogma when goddesses and priestesses were summarily replaced with male prophets and gods. [Karen Armstrong, *History of God: The 4000 Year Quest of Judaism, Christianity and Islam*, Vintage (2004).]. See also Judith Plaskow, "Feminist Anti-Judaism and the Christian God." *Journal of Feminist Studies in Religion* 7, no. 2 (1991): 99–108. Accessed August 18, 2020. www.jstor .org/stable/25002158. Nawal El Sadaawi, on the other hand, argues that religions do not cause women's exploitation and oppression. But rather, patriarchal societies cause this exploitation and oppression. Sadaawi argues that men use religious beliefs and ideas to control women. Nawal El Sadaawi, *Women at Point Zero*, Zed Books (2015). Feminists, such as Simone De Beauvoir, have long argued religion targets women with messages that

as evil and useless outside of procreation allowed men in power to solidify and expand their power and authority once 51% of the population was essentially neutralized. Early Christian theology proscribed obedient helper status to women whose primary purpose centered on her ability to produce viable male heirs. St. Jerome in the fourth century labeled women as "gate of the devil, the path of wickedness, the sting of a serpent." In other words, a woman was a "perilous object."[22] Similarly, Thomas Aquinas (c. 1239), referred to a woman as "a man's helpmeet" made expressly for procreation "since for other purposes men would be better assisted by other men."[23] These efficacious ideas for maintaining patriarchy permeated both Catholic and Protestant thought and came to influence cultural attitudes concerning contraception and women's bodies as objects to be controlled, while condoning intimate partner violence as a means of controlling females in the twentieth century.[24]

7 The Case Study Conclusion

As my mother's second marriage crumbled, she targeted me as the whipping post of least resistance. When my stepfather moved out of the house, his sexual assaults were soon replaced with my mother's ramped up physical abuse. Sleepless nights scrubbing floors often had me thinking about the best, least messy, methods of suicide. God forbid that I leave a mess behind when I died. If I did, she would probably follow me to hell and drag me back by my hair to clean up my mess.

And then my mother took a job outside of the house for the first time ever. She worked for a small company only a few miles away. I felt like I hit the jackpot. Of course, it meant more work for me after school, but my mother was often too tired to beat the daylights out of me in the evening. The night terror of being pulled by the hair to clean the kitchen floor stopped. I thanked God for allowing me to sleep through the night again. One by one my siblings returned

---

focus on their duty to cook, clean, have babies, and tolerate inequality and oppression in the hopes of a reward in heaven. [Simone De Beauvoir, *The Second Sex*, Vintage (2011).]

22 St. Jerome, "Woman," Retrieved from Statusquoteswishes.com website (December 2019). Retrieved from https://statusquoteswishes.com/st-jerome-quotes/.

23 Kristin Popik, "The Philosophy of Woman of St. Aquinas." Catholic Culture Website retrieved July 2020 https://www.catholicculture.org/culture/library/view.cfm?recnum=2793.

24 Approximately half of all rapes are perpetrated against females by someone they know. [NCADV, *National Statistics Domestic Violence Fact Sheet*. NCADV webpage retrieved August 19, 2020 from https://www.ncadv.org/statistics.]

from their banishment. It was good to have my brothers and sisters living in the house again. Nothing was said about their return. Life seemed good, perhaps for the first time. God had finally heard my prayers and Acts of Contrition.

My mother met a young handyman who worked for her employer. He was closer to my age than to hers, but she seemed quite happy with her new beau. I wasn't going to stick around to see what new kind of hell this would bring to my bedroom, so I moved out the moment that I graduated high school.

My mother, her five young children, and this handyman moved to Sodus, New York. It was a quiet little town where many people from Rochester owned summer cottages on Lake Ontario. Housing was old and cheap for the sturdy people who chose to live there year-round. The winters were brutal, but the summers were pleasant.

There were times when I felt like I had abandoned my younger siblings, but the new guy seemed OK and my mother appeared happy and less violent. I wouldn't find out how this third husband groomed one of my sisters for sex until years later.

I had very few employment options since I wasn't male, and I didn't have a family member who worked for Kodak that could get me into an entry level position on the night shift. So, I worked at a fast-food establishment. I worked hard and showed up for my shifts on time.

I felt free. Free from violence for the first time in my life. After only a few months, the manager asked if I would be interested in taking the assistant manager training. I thought long and hard considering my options carefully. I often closed the store with our assistant manager. She didn't work as hard as I did, but she stayed well beyond the time when I left the store and she closed every weekend. And while she did have to practically climb into the shake machine to clean it every night, she spent a good deal of her time counting inventory and filing paperwork.

I hated cleaning the public restrooms, scooping maggots from the meat discard container, and closing down the greasy hot fryer. But the worst part of my job was cleaning the slicer. It was so sharp, I never felt the deep cuts into my fingers—nearly down to the bone—until the blood was dripping profusely down my arm and onto my grungy, smelly uniform.

Clearly, an assistant manager's job was easier, but I wasn't willing to give up my new-found pleasure—bar hopping in the evenings. So, I declined my manager's kind offer. But the cost/benefit analysis left me contemplating my future for the first time. For the first time, I believed I *had* a future.

For sure, I didn't want to be shoveling fake roast beef sandwiches for the rest of my life and cleaning public toilets. Fortunately, one of the other servers at the store attended the local community college. She would go on and on about the difficult classes she was taking to become a dental hygienist. Without a working television most of the time while I was growing up and living in a blue-collar community where higher education wasn't an option for the majority of high school graduates, I never knew that there was a community college just 20 miles from my high school.

I began asking the community college student questions, soaking in all of the information. I drove to the college one morning before work in my less than dependable "rot box" car and I parked right in front of the center of a very long building. When I walked through the doors, it felt rather similar to the high school I had attended—similar enough that I could imagine myself coming to this place. I talked to one of the friendly office staff and immediately signed up for the mechanical technology program. No one discouraged me even though it was an overwhelmingly male program.

And no one discouraged me after looking over my transcripts *that didn't include any high school science.* My high school guidance counselor didn't think a girl like me was going to need science classes in high school and they weren't mandated by the state for graduation. I had a strange suspicion that I would regret not taking the science classes, but I was in too much of a hurry to graduate early to care about the details. Fortunately, I had all of the required math for this math and science focused program, and I was smart enough to pick up the science that I needed.

I finished this program in two years while working full time. This educational opportunity gave me a better income, a better life, and the promise of a better future. I had never dreamed of having a real future. I never dreamed at all. Now, I had a great career, a lovely townhouse, a new car, and a future. This community college saved my life.

8   Objectification and Sexualization: The Impact

Our case study suggests that females, despite the pervasive cultural objectification and sexualization of girls, can and do persist in our rape culture. Despite having lived through hell, our case study survivor never killed anyone (or even contemplated killing anyone other than herself), she never succumbed to addiction, and she did not end up living on the streets. But she did sever all ties with her parents and the siblings who did not live up to our survivor's expectations regarding trust and loyalty. When she heard that her mother and father had died decades later, she did not shed a single tear and she did not spend a second grieving. Not a second.

Since that pinnacle moment at the fast food store when she realized *that she had a future*, she never looked back. However, the scars of her objectification and sexualization remained. She has an unbounded empathy for the down-trodden and abused. Her life's work often focuses on helping single moms build their self-esteem and break the constraints of poverty through higher education. She also devotes herself to assisting domestic abuse victims and promulgating equal rights for the LGBTQ community. Her deep empathy propels her to work for social justice on many levels. Her social justice work often rests on her problem-solving skills and her ability to critically analyze verbal and nonverbal cues. All of these skills and character traits can be directly linked to survival strategies formed during an oppressive childhood of objectification and sexualization.

Needless to say, her negative character traits also have their antecedents in her destructive childhood experiences. While she takes an intense interest in listening to the problems and concerns of others, she rarely shares her own private thoughts and feelings. An administrator once told her that she would increase her chances of promotion if she socialized with and befriended her co-workers. Good advice to be sure, but if her continued employment depended on making friends, she was in real trouble. Making friends and trusting people with her vulnerabilities continues to be a challenge throughout her life's journey.

Additionally, our case study survivor's childhood experiences have prevented her from taking risks—risks with her career, her financial goals, as well as her family plans. Safe, reliable, predictable, and steady decisions rule her adult life. She does not take chances. Controlling her environment, her actions, and outcomes provides our survivor with the stability, safety, and peace of mind that eluded her throughout her childhood. Yet, her need for safety and control held her back from being the best that she could be and probably prevented her from encouraging her own children to take more chances. That is perhaps her deepest regret even though she recognizes that there was little she could change about her inability to embrace risk-taking given her childhood experiences.

Our case study survivor's early experiences helped her to create and hone analytic skills that have aided her in many ways, but they have also created a pesky and off-putting requisite to overthink everything—literally everything. Overthinking prevents our survivor from taking any risks at all when it comes to life-changing decisions, but it impacts even the smallest decisions to the point of preventing quick and decisive actions when circumstances demand immediate action.

But perhaps the most negative impact of our survivor's childhood has been her inability to feel happiness and satisfaction because of a sense of limited self-worth coupled with a sense of shame and guilt—all harkening back to her parent's Catholic upbringing and their imposition of the man-made dogma on their family that emphasized human wickedness and punishment.[25] Never having felt worthy of anyone's love, affection, or attention has been our survivor's biggest regret and perhaps the most unavoidable consequence of her lost youth.

The objectification and subsequent dehumanization of females, however pervasive around the globe, did not begin in the twenty-first century. Its roots lie in the previous century where we can see the effects in the 1970s clearly in our case study. Religious dogma formed the foundation for hypersexualized females in the media eons before our modern media materialized.[26] I have argued here that the sexual abuse of objectified and sexualized girls by older men stems from Christian doctrine's emphasis on females as evil and sexually promiscuous. Media normalizes the act of dominance and aggression against women by constantly showcasing them as objects of pleasure and associating them with commodity. This objectification often finds its genesis in all of the major religions.[27]

So, how do we move forward from this decidedly repulsive rape culture that objectifies and sexualizes girls? First and foremost, we need to educate. Everyone must acknowledge the objectification and sexualization of girls that creates the foundation for our social attitudes toward females stemming from Christian misogynist religious dogma. Next, we need to refuse to tolerate objectification and sexualization of girls in the media, in our religious beliefs, as well as our culture more generally. And finally, we need to provide healing for victims who might be our best hope for educating communities to bring this destructive patriarchy to an end.

---

25   Debra Meyers, "I Am Heartily Sorry: The Roman Catholic Church and Domestic Abuse," in Debra Meyers and Mary Sue Barnett, eds. *Crisis and Challenge in the Roman Catholic Church: Perspectives on Decline and Reformation*. Pittsburgh, PA: Rowman and Littlefield (2020) 223–244.

26   Ibid.

27   Michael J. Formica, "Objectification and Sexualization of Women," *Psychology Today* (June 2, 2008). Retrieved from https://www.psychologytoday.com/us/blog/enlightened-living/200806/objectification-and-sexualization-women.

Bibliography

American Psychological Association, "Report of the APA Task Force on the Sexualization of Girls" Retrieved from the APA website on August 5, 2020 https://www.apa.org/pi/women/programs/girls/report.

Armstrong, Karen. *History of God: The 4000 Year Quest of Judaism, Christianity and Islam*, Vintage (2004).

Aune, David. *The Blackwell Companion to the New Testament* (Blackwell Publishing, 2010).

Dunn, James and Rogerson, John. *Eerdmans Commentary on the Bible* (Eerdmans Publishing, 2003).

Formica, Michael. "Objectification and Sexualization of Women," *Psychology Today* (June 2, 2008). Retrieved from https://www.psychologytoday.com/us/blog/enlightened-living/200806/objectification-and-sexualization-women.

Gleeson, Hayley and Baird, Julia. " 'Their cross to bear': The Catholic women told to forgive domestic violence," *ABC News*, November 4, 2017, abc.net.au/news/2017-11-04.

Golsteyn, Bart and Schils, Trudie. "Gender Gaps in Primary School Achievement: A decomposition into endowments and returns to IQ and non-cognitive factors," in *Economics of Education Review* (Volume 41, August 2014) 176–187.

Gordon, Linda. *The Moral Property of Women: A History of Birth Control Politics in America*, Chicago: University of Illinois Press, 2002.

Hatch, Linda. "The American Psychological Association Task Force on the Sexualization of Girls: A Review, Update, and Commentary" in *The Journal of Treatment and Prevention* (Volume 18, 2011).

Jalilvand, Mahshid. "Married Women, Work, and Values" in *Monthly Labor Review* (Issue 8, August 2000) 26–31.

Kim, Marlene. "Women Paid Low Wages: Who They Are and Where They Work," in *Monthly Labor Review* (Issue 9, September 2000) 26–30.

Maseno, Loreen and Shabani Mligo, Elia. *Women within Religions: Patriarchy, Feminism, and the Role of Women in Selected World Religions*, Wipf and Stock (2019).

Meyers, Debra. "I Am Heartily Sorry: The Roman Catholic Church and Domestic Abuse," in Debra Meyers and Mary Sue Barnett, eds. *Crisis and Challenge in the Roman Catholic Church: Perspectives on Decline and Reformation*. Pittsburgh, PA: Rowman and Littlefield (2020) 223–244.

Miller-Perrin, Cindy and Wurtele, Sandy. "Sex Trafficking and Commercial Sexual Exploitation of Children," in *Women and Therapy* (Volume 40, issue 2, 2017) 123–151.

NCADV, *National Statistics Domestic Violence Fact Sheet*. NCADV webpage retrieved August 19, 2020 from https://www.ncadv.org/statistics.

Newsom, Carol and Ringe, Sharon eds. *Women's Bible Commentary*, Westminster John Knox Press (2012).

O'Brien, Jennifer E. and Li, Wen. "The Role of the Internet in the Grooming, Exploitation, and Exit of United States Domestic Minor Sex Trafficking Victims," in *Journal of Children and Media* (Volume 14, issue 2, 2020).

Plaskow, Judith. "Feminist Anti-Judaism and the Christian God." *Journal of Feminist Studies in Religion* 7, no. 2 (1991): 99–108. Accessed August 18, 2020. www.jstor.org/stable/25002158.

Rutledge, Martin Shawn. "Biological Father/Daughter Sexual Abuse and Step-Father/Step-Daughter Sexual Abuse Compared" thesis for Master of Social Work at the University of Manitoba (1991).

Sensus Fidelium, "Marriage & Incompatibility—Archbishop Fulton Sheen," (originally broadcast in 1964), YouTube video, December 29, 2012. Retrieved from https://www.youtube.com/watch?v=QtMKPaG7vVA.

Swift, Jaimee and Gould, Hannah. "Not an Object: On Sexualization and Exploitation of Women and Girls" (January 2020) Retrieved from UNICEF USA's website on August 5, 2020 https://www.unicefusa.org/stories/not-object-sexualization-and-exploitation-women-and-girls/30366?webSyncID=7b2514a7-6d5d-6ec1-a073-b5571d0576a8&sessionGUID=65879593-3442-144b-6887-053827d3ec94&_ga=2.1215 51435.2132436888.1596722461-858287951.1596722461.

Ward, L. Monique, "Media and Sexualization: State of Empirical Research, 1995–2015" in *The Journal of Sex Research* (Volume 53, 2016).

Welner, Michael. "Child Sexual Abuse: 6 Stages of Grooming" Retrieved from website on August 10, 2020 http://www.oprah.com/oprahshow/child-sexual-abuse-6-stages-of-grooming/all.

CHAPTER 5

A Squeegee in Your Path

Resisting Erasure

Johanna W.H. van Wijk-Bos

The hegemony of patriarchal thought in Western civilization is not due to its superiority in content, form or achievement over all other thought: it is built upon the systematic silencing of other voices.[1]

∴

A little more than six years ago I found myself listening to a sermon preached by a student in the chapel of our seminary focusing on her experience of being raped, engaging it with a difficult text from a psalm with denouncements of enemies and prayers for vindication against them through divine help.[2] In her searing account of being raped multiple times by three different men, this young woman showed not only her vulnerability but also her wisdom, her understanding of feelings of hatred and her slow regaining of trust in herself and in others. Through her testimony I learned a new language to approach this difficult topic in sacred scripture. As she told her own story, linking it to imagery used in the psalm, she tapped into the power of story to unlock buried pain and cries of distress from those with similar experiences. It was a personal story, and therefore unique, but also a story shared by many women. Recently the revelations made public by the #Me Too movement have once again brought to attention the frequency of women's molestation in our culture.

---

1 Gerda Lerner, *The Creation of Feminist Consciousness: From the Middle Ages to Eighteen-Seventy* (Oxford: Oxford University Press, 1993), 282.

2 Psalm 59 includes lines as the following: 2. Deliver me from my enemies, O my God, and from those who rise against me protect me. 3.Deliver me from the workers of evil and from men of blood save me. 4. For, look, they lie in ambush for my life; they attack me, those strong men, not for my offense, and not for my sin, Adonai! ... 7. They come back every evening, they howl like dogs and prowl around the city. 8. See, they froth at the mouth, daggers from their lips, for who is listening? ... 14. Make an end to them in wrath, make an end, so they be no more; may they know God is ruler in Jacob, to the ends of the earth.

In listening to our student's sermon what struck me most besides her story of the deeply wounding experience of violation was what happened in the aftermath. Few people in her environment were equipped to receive her story, so that she not only lost trust in herself and her judgment but also in those around her because she could not give voice to what had happened. Something this shameful and *dirty* had to wiped out. A devastating result of her rape was that she lost her voice. It was only through a long struggle and with the help of an unlikely biblical text that she was able to name what happened to her. Such instances, including my own less violent experiences, all examples of struggles against being erased, afford momentary views when the tip of the iceberg of patriarchal malfeasance against women becomes visible.

The title of this essay is a variation on the song "Un Violador En Tu Camino"/ A Rapist In Your Path.[3] Its lyrics directly confront the violence of patriarchy, which the perpetrator commits with impunity. Like the psalm cited by the preacher in our chapel, the women of the song state their innocence, declare that the violence against them did not happen because of something they did, how they appeared, or what they wore, which somehow would make it their fault.[4] The virus that is currently swamping the globe has put an end to live performances for the time being, but its thoughts and words are with us to stay, as they tear at the webs of patriarchal actions and ideologies that hold us imprisoned. With the "squeegee" of my title I have in mind the instrument that sponges dirt from a surface, a useful and seemingly benign tool. I chose it because what may appear benign and insignificant, even useful, in order to wipe away what is dirty and unwanted, in reality may abet the cover-up of inconvenient and even deadly truths.

Going back in my own history, I recall an incident when I was a young woman in graduate studies at my university in Europe in the 1960's. At that time all the professors in my department were male as were most of my peers. Although our classes were small, few professors engaged in any sort of dialogue with their students. Of twenty students in one class, five of them were perhaps women; in this particular class the professor was more generous than

---

3   The song with the accompanying dance was created by the Valparaiso Feminist Collective Las Tesis. First performed in Santiago, Chile, on November 25, 2019, it quickly became hugely popular. Its video became viral and both song and dance were performed all over the world. https://www.youtube.com/watch?v=mjhGYeKHkbQ

4   Psalm 59 also protests the speaker's innocence: 4. *Look, they lie in ambush for my life strong men plan an attack on me; not because of my fault and not because of my mistake, o God. 5. I have done no wrong yet they are ready to attack me.*

most in putting aside time for the attendees to make their voices heard. On one occasion, when we were invited to make an observation or pose an inquiry, I raised my hand to ask a question. Admittedly, this was a rarity, for I cannot recall any woman raising her hand in class at any time during those years. Of the question or the response nothing has remained with me, neither of the topic under discussion or the issue about which I was curious. Only the shockwave that went through the classroom once I opened my mouth has stayed with me clearly. Later, I heard that the professor had discussed the matter of my *boldness* with colleagues and administrators. I experienced no significant repercussions but clearly it was the exceptional nature of my gender rather than the content of my question that called for comment and attention. I was accepted as a student, allowed in the classroom, but with the unstated condition that I would not make my presence known by drawing attention to it through my voice. Making my gender the focus caused erasure of anything significant I might have brought to the discussion.

Many years later, living in the United States with a husband and our small son, when I had finished my doctoral studies, a position in my field was advertised in another state. The university that awarded me my degree had an administrative office, run by someone in charge of circulating my dossier, a privilege for which I paid a small fee. When I called the office to inquire if my Vita had gone out so I could apply for the opening for which I seemed suitable, she told me she had seen the posting of the position but judged the location to be too far away for me to commute. Again, all the attention was on my gender, defined as wife and mother, and constructed in a way to extinguish any professional life to which I might have aspirations. A bigger swipe of the squeegee occurred that time, potentially putting up a roadblock on the path toward the exercise of my vocation.

Compared to a story of violation, these two examples seem trivial, but even such seemingly insignificant cases serve to highlight the constant battering of misogyny a woman receives when functioning in a profession dominated by men. Once I set the wheels in motion to have the appropriate papers sent together with my application, I eventually received the position that I held for forty years. I had the luck to have an extremely supportive mate, whose watchful eye had initially discovered the advertisement for the position. Thus, a small crack, opened for me by a vigilant and encouraging husband, turned into an open door, and I got my job. It turned out that before a final decision was made by the faculty to recommend me to the Board as the new hire, a number of my colleagues, all of them male at the time, argued in favor of hiring two teachers for the same position, accepting me as the female and adding a male. Clearly someone of my gender needed the male half! Subsequently, there would be a great deal of sexist and misogynist comments and treatment that were wounding and made my work environment threatening and unpleasant. But, as one of my male colleagues used to point out with some frequency, it was so much worse in other schools! I did not know how good I really had it! So, be quiet already! The squeegee continued to do its work. Professional reviews of my early years regularly included comments about my physical appearance and demeanor. Apparently, I did not smile often enough.[5]

Those of us who came of age in the twentieth century grew up at the tail-end of modernity. In the modern age logic and reason were regarded as the tools to lead humanity to objective truth. Industrialization, technological innovation and capitalism are the hallmarks of modernity for the developed world. Within these frameworks male and female genders each have their place, and while the male is enough by himself, the female is not enough to be a person in her own right, to carry the load, do the job, in other words to exercise the function of a human being. Women were excluded from education, professions and politics because it was not in their *nature* to do so. In the words of Rosemary Radford Ruether: "Woman is ... defined as a *relative being* who exists only in relationship to the male, who alone possesses full autonomous personhood." She surmises that this view of woman may be the "ultimate core of misogynism"[6] Although this understanding of the female is rooted in classical periods it took on new shape and function in modernity. The stated conviction of my former colleagues in the mid-seventies that they were willing to settle for a female colleague if they could also hire a male is a testimony to the fact that this perspective was alive and well in American culture and religion in the late 1970s.[7] Because the exclusion of women became more visible in the modern age, this also became the period in which resistance took place and gains were made in terms of access to education, professions, and political power, albeit at the cost of physical and psychological suffering, and enormous consumption of time and energy. In the United States it goes without saying that patriarchy with its oppression and silencing of women has gone hand in hand with the practices of slavery, so that gains in

---

5 Such comments were not only sexist but xenophobic in that the critics took no account of my different cultural origins.

6 Rosemary Ruether, *Liberation Theology: Human Hope Confronts Christian History and American Power* (New York: Paulist, 1972), 100.

7 Since my institution was a theological seminary the irony of this position *vis a vis* the biblical story of humanity's creation is hard to ignore. In the classical creation story of Genesis 2, the male is not enough by himself so that the female is created as a corresponding half (Gen 2:18).

many places affected only white women and were made at the cost of dividing women from one another.[8]

In post-modernity which arrived somewhere around the middle of the twentieth century and which still defines contemporary modes of expression, everything, including reason and logic, is a construct.[9] Multiple truths define the landscape, and our understanding of the world becomes more fluid and diverse, also in terms of gender which is equally conceived of as a social construction. This era has presented openings for rights and privileges in regard to women's autonomy over their bodies, the freedom to live according to one's chosen rather than assigned gender, and to enter into marital relationships with persons of the same gender, for example. While in modernity religion was the guarantor of the moral sphere separated from that of the state, in post-modernity religion becomes an area of personal preference, which can lead to a mix and match approach, Christianity mixed with Zen Buddhism, or a search for rapprochement between religions that were heretofore hostile to one another. At the same time, steps that move cultures forward habitually unleash a virulent backlash, especially, although not only, from the direction of religious conservative strongholds. Once again, it serves to listen to Ruether as she observes that periods of serious backlash "are usually an indication that women are attempting to enlarge their sphere of activity and are colliding with male efforts to prevent it."[10]

Religious institutions are mainly "conserving" bodies, organizations that exist to uphold traditional values and mores, rather than to change them. Openings toward change may occur in the first stages of formation, including challenges to practices related to gender roles. Such "transgressive" impulses

---

8   Susan Thistlethwaite argues that "American patriarchy is inextricably interwoven with race and class as well as sex." *Sex, Race, and God: Christian Feminism in Black and White* (New York: Crossroad, 1989.)

9   It is a misunderstanding to conclude that truth does not matter in the post-modern context. Truth is as important as always, but it is arrived in complicated ways and through engaging different conversations.

10 Rosemary Radford Reuther, *Disputed Questions: On Being a Christian* (Nashville: Abingdon, 1982), 119. In her landmark book *The Creation of Patriarchy*, the Austrian-American scholar Gerda Lerner, who pioneered women's history as a field of academic studies, defines patriarchy as "the manifestation and institutionalization of male dominance over women and children in the family and the extension of male dominance in society in general." *The Creation of Patriarchy* (Oxford: Oxford University Press, 1989), 239. Sexism she defines as "the ideology of male supremacy, of male superiority and beliefs that support and sustain it." "... as long as sexism as an ideology exists, patriarchal relations can easily be re-established, even when legal changes have occurred to outlaw them." *The Creation of Patriarchy*, 240.

are often quickly opposed and wiped out for a variety of reasons, one of which is the desire to maintain status quo in areas where change is not absolutely required and maintaining well-established cultural norms.[11] Thus, early Christianity appears to have included women as full partners in support and evangelization, to ultimately deprive them of the claim to full humanity.[12] Times of change pose a particular challenge to religious institutions because of their nature to be conserving of tradition.[13] While the era of post modernity has ushered in profound changes in cultural and religious relations, it has at the same time created a yearning for a return to traditional values, bringing back periods of perceived stability and common understandings of oneself and the community in which one lives.[14]

On the other hand, religion is more than the standard bearer for traditional values and morality. Christian and Jewish traditions maintain a sacred text, which they confess to be a living document in which believers meet the spirit of the divine to help them negotiate paths forward out of current predicaments. While these texts contain regulations and instructions that continue to establish moral standards for contemporary believers, they also provide direction through telling powerful stories. The writers of the Hebrew Bible and

---

11   See Elisabeth Schüssler Fiorenza, especially *In Memory of Her: A Feminist Theological Reconstruction of Christian Origins* (New York: Crossroad, 1983) and *But She Said: Feminist Practices of Biblical Interpretation* (Boston: Beacon, 1993).

12   That women's voice is taken away in texts as 1 Corinthians 14; 33–35 and 1 Timothy 2: 11–15 also witnesses to the fact that women were indeed participating in supporting the apostolic evangelizing efforts. The most egregious example of the Scriptural voice arguing against women's full humanity is surely in 2 Timothy when the writer makes the declaration that women "will be saved through childbearing, provided they remain in faith, love and holiness, with modesty." (1 Timothy 2: 15) In other words, women are not saved through Christ but through bearing children and that only under certain conditions.

13   This is one reason why religion seldom leads the pack in the course of cultural change and reformation. Religious support for the institution of slavery in the United States can be cited as well as the latest struggles to accept gender identities other than the traditional heterosexual cis-gender in mainline Protestantism in the United States. My own denomination, the Presbyterian Church USA recognized same-sex marriage in the same year the United States Supreme Court ruled its legality, 2015. The church made its decision only after a long and divisive battle, lasting more than forty years, and other mainline churches are still not reconciled to full acceptance.

14   The ongoing and seemingly unbreakable support for Donald Trump's presidency in conservative Christian circles can only be explained from this desire to return to ways and relationships of the past, which must be achieved no matter whether their leader in his personal life gainsays everything their own lives reflect in terms of honesty, reliability and sexual libertinage. There is no question but that this past existence is illusory and unreachable. The dangerous part of the illusion is the support for a person who is in no way suited to be a head of state, who has the talent to tap into these fears and yearnings.

the Second Testament tell their histories for a great part in story-form. They understood how a people's past is most effectively told by relating historical events in ways that entertain as well as teach, providing information about a community's yesterday in order to engage the listener in their own day, and help them to find meaning in their world and chart a path for the future.[15] Like the young preacher in our pulpit with which I began, they knew that the story has the ability to shape an understanding of their own world for the listener making it possible to find a way through its difficulties and entanglements. Post-modern understandings of the sacred text enhance the possibilities of hearing and applying the stories in new ways, perceiving not only one voice, but the different voices that speak in them and finding coherent themes in the multi-voiced chorus.

If patriarchal arrangements and patriarchal ways of seeing the world is all one has known, even if we subject it to critique and scrutiny and resistance, it may escape us that these arrangements and ideologies have a history also and that they have not always been the same. Recently, the painter Artemisia Gentileschi of the Italian baroque period came to the attention of the art world through several exhibits, the most recent in the National Gallery of London. The lead-sentence of the online piece announcing the exhibit reads: "In 17th century Europe, a time when women artists were not easily accepted, Artemisia was exceptional."[16] It is a truth easily taken for granted that in previous eras, women in male dominated professions were rare because they did not belong in the art world. Actually, the acceptance of women in the world of art today is still limited, to go by the relative scarcity of artwork by women artists on display in major museums in the United States. As recently as 2019 the Museum of Modern Art in New York increased its percentage of paintings by women to 28% from its previous 3.8 percent. Julia Jacobs in a review published in the New York Times of September 25, 2019, concluded that only 11 percent of "art acquired by the country's top museums for their permanent collections

---

15   As a scholar of the Hebrew Bible, I consider the facts of ancient Israel's history to be important and in need of attention and the term "historical" to be appropriate for a great deal of biblical material. All the same the biblical text does not contain history writing as we recognize it today. "Taking the differences between the ancient world and the modern era into account, we may ascribe the category of historiography to the Historical Books of the Bible." Johanna W.H. van Wijk-Bos *The End of the Beginning: Joshua & Judges* (Grand Rapids: Eerdmans, 2020), 3. See also Rachelle Gilmour, *Representing the Past: A Literary Analysis of Narrative Historiography in the Book of Samuel* (Leiden: Brill, 2011).

16   https://www.nationalgallery.org.uk/exhibitions/artemisia.

is by women."[17] This percentage, contrary to expectations does not reflect an upward trend, but has "remained relatively stagnant." It is not surprising then that a general opinion of 17th century Europe, surely an age even less hospitable than our own (!), would judge it to be a climate that was unwelcoming to the woman painter. *Swish, swish goes the squeegee.*

In fact, the Italian art world of the late Renaissance and the early Baroque saw a flourishing of women as professional practitioners of the visual arts, Artemisia only one among them. It is not difficult to find the names and pictures of dozens of women painters of the period in Italy alone. As I wrote about Artemisia and other painters of her day:

> It is important to recognize Artemisia but it is equally important to remember her in the context of a period when the door for women opened to a world of possibilities beyond traditional expected roles. When Gentileschi is defined as the "only woman" painter of her time, making her the exception and an outlier, this recognition is established at the cost of ignoring her talented and productive sister artists. Also, erasing the memory of women's presence in a male dominated field of the past discourages participation in present times. If we cannot find ourselves by looking at the past it is going to be difficult to take on non-traditional roles in the present. A door that is wide open can become a door ajar and then a door that closes altogether. We do well to keep this in mind today. Vigilance in preserving her memory and that of the multitude of women who contributed to the visual arts through the centuries is always in order.[18]

Patriarchal arrangements and ways of seeing the world is what we know; erasure of women through violence and taking away their voices is what we know; thus we tend also to erase voices and presence of women in the past, when we assume things must have been so much worse than they are in our own day. Something happens in our view of the past that blocks us from recognizing our own presence there, perhaps the most pernicious result of the activity of the squeegee, for it robs us of a history, and therefore of seeking a way forward into

---

17   Julia Jacobs, "Female Artists Made Little Progress in Museums Since 2008, Survey Finds."
       New York Times, https://www.nytimes.com/2019/09/19/arts/design/female-art-agency
       -partners-sothebys-artists-auction.html#:~:text=The%20exhibition%2C%20called%20
       %E2%80%9CWomen%20Take,part%20of%20their%20permanent%20collection.
       Jacobs based her conclusions on an analysis done by Artnet.

18   http://johannabos.com, "The Art of Erasure."

the future. Our perspective is everywhere blinded by the patriarchal structures and ideologies that are a part of our current world.[19]

A word of caution then, before we step into the biblical world. The cultures in which the Hebrew Bible took shape are ancient; biblical literature was composed in the context of literary and cultural traditions of civilizations around the Mediterranean, far removed from today's western world in terms of space and time. It takes special effort and attention to listen to the voices that come to us from such a different place. Although in general the biblical text is unfamiliar territory, many people assume familiarity. If we state that world was a patriarchal world, we probably make an assumption of familiarity that leads us astray. Patriarchy does not always wear the same face, and patriarchal arrangements have undergone considerable changes in history. Biblical scholar Carol Meyers: "patriarchy may always be present but it is not always the same."[20] With Meyers I understand the dynamics of gender hierarchy to be context specific. The Hebrew Bible especially does not give evidence of imposing a gendered perspective on its world in depicting women as "other" and less human to explain their subordination. The position of women in ancient Israelite society was not supported by ideological underpinnings. This does not make of the biblical world a "feminist paradise" or imply that women were not at a disadvantage but at least "the Bible does not add insult to this disadvantage, does not claim that women need to be controlled or need to be directed because they are passive, or any other justifications for male domination that have been prevalent in Western culture."[21] Such claims are still powerful today notwithstanding the progress that has been made in terms of women's access

---

19   Gerda Lerner: "Human beings have always used history in order to find their direction toward the future: to repeat the past or to depart from it. Lacking knowledge of their own history, women thinkers did not have the self-knowledge from which to project a desired future. Therefore, women have, up until very recently, not been able to create a social theory appropriate to their needs. Feminist consciousness is a prerequisite for the formulation of the kind of abstract thought needed to conceptualize a society in which differences do not connote dominance." *The Creation of Feminist Consciousness* (Oxford: Oxford University Press, 1993), 281.

20   Carol Meyers, *Discovering Eve: Ancient Israelite Women in Context* (Oxford: Oxford University Press, 1988), 28–29 and *Rediscovering Eve: Ancient Israelite Women in Context* (Oxford: Oxford University Press, 2013), 180–202. Lerner in her comments on the definition of patriarchy: "It implies that men hold power in all the important institutions of society and that women are deprived of access to such power. It does *not* imply that women are either totally powerless or totally deprived of rights, influence and resources." *The Creation of Patriarchy*, 239.

21   Tikva Frymer Kensky, *Reading the Women of the Bible: A New Interpretation of their Stories* (New York: Schocken, 2002), xv.

to traditionally held male occupations and professions Binary gender codes are alive and well in our world and may also dominate our reading of a text that comes from a very different world. If it is taken as a given fact that 17th century Europe lagged far behind our more enlightened times in regard to participation of women in certain fields, surely this is even more true of eras that long preceded them! *Swish, swish goes the squeegee.*

From the ancient biblical world comes the story of princess Tamar, the daughter of Queen Ma'acah and King David, in the kingdom of Israel (full text located in the Appendix).[22] She was a daughter of royalty on both father and mother's side. Her mother was the daughter of king Talmai in Geshur, the current Golan Heights. At her introduction into the story, her name is wedged between her two brothers, adding an unnecessary double mention of her father's name. The note that she is beautiful is relatively rare in the Bible which only occasionally refers to the appearance of a person.[23] Her name means palm tree and she may have been named for her foremother Tamar on her father's side, through her great-great-grandparents Ruth and Obed.[24] Although David did not keep as large a harem as many kings did in that part of the world, the household was extensive with sizeable grounds and lodgings in the precinct of the palace for the grown-up members of the household; a busy place with a lot of coming and going of administrators, servants, and relatives other than the immediate family.[25] Absalom was Tamar's full brother and Amnon her half-brother by David's wife Ahinoam of Yezreel.[26] The piling on of male names around the beautiful Tamar bodes ill. Amnon was the oldest, David's

---

22   See Appendix for the complete text of 2 Samuel 13: 1–22. For theological and literary commentary see Johanna W.H. van Wijk-Bos, *Reading Samuel: A Literary and Theological Commentary* (Macon, GA: Smith & Helwy, 2011), 201–206 and Johanna van Wijk-Bos, *The Road to Kingship: 1–2 Samuel* Vol 2 in *A People and a Land* (Grand Rapids: Eerdmans, 2020), 291–95 and 337–41.

23   The observation about looks is made more often for the family of David than for others. David himself is spoken of as "ruddy," with "beautiful eyes," and his wife Abigail is also introduced as a "beautiful woman" (1 Samuel 25: 3). Bathsheba the mother of Solomon, who appears in the story with all its attendant drama just before the tale of Tamar, is called "very beautiful" (2 Samuel 11: 2) and later in the history his son Absalom is said to be more beautiful than anyone in all of Israel (2 Samuel 14: 2).

24   The story of that Tamar makes for an interesting tale as told in Genesis 38. See also Ruth 4: 12.

25   According to biblical record Solomon had 700 wives and 300 concubines (1 Kings 11: 3). Even though this number is likely an exaggeration of the reality in accord with exaggerated accounts of numbers at the time, a large harem was probably the norm, established both for diplomatic reasons and as a symbol of the status of the monarch.

26   The biblical text records a total of at least 17 children born to David by various wives (2 Samuel 3: 2–5 5: 14 and 12: 24).

presumptive heir, with Absalom third in line. Amnon is said to "love" his sister, which could mean that he lavished a great deal of attention on her, spoiled her as a younger sister, for example. To abuse the reader of that possibility the information follows immediately that something else is going on, for Amnon is making himself sick, not just about his feelings, or perhaps not at all about his feelings, but rather about the fact that there are rules about sex with a virgin among his people so he can't see his way to "do something to her."[27] There are also laws against sexual relations between family members, but this aspect does not arise yet.

A fourth male character pops up to get things moving, a cousin on Amnon's father's side, one Yonadav, by reputation a smart fellow. He invents a plan: Amnon will pretend to be ill, not too hard under the circumstances, and when his father, the king, comes to visit him on his sickbed he can ask him to allow Tamar to come and prepare him a special dish, something to comfort him, make him feel better while he is watching her.[28] Perhaps Tamar had a reputation for preparing special foods for the sick, or perhaps the idea is that the sight of a beautiful woman will revive his flagging health. Apparently, David's permission, as head of the household, is needed for Tamar to visit her half-brother, so the plan is set in motion. First, everything works as foreseen and Amnon does as his cousin advises. He asks King David if his sister Tamar, may come and prepare him some special food his presence. The delicacy he suggests inserts an interesting variation on the "comfort" food Yonadav had proposed. Amnon substitutes a word literally meaning *heart-cakes*. This is, after all, a matter of the heart![29] The king makes the request of Tamar, which, although politely framed, counts more as a command coming from her royal father. Thus far the story portrays patriarchal arrangements. Tamar is a secondary character, surrounded by powerful males, significant only in that she is used as a pawn on the chessboard, the means to solve a problem for the crown-prince.[30]

---

27   According to biblical law a man who had sexual intercourse with a virgin had to marry her. (Exodus 22: 16; Leviticus 21: 14; Deuteronomy 22: 19).

28   The term used in the Hebrew connotes such a diet rather than food in general. When you eat this kind of this you become healthy or fat. Robert Alter, *Ancient Israel: The Former Prophets: Joshua, Judges, Samuel and Kings* (New York, London: W.W. Norton, 2013), 496fn5.

29   The language of the scene reminds strongly of love language, especially as it appears in the Song of Solomon. Food as a comfort for lovesickness is appealed to in Song of Solomon 2: 5 and 5: 8. "Sister" or "my sister" is part of the Song's love language (Song of Solomon 4: 9, 10, 12; 5: 1, 2; 8: 8).

30   Although the line of succession does not get established by David until he is almost on his deathbed (1 Kings 1), being the oldest male descendant in a household counted for a

Unsuspecting, Tamar does the prince's bidding when he asked her for food since he is her half-brother after all and next in line to become the king. She comes prepared with her ingredients and as soon as she enters his house, we see everything in detail: he is lying down, she makes the dough, kneads it, shapes it into hearts and bakes the cakes with him watching. Then she hands him the food, but he refuses to eat and instead commands everyone else to leave so that they are alone, and invites her into his bedroom, a more intimate place, where he promises he will take the food. Perhaps her instincts tell Tamar that something is not exactly the way it should be with everyone out of the way while she remains alone with her brother in his bedroom; it may feel uncomfortable, but she still acts on trust. Food was demanded and food is what she prepares and offers. But, instead of taking the food, Amnon takes her, the language here is violent, and he tells her to sleep with him, then as now a euphemism for having sex. At this point all movement in the story stops because Tamar opens her mouth to speak.

Granting a character speech in a story enhances their presence and significance. Thus far the only characters who are quoted directly are two men, Yonadav and Amnon. Not only does Tamar receive a voice, but her words are powerful and true. What we know about Tamar is only that she is beautiful. We can figure out that she must have been young, but we do not know how young, because she still lives in her parents' house. A young woman who has come into her beauty. Fourteen? Fifteen? Sixteen? Amnon must have been a great deal older, mentioned in the text already before David is crowned king over all Israel.[31] He lives in his own house, and thus most likely has a family. Tamar so far has done everything an obedient daughter and sister of an older brother does. Nothing in the story creates the expectation that she will put up any resistance. But she does resist, strongly and wisely. First, she pronounces an unequivocal "No!" That one word should have been enough, but she has more to say. She calls Amnon "my brother," pointing to their family relationship. She points out that his abuse will shame her and Amnon himself will be disgraced as well. What would she do as a violated woman? Who would marry her? "Where would I go with my shame?" she demands. Finally, she is able to summon up the courage to offer counsel. Although there are laws that forbid brother and sister marriage, it is possible that especially for royal

---

lot and the rise of King Solomon, who was nowhere near the throne in the pecking order, takes place only after deliberate manipulation of the king by two court officials, one of whom includes his mother Bathsheba. It is also worth noting that Solomon's ascension goes accompanied by abundant bloodshed (1 Kings 2).

31   2 Samuel 3: 2.

offspring exceptions could be made, as was the case elsewhere in the world around Israel. So she urges Amnon to ask King David, the final authority in such things.[32] Tamar has the longest speech in the episode, a speech filled with strength and wisdom, showing her ability to think even when in great danger. It's about her, but also about her family, about her and Amnon as members of a people with an ethos, with norms. They are people of privilege, a part of the royal household, the king will be open to his son's request.

Her logical arguments and request do not help her, for Amnon refuses to comply and rapes her. The text piles up words that highlight his malfeasance: *he did not want to listen; he overpowered her and raped her.*[33] And it gets worse, because even at this point there might have been a turn in a different direction; but instead of repenting, instead of offering comfort, Amnon sends her out with harsh words. Although the prince is not polite in any part of the story and speaks mostly in command-form except when he talks to other men, overtly abusive words follow his abusive deed. Disgusted perhaps with himself and projecting his disgust onto Tamar, he orders her out, ignoring her protest that sending her away is worse than what he has already done! He asks a servant to throw her out of his house, locking the door behind her. While the insult of making one of his servants cast her out lends a particular egregious note to the proceedings, in addition, the politeness with which he addresses his attendant stands in contrast to the brutality of his tone to Tamar, to whom he refers now as "this one." Presumably, Amnon was himself entirely capable of bringing her to the door but in handing this task to an underling he shows both unwarranted cruelty, and cowardice.

Once again, we watch Tamar in vivid detail as the text in an extraordinary twist turns attention to her clothes. She was wearing a special dress, either long or especially colorful, to indicate her status in the royal household as a virgin daughter of the king.[34] Once outside, she shows obvious signs of mourning, putting ashes on her head and tearing her robe. In addition, she refuses to be a silent victim as she walks around crying aloud. She needs the world around

---

32   For an insightful article about this story see Anna Carter Florence, "Listening to Tamar: Pay Attention to the verbs and who controls them," *The Christian Century* 135, 2018, 26–29.

33   Literally the text reads: "he did not want to listen to her voice, he overpowered her and abused her and slept with her." A short sentence with five verbs to underscore the depravity of his action.

34   The detail is exceptional because the biblical text rarely affords insight into people's clothing. The adjective describing Tamar's robe occurs only twice in the Bible, with the other reference in respect to the robe of Joseph, given to him by his father (Genesis 37: 3, 23, 32). The meaning of the word describing the robe is not entirely clear.

her to know that she has been violated. According to biblical law, a "girl who cries out when she is attacked is considered innocent of sexual wrongdoing."[35]

Then the last, and not the least, significant moment in the drama happens: her brother Absalom encounters her although we do not hear how or when. The rumor about Amnon's infatuation was likely known around the court, since Absalom asks her if Amnon "was with her," and then goes on to tell her to be quiet. Absalom, another beautiful child of David, does not listen to his sister any more than Amnon did. Although on the surface his action is one of kindness, his words are inhibiting, and he makes light of what has happened to her by telling her not to not let it affect her too much, not to take it "to heart." Absalom does what those in the circle of the raped victim do best, be they friend or family: he shushes her. The last sounds we hear from Tamar is her crying out, for she becomes a "desolate woman," a description that in the Bible occurs in connection with destroyed and deserted land.[36] She moves into Absalom's house and never marries; the only member of the family she could count on offers her protection but no comfort. He trivializes her bereaved state of a single woman who drags the shame of her rape around with her, and while he affords her protection, he is busy pursuing an agenda of his own, one that will soon become evident in the story.

Amnon was the rapist in Tamar's path, her father became her brother's enabler, and Absalom is the one wielding the squeegee to erase Tamar's voice. She was correct in pointing out that the aftermath of the rape was worse than the violence itself. Her very presence was wiped from the board by the males in her family. King David is furious according to the storyteller, but he does not do anything about his daughter's suffering, then or later. Absalom's reaction is hatred for Amnon who is as of this moment marked for death. A tragic story, one familiar to our own context in which a woman finds no resolution than a continuing spiral of violence playing itself out in her circle of intimates; where she finds no ear to listen to her voice, to hear her tell the tale in order to find healing and regain trust. She is gone from the story.

Tamar was indeed a beautiful woman, not primarily because of her appearance or clothes, but because she resisted her rapist. The episode does not take place in a vacuum, of course. It follows on the heels of King David's rape of Bathsheba, condemnation by God's prophet, and the death of a husband and a child. In Anna Carter Florence's words since as of that time there is "the chilling sound of the predator sniffing the air."[37] After Tamar's violation, the story

---

35   Tikva Frymer-Kensky, *Reading the Women of the Bible: A New Interpretation of their Stories* (New York: Schocken, 202), 165–66.

36   Isaiah 1: 7; Ezekiel 23: 33; 35: 7; Joel 2: 20; Zephaniah 2: 9.

37   Carter Florence, "Listening to Tamar," 27.

continues with the murder of Amnon by Absalom, followed by palace intrigue and a political coup which sets King David on the run, causing more sexual violence, ending only with the death of David's treasured son in battle. Violence begot violence. The only wise words are spoken by women in this tale of kingship teetering on the brink of collapse, a household divided against itself and a people who are on the verge of complete disarray. Even for the storytellers of the Bible who do not shy away from severe critique of people and leaders, sparing few their merciless spotlight on deeds of human ugliness, these chapters in the histories called after the prophet Samuel paint a tragic tale of overweening pride and oblivion to moral responsibility. In the end, three of David's sons have died and equilibrium in the kingdom is hanging by a thread. The rape of Tamar is not quite the beginning, but it serves as another symbol of the disarray that marks David's kingship as of the time he first set eyes on Bathsheba.

Tamar lost her voice, as many victims of sexual and domestic violence lose their voice, forced into silence by the powers that be or the incapacity of the surrounding circles to hear the story, to accept the ugly facts, to hold the hand of a sister in solidarity. She comes out of the palace, goes into Amnon's house, is raped and ends up a desolate woman in the house of brother Absalom. Her cries of violation unheeded, unheard. It happened to her not because of anything she did, not because of the way she dressed or behaved, or what she ate or drank. She speaks eloquently and well to her rapist, she does what she is supposed to do and no one is willing to listen. It is a story that takes place in a patriarchal world of the Bible, but it is a world we recognize readily for a reason. It looks eerily like our own world. Anna Carter Florence writes "asking how a text might go differently is another way of asking how our lives might go differently." This text is one that makes her affirm that we can "claim the strength of standing together. We can claim the outrage of planting our feet. And we can claim the freedom of imagining new endings."[38] We can pick up the cry of Tamar of anguish and indignation and cry it out to the world with her.

I propose we go still further in continuing her voiceless presence and look again at the complete account of King David, from the time he violates Bathsheba and commits cowardly murder by ordering a hit on her husband, to the moment he comes home after Absalom is killed only to face another rebellion in his kingdom. David takes up a lot of space in the Bible, with a large presence that marks two biblical books. He was obviously one of those people to whom stories accrue, heroic tales of great and awesome defeats and clever manipulations. He is charismatic, everyone falls in love with him when he first

---

38   Carter Florence, "Listening to Tamar," 29.

comes on the scene and he outwits his powerful boss at every turn. King Saul never manages to catch him and dies an ignominious death on the battle-field. David is the proverbial character whose path is marked by good fortune. Above all David enjoys the favor of Israel's God. Divine guidance and counsel follow him wherever he goes, steering him right making his plans align with the Deity's design. It is a trusting relationship on David's side who consults God along his difficult road to kingship with great frequency. All of this can be said until the chapter in his life when he sees a beautiful woman bathing from the vantage point of his rooftop, from which moment events take a radical turn in the wrong direction.

Scholars put the boundaries of these stories and their markers at different places, but they always include chapters 9–20 in Second Samuel.[39] Generally, commentators assume that the material came from one hand, someone with a clear eye for David's foibles and the less admirable parts of his nature.[40] The chapters show cohesion of subject and style and depict a king in stark con-trast to what came before. They can be read as one story with a king who takes a wrong turn at the beginning, in the course of events jeopardizing both his kingship and his realm, and at the end regaining a fragile stability. Unlike the depiction that led up to them in 1 and 2 Samuel, the narratives paint a David who takes unnecessary risks on behalf of his own needs and desires, a fond father who indulges his sons, and condones the rape of his daughter by not calling the perpetrator to account. He turns a blind eye on the machinations of another son who first murders his brother, then manages to stage a revolt, and he leaves the women in the palace behind to be raped by his rebel son. He is no longer with his soldiers on the battlefield but sits impotently waiting for news about the death of his sons, first Amnon, then Absalom. It is hard to imagine anyone farther from the young hero who stole everyone's heart at the start of his career. Above all, there is no question of divine guidance in this material. David does not ask the deity for counsel, in regard to his family or his kingdom, nor does he receive any beyond an announcement of consequences for what he has done. God is for the greatest part absent from this part of David's life.

Already in the late nineteenth century American biblical scholar Henry Preserved Smith considered this part of 2 Samuel to be a "homogenous and

---

39   The perimeter of this material sometimes identified as the Court History of David are variously defined as consisting of 2 Samuel 9–20+ 1 Kings 1+2 or 2 Samuel 9–20.

40   For two treatments of King David that put him in a more negative light see Joel Baden. *The Historical David: The Real Life of an Invented Hero* (New York: Harper Collins, 2013) and Baruch Halpern, *David's Secret Demons; Messiah, Murderer, Traitor, King* (Grand Rapids: Eerdmans, 2001).

continuous narrative of David's life."[41] He and other scholars proposed various possible authors, all of them male. Smith also argued that the original author was someone close to the events, but that it would be the "height of temerity to determine a setting" for these texts. The prophet Nathan or Gad, each having a place in the account, have both been candidates for authorship. Taking all these suggestions into consideration and agreeing that the author likely was someone close to the events, I assume also that the story was originally in *written* form. The literary skill of the story is striking to everyone who comments on it.[42]

Are we taking part in the erasure of women by ruling out possible authorship by a woman? Are the arguments against this possibility much like those of the reviewer who judged a bygone era to be an unwelcome place for a woman artist? Is it possible to escape our patriarchal reading of the world of the past? That women composed text is recorded in the Bible itself.[43] Is there anything that holds us back from assigning this story to a female author? Bathsheba and Tamar both come to mind as candidates, but my preference goes to Tamar. Unlike Bathsheba, she has a voice in the story and her reasoning is complex and sturdy. If with Carter Florence we want to claim the freedom of "imagining new endings," are we not free to imagine this new ending?

The ancient world was indeed patriarchal but not exactly in the same way as our world; it was a less gendered world and women in biblical culture filled a great number of professions. Biblical scholar Carol Meyers lists textile work, food-processing, healthcare, cultic activities, prophecy and musical composition and performance among the professions open to women in that time and place.[44] Biblical scholar Wilda Gafney has convincingly argued for membership of women among scribal guilds, both in the larger ancient Mediterranean world and Israel.[45] Much of the biblical material is anonymous, authorship can only be surmised. I suggest that the assumption of an all-male authorship for the Hebrew Bible stems from persisting patriarchal prejudice. The sanest voices in the stories of 2 Samuel 9–20 are those of women: Tamar in chapter 12, the wise woman of Tekoa in chapter 14 and the wise woman of Abel

---

41   Henry Preserved Smith, *The Books of Samuel* (Edinburgh: T&T Clark, 1899), 310.

42   For more extensive comments on literacy in the biblical world, see van Wijk-Bos, *The End of the Beginning*, 31–32 and 150.

43   Exodus 15: 20–21, and Judges 5: 1–31, for example.

44   Carol Meyers *Rediscovering Eve: Ancient Israelite Women in Context* (Oxford: Oxford University Press, 2011), 171–79.

45   Wilda C. Gafney, *Daughters of Miriam: Women Prophets in Ancient Israel* (Minneapolis: Fortress, 2008), 123–30.

in chapter 20.[46] It is very possible that Tamar was a literate woman, trained in the schools common at royal courts. Living in the house of her brother did not mean she was imprisoned; she may have congregated with other clever women at the court, including Queen Bathsheba, her own mother Ma'acah, and Abigail, one of David's wives who is called "insightful."[47] She did not have the preoccupations of most women with family and teaching of children, which would have left her more freedom and the opportunity to write down the story of her father and his court as she saw it. In doing so, she reclaimed the voice her brother had taken away, and our acknowledgment of her authorship returns her voice to her.

I began this essay with a reflection on events that illustrate the erasure of women's presence and their voice in current contexts dominated by patriarchal ideologies. I argued that such perspectives not only influence modes of perceiving the present world, but also our reading of the past. One way to reclaim our presence is to resist the erasure of women's voices in history. Tamar, granddaughter and daughter of kings, wrote it all down, including the story of Bathsheba and Uriah and the story of her own rape and humiliation, drawing on material she knew from earlier traditions.[48] Her view of the world around her, permeated by male violence that she wanted to bring to light, does not make for a lifeless or a loveless story. On the contrary it pulses with all the profound feeling of which the human heart is capable. We have no proof of her authorship of course, but that can be said of much of the biblical text. We may have it all wrong, but we could do worse than taking our stance here, resisting the squeegee of erasure and listening to Tamar's story. By assigning to Tamar the creation of the work of art that became the Court History of David, we raise up her voice and not only cry together with her the cry against the misogynist violence, but also stake a claim against erasure of the female voice in contributing to the writing of sacred history.

Appendix

2 Samuel 13: 1–22:[49]

2 Samuel 13: 1–2: Afterwards, this happened: Absalom, the son of David, had a beautiful sister, whose name was Tamar, and Amnon, the son of David, loved her. Amnon

---

46   Following this line of thinking I have in the past argued for female authorship of Genesis 38 Ruth, and Ecclesiastes.

47   See 1 Samuel 25: 2.

48   Van Wijk-Bos, *The Road to Kingship*, 341.

49   Author's translation based on the traditional Hebrew text.

was so distressed that he became sick on account of his sister Tamar, for she was a virgin. It seemed impossible in Amnon's eyes to do something to her.

2 Samuel 13: 3–5: Now Amnon had a friend whose name was Yonadav. He was the son of Shimah, David's brother. Yonadav was a very clever man. He said to Amnon: Son of the king, why are you so down every morning? Won't you tell me? Amnon answered: I love Tamar, the sister of my brother Absalom! Yonadav said: Stay in your bed and fake illness, so your father will come to see you. Then say to him: Please, let my sister Tamar come and comfort me with food. Let her make the comforting dish before my eyes, so I can watch and eat from her hand. So Amnon went to bed and faked illness and the king came to see him. Amnon said to the king: Please, let my sister Tamar come, and let her bake some heart-shaped cakes in my presence, so I can take this comfort from her hand. David sent word to Tamar at home: Please, come to the house of your brother Amnon and make him some comforting food.

2 Samuel 13: 8–14: Tamar went to Amnon's house and he was lying down. She took dough, kneaded it, and shaped it into hearts with him watching; then she baked the cakes. She took the pan and set it before him and he refused to eat them. Amnon said: Everyone out! And everyone left. Amnon said to Tamar: Bring the comfort-food to the bedroom so I can eat it out of your hand. Tamar took the heart-shaped cakes she had made and brought them to her brother Amnon, in the bedroom. When she brought them to him to eat, he grabbed her and said: Sleep with me, sister! She said to him: Oh no, my brother, don't force me, for we don't do things like that in Israel. Don't do something so disgraceful! Where would I take my shame? And you! You would be disgraced in Israel. Why don't you speak to the king, for he will not keep me from you. But he did not listen to her; he overpowered her and raped her.

2 Samuel 13: 15: Then Amnon came to hate her deeply. The hate with which he hated her was greater than the love with which he had loved her He said to her: Get up! Out! She said to him: Oh no, don't do that! Sending me away is worse than what you did to me! But he did not want to listen to her. He called one of the men who waited on him and said: Please, send this one away from me. Outside with her and close the door behind her! Now she was dressed in a fancy robe, the way the virgin daughters of the king were dressed. His man led her outside and closed the door behind her. Tamar put ashes on her head, and tore the fancy dress she wore and put her hand on her head, walking around crying out loud.

2 Samuel 13: 20: Her brother Absalom said to her: Has your brother Amnon been with you? Now be quiet, my sister; he is your brother; don't break your heart over it. Tamar stayed desolate in the house of her brother Absalom. When King David heard all this he was furious. Absalom did not say anything to Amnon either good or bad, for Absalom hated Amnon because he had raped his sister Tamar.

Bibliography

Alter, Robert. *Ancient Israel: The Former Prophets: Joshua, Judges, Samuel and Kings* (New York, London: W.W. Norton, 2013).

Baden, Joel. *The Historical David: The Real Life of an Invented Hero* (New York: Harper Collins, 2013).

Carter Florence, Anna. "Listening to Tamar: Pay attention to the verbs and who controls them," *The Christian Century* 135, 2018, 26–29.

Gafney, Wilda C. *Daughters of Miriam: Women Prophets in Ancient Israel* (Minneapolis: Fortress, 2008).

Gilmour, Rachelle. *Representing the Past: A Literary Analysis of Narrative Historiography in the Book of Samuel* (Leiden: Brill, 2011).

Halpern, Baruch. *David's Secret Demons; Messiah, Murderer, Traitor, King* (Grand Rapids: Eerdmans, 2001).

Frymer-Kensky, Tikva. *Reading the Women of the Bible: A New Interpretation of their Stories* (New York: Schocken, 2002).

Lerner, Gerda. *The Creation of Feminist Consciousness: From the Middle Ages to Eighteen-Seventy* (Oxford: Oxford University Press, 1993).

Lerner, Gerda. *The Creation of Patriarchy* (Oxford: Oxford University Press, 1989).

Meyers, Carol. *Discovering Eve: Ancient Israelite Women in Context* (Oxford: Oxford University Press, 1988).

Meyers, Carol. *Rediscovering Eve: Ancient Israelite Women in Context* (Oxford: Oxford University Press, 2013).

Ruether, Rosemary Radford. *Liberation Theology: Human Hope Confronts Christian History and American Power* (New York: Paulist, 1972).

Ruether, Rosemary Radford. *Disputed Questions: On Being a Christian* (Nashville: Abingdon, 1982).

Schüssler Fiorenza, Elisabeth. *In Memory of Her: A Feminist Theological Reconstruction of Christian Origins* (New York: Crossroad, 1983).

Schüssler Fiorenza, Elisabeth *But She Said: Feminist Practices of Biblical Interpretation* (Boston: Beacon, 1993).

Smith, Henry Preserved. *The Books of Samuel* (Edinburgh: T&T Clark, 1899).

Thistlethwaite, Susan. *Sex, Race, and God: Christian Feminism in Black and White* (New York: Crossroad, 1989).

van Wijk-Bos, Johanna W.H. *The End of the Beginning: Joshua & Judges* (Grand Rapids: Eerdmans, 2020).

van Wijk-Bos, Johanna W.H. *Reading Samuel: A Literary and Theological Commentary* (Macon, GA: Smith & Helwys, 2011).

van Wijk-Bos, Johanna W.H. *The Road to Kingship: 1–2 Samuel* Vol 2 in *A People and a Land* (Grand Rapids: Eerdmans, 2020).

CHAPTER 6

Resistance to Gender-Based Violence and Femicide

Mary Sue Barnett

It was a bright, summer afternoon with the warm wind flowing through the open windows of the car. I heard, *"Where are you going?"* so distinctly that I thought my friend in the car had asked me a question. But she was looking out her window without having said a word. The words so clearly spoken, and heard, I was briefly startled to realize no person in the car was speaking to me. In a few moments I realized I was experiencing something from my own intimate depths—so quiet and still I had been at the retreat center, I was deeply attentive. To experience such a lovely query, so undeniably personal while at once transcendent, my heart began to hold the question, the very sound of the words, on that day and into my future. My listening heart, or mystic heart, is what guides my priesthood, chaplaincy, and human rights advocacy for women and girls today. As this chapter's focus is an exploration of a mystical healing[1] response to women and girls traumatized by misogynist violence, woven throughout are accounts of my inner experiences, poetic outreach, and embodied resistance that followed that day of hearing, *Where are you going?*

1 Inner Experiences

Hiking along a remote forest trail in early spring, blackbirds and bluebirds singing into the silence, I suddenly perceive a wailing in the woods. I feel it within my being. It rises from my core while also rising from over there, off the trail, down in the woods, in a clearing. The wailing comes from a horrified woman, a victim of violence. Though fiercely wanting to live, she is dying. Desperate to be heard, she

---

1   Mystical Christianity is a secret well-kept and does not serve empire, or patriarchy, or churchiness, says Matthew Fox. Mysticism is a launching into the depths of the unconscious, into the deep feminine, wisdom, compassion, and heart. It is a deep dive into one's self/Self where one travels an intimate path toward and with the Divine. I agree with Fox that deep down, each person is a mystic and every mystic is a healer, a conviction that is central to this author's invitation to the reader. I will use the terms mystic and contemplative interchangeably. For more on mystical Christianity, see Matthew Fox, *Christian Mystics: 365 Readings and Meditations* (Novato, California, 2011).

screams from a crouched position, her cries carried by the wind upward and out-
ward. Though terrifying, I am deep at peace as I walk among the prairie bluestem
and periwinkle, purple ground blossoms rising through a blanket of dried leaves,
enjoying dappled shade under a wide blue horizon. Tranquility is in knowing that
the wild cry of the Holy is sounding from within the very heart of the woman's
wailing, summoning, "Step off the trail, descend into the clearing, draw near!"
Spring 2020

A victim and survivor of misogynist violence may be like a female Eastern
bluebird that sits at the top of a dead tree—from her barren, lonely perch she
sings a distress song. She longs for an end to her isolation and for the dawning
of human connections when love can reach her traumatized depths. I open
with my experience recounted above to share an available mystical path for
healing and resistance in a world that normalizes the ontological inferiority of
females, a global landscape where women and girls are terrorized by harassment, sexual assault, stalking, rape, domestic violence, trafficking, and femicide. I invite readers, particularly Christian religious leaders, to turn inward
and follow a path of descent into one's own being. In sharing this mystical
experience, I hope to herald a way of plumbing the traumatized depths of the
soul for redemption, not yet seen nor heard, but longed for. I see it as a gateway into an individual and communal soul space where the female victim and
survivor is centered, where healing presence and voices are called to gather
around her, and where mystical hope draws hearts to transcend misogynist
devaluation of female humanity. This chapter will include guideposts for this
inward sojourn including biblical lament, the early Christian desert dwellers,
insights from Beverly Lanzetta's via feminina, and the wisdom of victims and
survivors.

Misogynist physical, sexual, and spiritual assaults perpetrated on a female
human being in the world today cause extreme suffering. Biblical lament literature can open doorways of the heart and can shine light on the extremities of female suffering in a misogynist world. If one listens deeply, the
multimillennial-old holy words can awaken one to crucial, sacred feminine
truths today. The ancient psalmist cries deeply inward to the self, "Why are you
cast down, O my soul, and why are you disquieted within me?"[2]

Today, how lonely it is for a female human being, raped by a man, to shriek
within herself as she feels reduced to a shadowy abyss. The psalmist's plea is
also directed to the Holy, "O God, you are my God, I seek you, my soul thirsts
for You; my flesh faints for You, as in a dry and weary land where there is no

---

2 Psalm 42:5 (New Revised Standard Version).

water."[3] Today, how painful it is for a female human being trafficked and raped by men, to yearn for Divine Presence as her body, her life, is stolen from her control, from her rightful place in the land of the living.

The ancient city of Jerusalem, personified as Daughter Zion, "weeps bitterly in the night with tears on her cheeks" for "all her gates are desolate."[4] Today, how terrifying it is for a female human being brutalized by an intimate partner, to feel completely closed in on herself with no horizon toward which her being can breathe, stretch, and become. Daughter Zion cries out to the people, "Is it nothing to you, all who pass by? Look and see if there is any sorrow like my sorrow."[5] Today, how agonizing it is for a female human being stalked like prey by a man, to feel cut off from safety, untethered in a chaotic existence. Daughter Zion cries directly to the Holy One to see her to see, "how distressed I am, my stomach churns, my heart is wrung within me."[6] Today, how horrifying it is for a female human being suffering misogynist assaults to her mind, body, and soul, that she feels contemptible to her God.

The writing of this essay coincides with the 2020 Covid-19 global pandemic when on Sunday, April 5th, Palm Sunday, United Nations Secretary-General Antonio Guterres called for a ceasefire in the horrifying global surge in domestic violence directed towards women and girls following global Covid-19 lockdowns. Guterres said, "Peace is not just the absence of war. Many women under lockdown for Covid-19 face violence where they should be safest: in their homes."[7] He urged all governments to put women's safety first as they respond to the pandemic. Executive Director of UN Women, Phumzile Mlambo-Nguka announced that as countries around the world locked down, women's shelters and domestic violence helplines were reporting record calls for help. Women of diverse ethnicity, race, and class sought relief from the terrors of violent men. Government authorities, women's human rights activists, and civil society partners have flagged increasing reports of domestic violence during this crisis, and heightened demand for emergency shelter. She stated, "We see a shadow pandemic growing; violence against women ... Even before COVID-19 existed, domestic violence was already one of the greatest human rights violations."[8]

---

3   Psalm 63:1 (New Revised Standard Version).

4   Lamentations 1:2,4 (New Revised Standard Version).

5   Lamentations 1:12 (New Revised Standard Version).

6   Lamentations 1:20 (New Revised Standard Version).

7   Daniel Klapper, "UN SG calls for domestic violence 'ceasefire' after surge related to COVID-19 lockdowns," April 7, 2020. jurist.org.

8   Phumzile Mlambo-Ngcuka, "Violence against women and girls: the shadow pandemic," April 6, 2020. unwomen.org.

Gender based violence and femicide is a global scourge rendering the world a parched and weary land for so many women and girls. During the spring and summer months of 2020, terror struck women and girls. Rebekah Workman was murdered in her home by her husband,[9] Karleigh Miller was murdered by her boyfriend in her car,[10] Breonna Taylor was murdered in her home by police;[11] three femicides perpetrated in Louisville, Kentucky. Nineteen year-old Black Lives Matter activist, Oluwatoyin Salau was sexually assaulted and murdered in Florida.[12] Fort Hood soldier Vanessa Guillen, who had been sexually harassed, went missing and was later found murdered (#IAmVanessaGuillen movement surges online with hundreds sharing stories of sexual trauma in the military).[13] A sixteen year old girl was gang raped in Israel while on vacation.[14] Daisy Coleman committed suicide at twenty three after suffering for years with the nightmare of having been sexually assaulted at fourteen years old in Missouri while unconscious and discarded afterwards on her front lawn where she lay lightly clothed for hours in twenty-two degree weather.[15] A thirteen year old girl in Malawi was found screaming for help in a bathroom after she was sexually assaulted by a Catholic Church catechist.[16] Brayla Stone, a seventeen year old transgender girl was murdered in Arkansas, a victim of transmisogynoir femicide. Advocates continue to raise their voices that transgender women of color face multiple forms of discrimination.[17] Sydney Sutherland, a twenty-five year old nurse, was abducted, sexually assaulted, and murdered in Arkansas while out jogging near her home.[18] Nineteen year

9   Gil Corsey, "Louisville murder-suicide case underscores city's fears of uptick in domestic violence," April 14, 2020, wdrb.com.

10   Billy Kobin, "Police: Louisville man charged with fatally shooting woman at Seventh and Hill streets," June 5, 2020, courier-journal.com.

11   Darcy Costello and Tessa Duvall, "Minute by minute: What happened the night Louisville police shot Breonna Taylor," September 15, 2020, courier-journal .com.

12   Giulia McDonnell Nieto del Rio, "Oluwatoyin Salau, Missing Black Lives Matter Activist, Is Found Dead," June 15, 2020, nytimes.com.

13   Johnny Diaz, Maria Cramer, and Christina Morales, "What We Know About the Death of Vanessa Guillen," August 14, 2020, nytimes.com.

14   David M. Halbfinger, "Vacationing Israeli Teen Says She Was Gang-Raped, Shocking the Nation," August 20, 2020, nytimes.com.

15   Lili Loofbourow, "Why Do We Think 'Believing' Rape Victims Is Enough?" August 13, 2020, slate.com.

16   Nyasa Times Reporter, "Catholic catechist arrested for sexual assault on 13-year-old church choir member," August 20, 2020, nyasatimes.com.

17   Elliott Kozuch, "HRC Mourns Brayla Stone, Black Trans Girl Killed in Arkansas," July 1, 2020, hrc.org.

18   Steve Helling, "Suspect in Killing of Ark. Jogger Allegedly Saw Her While Driving, Then Doubled Back to Abduct Her," August 25, 2020, people.com.

old sex trafficking victim Chrystul Kizer awaiting trial for killing her perpetrator was finally released on a $400,000 bond after spending two years in a
Wisconsin jail.[19] Amnesty International reports that women and girls in Sub-
Saharan Africa are at increased risk of suffering violations of their rights.[20]
Tatyana Moskalkova, Russia's High Commissioner for Human Rights, reported
the number of calls to domestic abuse hotlines jumped from just more than
6,000 in March 2020 to more than 13,000 in April 2020.[21] Isabel Cabanillas, a
twenty-six year old women's rights activist was murdered in Juarez, Mexico
and feminist collectives chanted in the streets, *Ni una más, ni una más, ni
una asesinada más, Not one more, not one more murder.*[22] And twelve year old
Napali, Samjhana BK, was kidnapped then raped and murdered inside a temple near her house.[23] In the first six months of this year, hundreds of thousands
of females around the world have been shaken to their core and continue to
suffer traumatic reverberations caused by misogynist violence, sorrowing in
their depths and crying for relief and compassionate connection. So many
have been stolen from the earth, leaving painful voids to be reckoned with.

Misogynist violence is an attack on female humanity and divinity. In a
female's spiritual depths where she suffers the trauma, God as a female suffers there with her. Christian leaders around the world today can boldly avail
themselves to the safety, relief, and healing of women and girls. Nothing less
than a radical spiritual response will reach the suffering depths and losses, and
nothing less than a radical spiritual response will drive out the evils of misogyny. This radical spiritual response begins with a hitherto unknown sojourn
into one's inner self. It is a path of significant personal risk where the Holy
leads one along the terrible way of undoing. Although it is a path leading into
new depths of Holy mystery and love, the misogynist world, including male-
dominant Christianity, will disparage and reject those who embark on this
sacred sojourn.

As stated in the description of my mystical experience above, the wailing
comes from my experience of the Holy, the Holy Who hears the cries of women

---

19   Ryan Brooks, "Chrystul Kizer, A 19-Year-Old Sex Trafficking Victim Who Killed Her Abuser,
      Has Been Released From Jail," June 23, 2020, buzzfeednews.com.

20   Amnesty International, "Sub-Saharan Africa: Government Responses to COVID-19 should
      guarantee the protection of women and girls' rights," May 7, 2020, amnesty.org.

21   Moscow Times Reporter, "Domestic Abuse in Russia Doubles Amid Virus Lockdown:
      Official," May 5, 2020, themoscowtimes.com.

22   Ecleen Luzmila Caraballo, " 'Ni Una Mas': Hundreds Demand Justice for Isabel Cabanillas
      and Countless Other Femicide Victims," January 27, 2020, remezcla.com.

23   Jagat Khadka, "Victim's family does not wish to see her body before culprit is arrested,"
      September 27, 2020, myrepublica.nagariknetwork.com.

and girls and knows intimately their suffering (Exodus 3:7), Who, compared to light, is found more radiant (Wisdom 7: 30), Who bears sufferings, and through Whose wounds, healing happens (Isaiah 53: 3–5). It is the Holy in female cruciform that echoes the terrifying scream from within the bodies and souls of women and girls who are diminished, desperate, and ravaged. It is the Holy in female cruciform Who calls for courageous, sacred sojourners *to step off the trail and to descend into the clearing,* to walk a steep path of descent into one's inner life. This path of soul wilderness, though likely a fierce unsaying of one's life and vocation as it is, holds within it a broad horizon. In heeding the call of the Holy in female cruciform, one becomes uniquely opened to a radical communal love with power to transform deserts of misogynist terror so that man who is of the earth may strike terror no more (Psalm 10:18). Rather than deserts of sexual assault, rape, and femicide, landscapes will become lush forests and gardens of vivid color where women and girls breathe, speak, sing, and dance as fully safe and fully free in their female selves. The Holy in female cruciform sounds a sharp, seemingly impossible, paradoxical call; enter female terror with her/Her to heal it.

In my young adulthood I volunteered for a Rape Crisis Center in Louisville. I sat with sexual assault, molestation, and rape victims in hospital emergency rooms and responded to calls on the crisis line. Called at any hour of the day or night, I was present, bearing witness to her trauma while allowing inner space for my own. It was my hope to bring a perceivable gentleness and respect into the hospital room or over the phone. The muteness of victims was consistently haunting. Even over the phone, I would often simply offer a listening presence to someone who needed loving human connection as she fought to survive. I would hear breathing, soft cries, and so few words. In this I witnessed how misogynist violence, its terror and shock, thrust women and teen girls into inner chaos where their voice, once a vibrant expression of their unique selfhood and deepest being, was submerged, by force, somewhere deep inside.

It was during these years that my understanding of *Wisdom Sophia,*[24] began to shift. For some years prior, I had experienced an awakening to the Divine Feminine as overwhelmingly liberating mystery and personal joy. At one point in my young adulthood I experienced a vivid image of an inner door. Upon choosing to open this door into the soul, I felt my existence affirmed with benevolent expansiveness. There are no words for this joy. The divine benevolence

---

24 Biblical Wisdom, Sophia in Greek, is "simply God, revealing and known," and "an expression of the most intense divine presence in the world." Elizabeth A. Johnson, *She Who Is: The Mystery of God in Feminist Theological Discourse* (New York, NY: Crossroad, 1992), 91, 92.

of expansive light and possibility within my being was a beautiful grace. In my being I felt profoundly *summoned by Her* as though my own female face and body were enfolded within an inexplicably *intimate*, female divine presence. And then the comfort of this intimacy began to evolve into something new. As I grew into this grace, I began to feel more deeply over time an irreconcilable dissonance between the freedom of the Divine Feminine dwelling within and the caustic misogyny of the world with its male-dominant Christianity. The following lines are woven throughout a poem I wrote during those years; *Clenched firmly and fiercely in Her fist is my red, fleshy heart—and the shift is realized—Wisdom is Struggle, is War, is the Feminine on the Battleground—She blinds from the inside out, from the outside in, all worlds are suddenly, rudely different—in this irrevocable cocoon—the force of Her fight terrifies my life.*

To live into this quaking within my own soul meant becoming distanced from the church where pervasive extremities of female suffering are silenced and perpetuated. Many of my horizons in the world closed, my inner light went dim, and my inner spaciousness constricted painfully. I was left with a solitary cry at my center, at one moment a cry for myself, another moment a cry for another woman's trauma, and another moment, a cascade of weeping that seemed to come from everywhere. It was indeed a wilderness, a barren cathedral, a lone female Eastern bluebird singing a distress song from a lifeless tree. Sitting with female victims during rape exams was my contemplative ascent to the Divine Feminine roaring Her call through my marrow. It was my gradual undoing, a preparation for the strengthening of my heart.

The Divine Feminine is the crucible of munificent and sublime care of female humanity. She Who Is configured to victims of gender-based violence and femicide, invites Her people into the fire. With unimaginable fierceness, She wails from the woods, summoning healers to be near her/Her. Desert Christians in the early centuries of the church chose to dwell in desert landscapes to find God in their center. They detached themselves from the influence of culture and institution. Desert landscapes of rocky terrain, dangerous clefts, and frightening nothingness provided the opportunity for Desert Mothers and Fathers to be still and to hear the Holy speak to the heart. Belden Lane writes that amazing things happen on the edges; "Demons are cast out, lepers are healed, the blind are given sight. Who knows what might happen out there on the boundaries, in the "wilderness," in the wild unpredictability of desolate places?"[25] As early Christian mystics settled in the dust of the desert

---

25   Belden C. Lane, *Desert Spirituality and Cultural Resistance: From Ancient Monks To Mountain Refugees* (Eugene, Oregon: WIPF & Stock, 2011), 22,23.

to become attuned to the stark call of the Holy, feminist contemplatives today can pitch a tent in their own hearts to become attuned to the wailing of the Holy in female cruciform, she/She who is crouched over in anguish. This is the edge, the desolate place, the liminal space. This is the chaotic unknown where the Holy calls for radical trust, trust that in surrendering one's heart to the suffering, this liminal space of deep interiority will unearth the profound worthiness of femaleness and the feminine, finally unburied from misogynist ruins.

As a young woman making the inner descent, my extended times of solitude and silence led my heart to edges where I *pitched a tent*. For instance, during the early 1990's when Bosnian women and girls were targeted with systematic gang rape, "some as young as twelve or fifteen years old—who endured unimaginable horrors around them,"[26] I listened in silence. I felt the horror in silence. The stillness of my heart opened me to their devastation. With full respect for their Muslim faith, the spiritual impact of their suffering in my core, took the form of my faith. These words are woven through a poem I wrote then; *Her Body is in the Garden where the olives grow. Her body is on the kitchen floor, in the desert, in the emergency room, on the dirt floor, in the desert. It is Her. It is You. It is Me—Her Body is on the tree—to reach Her grave in moments prematurely, unnaturally—the girl, the young woman, the old woman—Her feet have memorized the terrain of Golgotha.* Connecting in femaleness, and cleaving in spirit across faith traditions, one can *be* for another.

For women particularly who feel called to embark on an inner descent into the wilderness seeking spiritual nearness to female victims of gender-based violence and femicide, it is important to point out Beverly J. Lanzetta's book *Radical Wisdom: A Feminist Mystical Theology* as a rich resource. She writes of the Divine Feminine as breaking into history unveiling a gift for women; "the feminine heart of divinity and the spiritual equality of women."[27] She describes the *via feminina,* as a new mystical path in which the undoing or the unsaying of a woman's life involves the explicit work of pulling up "the sources of misogyny imbedded in their souls."[28] It is a holy negation of misogynist falsehoods and distortions planted in a woman's and girl's soul. The self-emptying of misogynist toxins is a path of powerful self-discovery in which a woman can begin to see her own face, her own soul held in the light of the Divine Feminine. The light is also a darkness as the process of deep healing

---

26   Ian Black, "Serbs 'enslaved Muslim women at rape camps,' " March 21, 2000, the guardian
      .com.
27   Beverly J. Lanzetta, *Radical Wisdom: A Feminist Mystical Theology*, (Minneapolis: Fortress
      Press, 2005), 13.
28   Lanzetta, *Radical Wisdom*, 13.

is strenuous and undergoing transformations is disorienting. Related to this, Lanzetta writes, "A woman's dark night requires a breaking and tearing of thought patterns and ways of knowing and loving that perpetuate a fundamental falsehood that women *by nature* are less."[29] Ursula King lauds Lanzetta's *Radical Wisdom* as innovative, pointing out that the *via feminina* necessarily transforms or subverts "the traditional spiritual journey, by turning in two directions," "inward toward the divine center of the self, and outward toward the world."[30] King and Lanzetta agree that the *via feminina* must include the naming and eliminating of spiritual oppression and myriad forms of gender-based violence against women. The via feminina is the mystical pathway to union with the Holy in female cruciform.

Philosopher Ann J. Cahill explores the concept of derivatization in her book, *Overcoming Objectification: A Carnal Ethics,* as portraying, rendering, understanding, or approaching "a being solely or primarily as the reflection, projection, or expression of another being's identity, desires, fears, etc. The derivatized subject becomes reducible in all relevant ways to the derivatizing subject's existence—other elements of her being are disregarded, ignored, or undervalued."[31] A derivatized woman is required to mirror men's desires, actions and choices. Beyond those desires, she explains, "a derivatized woman cannot exist, cannot speak, and cannot act."[32] If a woman resists derivatization by claiming a subjectivity beyond the male derivatizer, she is met with male anger and retribution. In sexual derivatization of women, a woman's body is not targeted and exploited as a *thing,* but "as the sight of her sentience and her potential for agency."[33] Cahill states that as derivatization involves reducing one being to the subjectivity of another, "then non-derivatization as an ethical imperative demands a mutual, dynamic interaction."[34] Any person traveling the mystical path of inner descent toward nearness with the Wailing Woman, the female Holy in cruciform, will necessarily undergo a profound undoing of sexual derivatization where female subjectivity is never subjected to male subjectivity. The summoning power of the Divine Feminine is the evocation of love and respect for femaleness and the feminine.

---

29   Ibid., 134.

30   Ursula King, "Pneumatophores for Nurturing a Different Kind of Love," in *Through Us, With Us, In Us: Relational Theologies in the Twenty-First Century,* ed. Lisa Usherwood and Elaine Bellchambers (London: SCM Press, 2011), 57.

31   Ann J. Cahill, *Overcoming Objectification: A Carnal Ethics,* (New York: Routledge, 2011), 32.

32   Cahill, *Overcoming Objectification,* 34.

33   Ibid., 35.

34   Ibid., 54.

2   Poetic Outreach

Because of my loud groaning my bones cling to my skin.
I am like an owl of the wilderness, like a little owl of the waste places.
I lie awake; I am like a lonely bird on the housetop.
All day long my enemies taunt me; those who deride me use my name for a curse.
For I eat ashes like bread, and mingle tears with my drink.[35]

In her book, *Is Rape a Crime? A Memoir, an Investigation, and a Manifesto,* Michelle Bowdler describes herself in a police car after being raped by two men; "That I am dead seems completely probable."[36] She then describes her rape trauma during the rape kit exam at the hospital emergency room; "I am above my body on the ceiling once more, looking down on a person I do not recognize. She is a tiny girl with no control, eyes covered, feeling like nothing more than an object for the second time in less than a few hours."[37] Equally courageous, Karyn L. Friedman shares in her memoir, *One Hour In Paris: A True Story Of Rape And Recovery,* that years after being raped she continued to feel unsafe in her body as though her body was always under threat. And further, "I was having trouble breathing. I have been plagued with this affliction ever since I was raped."[38] She explains that not being able to catch a deep breath, "remains one of my clearest indications that my body is in distress." Friedman points to the pervasiveness of rape and the subsequent distress of sexual violence survivors who are pressured to remain anonymous and closeted in a society that blames and shames them. A profoundly generous survivor, she writes, "My hope is that through focusing intimately inward I am able to relate something that others can connect with."[39]

Chanel Miller writes of the understanding experienced among survivors in, *Know My Name: A Memoir,* as a connection forged in the haunting aloneness following the assault. For her, it was, "Something slipping out of you. Where did I go. What was taken. It is terror swallowed inside silence."[40] She describes

---

35   Psalm 102: 5–9 (New Revised Standard Version).
36   Michelle Bowdler, *Is Rape A Crime? A Memoir, an Investigation, and a Manifesto* (New York: Flatiron Books, 2020), 16.
37   Bowdler, *Is Rape A Crime?*, 23.
38   Karyn L. Freedman, *One Hour In Paris: A True Story of Rape and Recovery* (Chicago: The University of Chicago Press, 2014), 46.
39   Freedman, *One Hour in Paris*, ix.
40   Chanel Miller, *Know My Name: A Memoir*, (Viking, 2019), 6.

this aloneness not as pain, hysteria, or crying, but rather, "It is your insides turning to cold stones."[41] Miller, sexually assaulted behind a dumpster while intoxicated, writes courageously, sharing with her readers details of the intimate harm done to her. Delicately she explains, "After the assault, I felt this need to be touched, but wanted nothing to do with *invade, inject, insert, inside,* only wanted the intimacy of being wrapped up safely in something."[42]

In her essay, "Dead to the World: Rape, Unconsciousness, and Social Media," Cressida J. Heyes offers a philosophical response to society's trivialization of sexual assault and rape committed against unconscious women. She says for women, sleep "can be a state where we are not self-conscious or surveilled and where we can get a respite from the anxieties of bodily exposure,"[43] and she argues "that the sexual assault of a *sleeping* woman threatens her most vulnerable state of anonymity, and her ability to retreat into the night."[44] When raped while unconscious, drugged, or sedated, it "exploits and reinforces a victim's lack of agency and exposes her body in ways that make it especially difficult for her to reconstitute herself as a subject."[45]

Words of hope and strength spoken by survivors are words that "have been forged in the crucible of scorching turmoil."[46] Bowdler, Friedman, and Miller are three survivors, who from the depths of human bravery, have chosen to open themselves to the world. In telling their unique experiences of sexual trauma and the vicissitudes of the healing process, they add vivid, sacred testimony to a global desert landscape of profound body/soul suffering of women and girls. Sharing their inner geography of terror and trauma, survivors are *the* wisdom figures, *the* spiritual leaders, *the* desert mothers with power and knowledge to guide twenty-first century Christian leaders who hear the divine call to pitch a tent near the Wailing Woman.

Cressida describes rape as penetration of the body's depths that damages a woman's or girl's bodily integrity. Within the violated bodily and spiritual depths of women and girls, within the intimate flesh, sinew, blood, and marrow, and within the shallow breath of the soul lying in waste, the Holy is there, in love. Into the deathly stillness and silence, One's mystic heart can hear Her

---

41   Miller, *Know My Name*, 7.
42   Ibid., 58.
43   Cressida J. Heyes, "Dead to the World: Rape, Unconsciousness, and Social Media," *Signs* 41:2, (January 2016): 378, http://www.journals.uchicago.edu/t-and-c.
44   Heyes, "Dead to the World: Rape, Unconsciousness, and Social Media," 378.
45   Ibid., 365.
46   Matt Atkinson, *Letters To Survivors: Words of Comfort for Women Recovering From Rape* (Oklahoma City, OK: RAR Publishing, 2011), 8.

say to Her daughter, *I love you. I love you. I love you,* who in turn may not hear for the all the pain. Her presence is Holy dynamism in the chaotic, lonely depths. In Her power, She raises the violated female up to a crouched position, wailing with her and for her. The wail is the beginning of healing. Soothing balm and gentle light will wrap her round and walk with her toward restoration of her beautiful human integrity and agency, woven back into her divine center. Simultaneously, in the spirit of the Mighty One of the Magnificat, the Divine Feminine holds male supremacy by the jugular. Because it is into these very female bodily, spiritual depths that male-dominant Christian leaders so often force their pronouncements of female ontological inferiority in the name of Father God, nothing less than the Holy, in intimate female cruciform, has the power to drive out the masculine evil of rape upon rape.

As a feministic contemplative, my heart is gripped by the pain of female trauma. Noa Pothoven was raped at eleven years of age and then again by two men when she was fourteen. She suffered from depression, anorexia, and attempts at suicide. She was treated in mental hospitals numerous times, having to be placed in a coma in order to feed her when she was dangerously thin. She wrote a book to help others suffering similarly. At age fifteen she went on her own to the end-of-life clinic at The Hague to request euthanasia but was turned down because of her age. She said she could not wait until she was twenty-one to be evaluated for euthanasia. Her parents, family, and doctors tried desperately to help her. She would not eat and drink and finally they decided not to intervene. Noa died on June 2, 2019 in Holland at the age of seventeen. The mystical poem, "Beautiful Noa," created from a captive heart—my being drawn fiercely into resistance against the sexual violence that brutally severed Noa from the earth while at the same time alighted in the Divine words, *I love you, I love you, I love you,* words imprinted on the wings of mystery bearing a tortured soul into an endless future. The Wailing Woman, within me, near me, and beyond me, is felt to rise upward from a crouched position in the forest, lifting the indescribable suffering into the expanse of divine light and fecundity. Though no longer intimate flesh, sinew, blood, and marrow of the earth, the voice of a femicide victim, *forged in the crucible of scorching turmoil,* can be heard in the wilderness tent pitched within one's own depths. When we gather as desert dwellers, we are emptied to be paradoxically filled with the Divine mystery holding female humanity lost to misogynist violence. "Beautiful Noa," rising from the desert transcendence within my own being, compels me to reach outward and to share in the communal *pitched tent,* my verses, so that together we can bring our love to the trauma, assist in the healing, and be in awe of the Holy One's unfailing powers of recreation against evil. *Come circle now around the mountaintop* is the future, the locus of new redemptive power, to be founded by feminist contemplatives.

Beautiful Noa
Tell it!
Tell it to
the world,
to countries,
courts,
religions.
Yes, tell it
to The Hague—
Rape is evil.
Shout it down.
Pray it down.
Stalk it.
Exorcize it.
Annihilate it.
It burst into
your "house,"
your body,
Noa.
A fatal toxin
seared your soul,
the sanctuary
of your selfhood,
crushing your girlhood,
stealing your joy.
"I'm still breathing,"
"but no longer alive,"
you explained
as rape trauma
defaced your spirit,
afflicted your being,
though you labored
to heal,
fought to
survive.
Women,
men,

humanity,
Come!
'Tis the hour
to scale the
mountain,
'Tis the moment
to trek
the sharp
ascent.
Fueled with
compassion
for her
unbearable suffering,
take the arduous steps.
Driven by
her tragedy,
seek the distant skies.
Drawn into future,
chant the truth—
"Rape is evil."
"Shout it down."
"Pray it down."
"Stalk it."
"Exorcize it."
"Annihilate it."
Women,
men,
humanity,
Come, circle now
round the
mountaintop!
Shhh, listen,
be silent.
You can
sense Noa
in the expanse
of sun
and clouds.
You can
feel Noa

in the softness
of the breeze.
You can
know Noa,
in shining foliage
everywhere.
She is being free.
She is being created.
She is being beautiful.
Beautiful as the sun!
Shhh, listen,
be silent.
'Tis only an
eternity to
hear her song.
Tell this
to the
world too. [47]

In the beginning of her riveting speech to an audience of five hundred men titled, "I Want A Twenty-Four-Hour Truce During Which There Is No Rape," feminist activist and writer Andrea Dworkin said she wanted to scream, a scream that would include the cries of the raped and battered and at the center of the scream is women's silence. She pleaded with the men in the audience to understand that women don't have time, some women don't have another day or another week: "we are very close to rape and very close to beating. And we are inside a system of humiliation from which there is no escape for us."[48] She insisted that if the men were opposed to violence against women then they ought to, "Tell the pornographers. Tell the pimps. Tell the warmakers."[49] If the men were sincerely opposed to gender-based violence, she persisted, then there are streets in which to go out and organize political opposition. With unwavering strength, she told the men, "I want to see the men's movement

---

47   Mary Sue Barnett, "Beautiful Noa," *The Feminist Voice* 1, no. 1 (2019): 25. [Printed with permission from the copyright holder.]

48   Andrea Dworkin, "I Want A Twenty-Four-Hour Truce During Which There Is No Rape," in *Transforming A Rape Culture*, ed. Emilie Buchwald, Pamela R. Fletcher, and Martha Roth (Minneapolis, MI: Milkweed Editions, 2005), 14.

49   Dworkin, "I Want A Twenty-Four-Hour Truce During Which There Is No Rape," 18.

make a commitment to ending rape because that is the only meaningful commitment to equality ... Ending it. Stopping rape. No more. No more rape."[50]

As a chaplain in a psychiatric hospital, I witness the suffering of women. I hear their cries. Some raped. Some beaten. Some molested. Some sex trafficked. Their PTSD is often severe. Some self-harm. Some have attempted suicide. When I am called to her side, I go carefully. I see her cower, tremble, weep. Some are mute. Some scream. Some are guarded, hypervigilant. Some hide beneath a bed sheet. When I am near, there is often silence at first. In the silences, I breathe peace into the space. When I speak, I do so softly. And I say, "My heart is with you." Her healing process is arduous. It is step-by-step. I will walk step-by-step alongside as she paces the halls. As she begins to speak, I listen. There is often despair—*I am not me anymore.*

The spiritual thirst that follows sexual traumatization is profound. It truly is as if the women *eat ashes*. In response to this thirst, I create poetry and prayer to share when there is readiness. Where it is appropriate to the faith tradition of the woman, I share with her my poem, "Mary Magdalene." As female, Mary Magdalene would have suffered sexual derivatization in her patriarchal context. She knew illness, pain and, grief. Catholic poet and mystic, Edwina Gateley, has written a poem titled "Mary Magdalene," in her book, *Soul Sisters: Women in Scripture Speak to Women Today.* In the poem she speaks to Mary Magdalene as a soul sister asking her about her suffering; "What sickness wracked your woman body, Mary," "your spirit was battered in a society that had no place for you. Was your sickness then a soul-sickness, Sister?"[51]

Meggan Watterson, in her book, *Mary Magdalene Revealed: The First Apostle, Her Feminist Gospel & the Christianity We Haven't Tried Yet,* shares her lovely personal experience of the impact of discovery of Mary Magdalene's *voice.* She said it was like finding a church that she had always imagined as a little girl, "a place where we're not trying to be better than anyone else, or to be better than who we are in the moment. Everyone, no matter who we are, and everything, is included, especially the body."[52] Jean-Yves Leloup, in his book, *The Gospel of Mary Magdalene,* writes that Mary Magdalene "represents a human being who is open and available to true 'inner knowing,' and who can 'see' in a deeper, clearer way."[53] In her beautiful book, *The Meaning of*

50   Ibid., 19.

51   Edwina Gateley, *Soul Sisters: Women in Scripture Speak to Women Today* (Maryknoll, New York: Orbis Books, 2010), 118.

52   Meggan Watterson, *Mary Magdalene Revealed: The First Apostle, Her Feminist Gospel, & the Christianity We Haven't Tried Yet* (Carlsbad, CA: Hay House, Inc. 2019), 18.

53   Jean-Yves Leloup, *The Gospel of Mary Magdalene,* (Rochester, Vermont: Inner Traditions, 2002), xxiii.

Mary Magdalene: Discovering the Woman at the Heart of Christianity, Episcopal priest Cynthia Bourgeault writes that Mary Magdalene walked a "path toward inner integration,"[54] and "is a *transformed* woman,"[55] and a "wisdom bearer."[56] Desert mystics can make accessible the spiritual power of Mary Magdalene to the hearts and bodies of traumatized women today.

When bringing my own "Mary Magdalene" poem to the delicate healing hours of a sexually traumatized woman who is hospitalized, the air lightens, the space expands, and breathing deepens—a space for her to be herself. The dynamism, strength, and resistance of Magdalene in my poem is explored with her as possibility for her own strength of resistance and is given to her as a blessing upon her life. If she is open to touch, I hold her hands. When her trust increases, I bring anointing oil for her embodied *whole self.* Mary Magdalene is a *wisdom bearer* not only for the traumatized woman, but for the Christian leaders pitching a wilderness tent in support of her healing. Because Mary Magdalene is still maligned and marginalized by male-dominant Christianity, it is a double-layered act of religious resistance to centralize both her and a female victim of misogynist violence. The wilderness tent is a place for boldly inviting, uncovering, and integrating rejected, buried feminine wisdoms of the Christian tradition, to listen to the scholars, poets, prophets, and mystics in their own inward depths, and to share these riches in trust and love. I once shared my Magdalene poem with a woman who had just escaped a near lethal domestic violence attack. She announced, *I understand every word!*

> Mary Magdalene
> Violence would quell
> your soul
> but you walked
> step-by-step
> away from evil
> Trauma would rout
> your heart
> but you walked
> moment-by-moment
> into the next day
> Tears would becloud

---

54   Cynthia Bourgeault, *The Meaning of Mary Magdalene: Discovering the Woman at the Heart of Christianity* (Boston: Shambhala, 2010), 185.

55   Bourgeault, *The Meaning of Mary Magdalene,* 175.

56   Ibid., 168.

your path
but you walked
breath-by-breath
into the unknown
Grief would avert
your courage
but you walked
pulse-by-pulse
into the vision
Doubt would rescind
your mission
but you walked
pace-by-pace
into the blaze
Loneliness would shroud
your purpose
but you walked
leap-by-leap
into the luminescence
Trepidation would enervate
your passion
but you walked
caper-by-caper
into the joy
Depression would thieve
your hope
but you walked
glide-by-glide
into the tenderness
Death would dissolve
your being
but you walked
wingbeat-by-wingbeat
into the furthermost
from within
your inmost
through all dark
into all light
with truth
on your lips

with Christ
as your shield
with oil dripping
upon the world
from your ancient
holy hands
its blessed fragrance
reaching every
thirsty soul
from the garden
into this moment
the inmost heart
of this moment
now and forever
amen.[57]

3   Embodied Resistance

In December of 1993, I visited the Motherhouse chapel of the Dominican Sisters in Springfield, Kentucky. I had been invited by the Sisters to preach on a Sunday in Advent about my advocacy work for women and girls. Several days prior, a young woman in Louisville lost her life to misogynist violence. Mary Byron, on her twenty-first birthday, was ambushed while in her car in a Mall parking lot. At point blank range, she suffered seven gunshots to her head and chest. The murderer, who had previously raped, assaulted, and stalked her, was an estranged boyfriend who hunted her down immediately after being released from jail. From the pulpit, I spoke Mary's name and lamented the injustice. The tragedy of her rape and femicide was far too profound to be embraced on one night, in one pulpit, in one small chapel. The terror that Mary experienced, the enormity of trauma to her body, to her whole being, could never be contained in one preaching event. The depth and weight of it in my voice felt as though it must push through the chapel walls and ceiling, out into the darkness, over the empty hills of rural Kentucky, and then beyond, so that it could be heard, felt, and carried in communal solidarity to heal it and to cry out together, "Stop!"

---

57   Mary Sue Barnett, "Mary Magdalene," *The Feminist Voice*, 1, no. 1 (2019): 22. [Printed with permission from the copyright holder.]

Following the formal chapel service that evening, the Sisters and I gathered for interpersonal dialogue. One of the Sisters told a story that has continued to stir with vivid resonance within me over the decades. She shared that years earlier when she preached a homily, a male Catholic priest severely criticized many aspects of her content and delivery. Speaking slightly above a whisper, reluctant to share eye contact, I could see her suffering. The male priest, a representative of a male-exclusive church hierarchy, accosted her personhood, her soul, besieging the holy place within her female self where depth words[58] are formed and rise to consciousness to share with others. Those who walk the way of the Wailing Woman are desert contemplatives with communal power to rise in word and in body against misogynist forces that aim to silence the holy wisdom of female humanity and their allies.

The path of descent into one's inner desert to hear the Wailing Woman, the path of drawing near to the Holy Who bears the wounds of sexually violated and murdered women and girls, is a path of radical empathy. It calls one to viscerally know the female wounds, to become the one living the *crucible of scorching turmoil* and the one who *eats ashes*. It is from this inner wilderness that one's soul has space to be filled with the wisdom spoken by victims, survivors, and the resistance. It is to hear their longing hearts deeply enough to become a bold embodiment of comfort and resistance in the world. *Stop Rape,* Andrea Dworkin's plea before an audience of five hundred men, becomes a spiritual command that echoes through the soul's loneliness for the love of oneself and others.

In her anthology, *Not That Bad: Dispatches from Rape Culture,* Roxane Gay gathers voices of victims and survivors across the gender spectrum telling their stories of how they have been marked by rape culture. "When I was twelve years old, I was gang-raped in the woods behind my neighborhood by a group of boys with the dangerous intentions of bad men. It was a terrible, life-changing experience,"[59] she writes in the opening paragraph of her introduction. For a long time she told herself it was *not that bad* but eventually realized that what she and others experienced was indeed *that bad*. In the chapter titled, "Why I Stopped," Zoe Medeiros writes about what helps her as a rape survivor; she chose a therapist who laughs at her jokes and whose office is located by the

---

58   According to Karl Rahner, God's word is located in primordial words that emerge from the depth of the human heart. Depth words, spoken from the center of a person, have potential to become sacraments of divine love. See Mary Catherine Hilkert, *Naming Grace: Preaching and the Sacramental Imagination,* (New York: Continuum, 1997).

59   Roxane Gay, *Introduction in Not That Bad: Dispatches from Rape Culture,* ed. Roxane Gay (New York: Harper Perennial, 2018), viiii.

sea so that following a session, she could, "go stare at something bigger than me."[60] About her comfort, she touchingly writes, "Sometimes I imagine black wings. Specifically, I am lying on my bed at night, on my left side, and I imagine someone climbing in next to me and wrapping long black wings over me."[61]

As Roxane Gay's anthology of rape survivors' testimonies provide heart-rending content for the responsive desert soul, so Diana E. H. Russell's anthologies of voices on femicide provide poignant insight. In *Femicide in Global Perspective,* edited with Roberta A. Harmes, she describes femicide as a lethal hate crime that "is on the extreme end of a continuum of the sexist terrorization of women and girls."[62] It becomes a femicide whenever a form of sexist terrorism results in death. She identifies the following on the continuum: rape, torture, sexual slavery, incestuous and extrafamilial sexual abuse, physical and emotional battery, and serious cases of sexual harassment. The goal of violence against women, she writes, is to preserve male supremacy. Joining voices with Jane Caputi in her volume edited with Jill Radford, *Femicide: The Politics of Woman Killing,* Russell and Caputi hold that if the United States were to become sensitized to all the femicides, nonlethal sexual attacks, battery, and pornography and gorenography as hate literature, then this country would have to "acknowledge that we live in the midst of a reign of sexist terror comparable in magnitude, intensity, and intent to the persecution, torture, and annihilation of European women as witches from the fourteenth to the seventeenth centuries."[63]

Dawn Wilcox provides databases of women and girls lost to femicide in the United States. At womencountusa.org, *her femicide accountability project,* she writes, "This is a sacred victim-centered space. Every woman or girl remembered here was precious and irreplaceable. Their absence continues to cause pain for family and friends who loved them."[64] It is a prayer of lament to quietly see pictures of their unique and diverse faces, read their names, and learn about their stories—thousands in just the last couple of years. The databases will be a shock

---

60   Zoe Medeiros, "Why I Stopped," in *Not That Bad: Dispatches from Rape Culture,* ed. Roxane Gay (New York: Harper Perennial, 2018), 245.

61   Zoe Medeiros, "Why I Stopped," 246.

62   Diana E. H. Russell, "Introduction: The Politics of Femicide," in *Femicide in Global Perspective,* ed. Diana E. H. Russell and Roberta A. Harmes (New York: Teachers College Press, 2001), 4.

63   Jane Caputi and Diana E. H. Russell, "Femicide: Sexist Terrorism against Women," in *Femicide: The Politics of Woman Killing,* ed. Jill Radford and Diana E. H. Russell (New York: Twayne Publishers, 1992), 20.

64   "The Databases." Women Count USA Femicide Accountability Project. Accessed August 1, 2020, womencountusa.org.

to one's internalized normalcy of misogynist violence and will stir heart break in a contemplative desert dweller. Black women are 2.5 times more likely to be murdered by men than white women and disproportionately at risk for intimate partner femicide.[65] The Coalition to Stop Violence Against Native Women (#MMIWG2S Missing and Murdered Indigenous Womxn, Girls, and Two Spirit), whose mission is to stop violence against Native women and children, reports on its website that the U.S. Department of Justice finds that American Indian women face murder rates that are more than ten times the national average.[66]

In Juarez, Mexico, mothers of murdered daughters paint pink crosses on telephone poles. In painting them pink, they are "overtly associating crosses with female humanity."[67] Nancy Pineda-Madrid, in *Suffering and Salvation In Ciudad Juarez,* explains that the pink crosses painted with the victim's name on the crossbar "signals an assault on patriarchal ideology, which has left its imprint on Christianity."[68] The mothers are issuing "an indictment against the complicity of the church and state in the evil of feminicide."[69] The mothers refuse to be silent and risk suffering to embody public resistance. Marking public places with pink crosses that connect crucifixion and female humanity, the mothers are waging a battle against Christianity that remains passive in the face of horrific evil perpetrated against their daughters. They are summoning collective consciousness into the desert to struggle in solidarity for emancipatory space for females, to end the crucifixions, to wrench life from death, and to "insist on hope even in the face of terror."[70]

When the United Nations sent out a global message about the shadow pandemic of violence against women during COVID-19 lockdowns and called for a global ceasefire of this violence, a small group of Louisville clergy pitched our tent on the sidewalk in front of Central Presbyterian Church. Knowing well there are wailing women and girls in our own city, as in every city, and aware of the added obstacles to reaching them, we went out in the open. On Good Friday 2020, we stood together on the public sidewalk, collectively embodying hope and resistance via Facebook live. Speaking into an iPhone held by my young adult son, I prayed,

---

65   "Black Women & Domestic Violence." *Blackburn Center: Standing Together to End Violence.* Accessed August 1, 2020, blackburncenter.org.

66   "MMIWG2S." Coalition to Stop Violence Against Native Women. Accessed August 1, 2020, csvanw.org.

67   Nancy Pineda-Madrid, *Suffering and Salvation in Ciudad Juarez* (Minneapolis: Fortress Press, 2011), 115.

68   Nancy Pineda-Madrid, *Suffering and Salvation in Ciudad Juarez,* 115.

69   Ibid., 115.

70   Ibid., 115.

Eternal One, Who dwells deep within each one of us, open our hearts and ears to hear the cries for help. Open our eyes to see the signs of violence and oppression. Disturb our souls that we feel the pain of women and children who are frightened, in danger, and dehumanized. Give us the courage to learn and respond, to provide safety and relief, and to help rebuild lives. Breathe the power of Your love into those who cry out and help them to know that You are near and You are guiding them.

Rev. Chrisopher Elwood sang his song "Still Night,"

> There's a war
> in the neighborhood
> behind smiling faces
> and picture-pure childhood
> Hide the bruises
> Don't mind the stifled cries
> Avert your gaze
> Compartmentalize.[71]

Rev. Johanna Van-Wijk Bos prayed, *Let us walk in trust then, trust in the Holy Creator who walks with us as the mother shepherd, who takes her children to her bosom when they falter, who guides us to a place on the other side of patriarchal violence. We join hands with Woman Wisdom who danced at the dawn of creation because of her delight in the earth, in woman and in all human beings. We take the hands of wounded sisters in hope that our weeping at the end of the day will be turned into joy at dawn. Together we take refuge under the wing of the Sheltering Spirit, whose love endures forever, whose favors never fail.*

And Rev. Chris Elwood, sang his song "Pulse of Love,"

> Beating with the pulse of love
> Breathing in the wind of justice
> Walking to the rhythm of hope
> Together we will all make a way
> Love one another
> Just as I have loved you
> You are never left alone.[72]

---

71   Words and music by Christopher Elwood, © 2020, https://soundcloud.com/mundobrewhorizon/pulse-of-love-w-congas.

72   Words and music by Christopher Elwood, © 2020, https://soundcloud.com/mundobrewhorizon/pulse-of-love-w-congas.

To step off the trail, to descend into the clearing, to draw near to the Wailing Woman, is a risk to self, especially to women and other marginalized groups. An inner desert sojourn to hear a woman's and girl's lonely cry from a barren perch, to courageously empty oneself to become filled with healing energy to resist misogynist violence, ironically renders women more vulnerable to violence. Backlash is not only real, but a most virile form of misogyny. As such, it is naïve to expect male dominant Christian leaders to respond amicably to women contemplatives who, following their inner authority, challenge them to their core about gender-based violence. The bold wilderness path that draws one into interbeing with the traumatic wounds of women and girls must be done in physical solidarity. Physical solidarity provides not only protection, but presence to one another in the hoped for unfolding of healing light and joy. Men who walk this path are profoundly needed as women's intimate friends and allies whose kenotic, attentive hearts are central to the transformational work.

In this chapter I have compared the distress call of a bird to a sexually traumatized woman to highlight the loneliness and remoteness of her suffering. Another metaphorical step into the ornithology world, that of female birders, will aid in demonstrating both the vulnerability and power of female contemplatives going the way of the Wailing Woman. Female birders often do not have the needed space and safety on the hiking trails to listen, explore, watch, and work. Purbita Saha writes that many female birders experience dismissive comments and sexual harassment; "I've had men touch my hips to correct my perfectly fine birding stance. A ranger at a national wildlife refuge winked and told me about his 'big, loaded gun.' My friends have been propositioned in parks and stalked by drivers along country roads. Not even a 16-year-old can bird in peace without commenters attacking her abilities."[73] In response to this, The Phoebes were born. Named after a Titan from Greek mythology whose name signifies brightness, they are a female centric birding group founded in 2017 by Judith Mirembe, Kimberly Kaufman, and Molly Adams, that seeks to "transform the community from its core."[74] They report that they do not want to separate the birding world by gender, rather their serious resistance to misogyny is grounded in gaining "parity, educating about prejudices,"[75] and bringing, "men

---

73 Purbita Saha, "When Women Run the Bird World," Audubon. May 3, 2019, audubon.org.
74 Purbita Saha, "When Women Run the Bird World," Audubon. May 3, 2019, audubon.org.
75 Purbita Saha, "When Women Run the Bird World," Audubon. May 3, 2019, audubon.org.

along with us as we try to create a better, safer culture for everyone."[76] Relevant here is Kenn Kaufman's perspective as a male birder, who writes, "When species have descriptive names, they always describe males. The female Scarlet Tanager wears no scarlet; the female Blue Grosbeak shows hardly a hint of blue."[77] Kaufman's powers of observation sharpened, and he became awed by what he saw as he transcended the male-controlled ornithology field, where birds are classified by male characteristics, by men who are the power-holders with the loudest voices.

Like the feminist Phoebes leading the forest hike in solidarity, donning high powered binoculars and paying close attention to the oft ignored appearance and behavior of female birds, women desert dwellers are the spiritual leaders in physical and spiritual solidarity, gathering in ground zero *tents* to grow radical empathy and public, embodied resistance in and through one another. Together they will search, they will hone their listening for distress calls from the woman beaten in her home, the young woman raped on her college campus, and the girl violated in her bed. Beverly Lanzetta writes that "women contain the salvific potency and enlightening potential of being bearers of the holy. They know and understand She who is 'not the Remote One, but the One Who is involved, near, and concerned.'"[78] To draw near the Wailing Woman is to stand at the edge of life and death, where one begins to look into the abyss of misogynist violence, where one becomes aware of the Divine in one's own flesh as shared with one's traumatized sisters, and where most of all, Divine Love is felt pulsing through heart, sinew, blood, and marrow. This Divine Love energy, found by way of emptying oneself of the deathly sexual derivatization of women and girls, illumines one's vision for seeing the long-hidden faces, and sharpens one's listening for hearing the long-silenced distress calls of victims and survivors. The Divine Love energy is a gathering force for the centering of their truths where the transformational work begins in the world, especially in male-dominant Christianity.

To enter the terror with her/Her to heal it is a radical spiritual response with soul-quaking empathy—a path filled with unknowns in liminal space, it requires deep trust. The global landscape of misogynist violence necessitates feminist contemplatives who will become warriors in solidarity, gripping male supremacy by the jugular and driving out the evil. The Holy, in female cruciform is a force of resistance to *end the crucifixions*. Feminist desert

76   Purbita Saha, "When Women Run the Bird World," Audubon. May 3, 2019, audubon.org.

77   Ken Kaufman, "I Became a Better Birder When I Stopped Focusing on the Males," Audubon. March 14, 2018, audubon.org.

78   Lanzetta, *Radical Wisdom: A Feminist Mystical Theology*, 165.

contemplatives willing to take on Her mantle of female terror are powerful, as their communal soul will be wide awake. The world awaits the unleashing of this fierce Love when female centric desert mystics come face-to-face with traumatized women and girls. They will see in one another's faces, bearers of the Holy. Feminine Divine Immanence will compel them forward as intimate companions on a desert path that will be transformed into lush landscapes. And they will herald the call *Come, circle now round the mountaintop,* where women and girls will breathe, speak, sing, and dance as fully safe and fully free.

Bibliography

Amnesty International, "Sub-Saharan Africa: Government Responses to COVID-19 should guarantee the protection of women and girls' rights," May 7, 2020, amnesty .org.

Atkinson, Matt. *Letters to Survivors: Words of Comfort for Women Recovering from Rape* (Oklahoma City, OK: RAR Publishing, 2011).

Barnett, Mary Sue. "Beautiful Noa," *The Feminist Voice* 1, no. 1 (2019).

Barnett, Mary Sue. "Mary Magdalene," *The Feminist Voice*, 1, no. 1 (2019).

Bourgeault, Cynthia. *The Meaning of Mary Magdalene: Discovering the Woman at the Heart of Christianity* (Boston: Shambhala, 2010).

Bowdler, Michelle. *Is Rape A Crime? A Memoir, an Investigation, and a Manifesto* (New York: Flatiron Books, 2020).

Brooks, Ryan. "Chrystul Kizer, A 19-Year-Old Sex Trafficking Victim Who Killed Her Abuser, Has Been Released from Jail," June 23, 2020, buzzfeednews.com.

Cahill, Ann J. *Overcoming Objectification: A Carnal Ethics*, (New York: Routledge, 2011).

Caputi, Jane and Diana E. H. Russell. "Femicide: Sexist Terrorism against Women," in *Femicide: The Politics of Woman Killing*, ed. Jill Radford and Diana E. H. Russell (New York: Twayne Publishers, 1992).

Caraballo, Ecleen Luzmila. " 'Ni Una Mas': Hundreds Demand Justice for Isabel Cabanillas and Countless Other Femicide Victims," January 27, 2020, remezcla.com.

Costell, Darcy and Tessa Duvall. "Minute by minute: What happened the night Louisville police shot Breonna Taylor," September 15, 2020, courier-journal.com.

Diaz, Johnny, Maria Cramer, and Christina Morales, "What We Know About the Death of Vanessa Guillen," August 14, 2020, nytimes.com.

Dworkin, Andrea Dworkin "I Want A Twenty-Four-Hour Truce During Which There Is No Rape," in *Transforming A Rape Culture*, ed. Emilie Buchwald, Pamela R. Fletcher, and Martha Roth (Minneapolis, MI: Milkweed Editions, 2005).

Fox, Matthew. *Christian Mystics: 365 Readings and Meditations* (Novato, California, 2011).

Freedman, Karyn L. *One Hour In Paris: A True Story of Rape and Recovery* (Chicago: The University of Chicago Press, 2014).

Gateley, Edwina. *Soul Sisters: Women in Scripture Speak to Women Today* (Maryknoll, New York: Orbis Books, 2010).

Gay, Roxane. *Introduction in Not That Bad: Dispatches from Rape Culture*, ed. Roxane Gay (New York: Harper Perennial, 2018).

Halbfinger, David M. "Vacationing Israeli Teen Says She Was Gang-Raped, Shocking the Nation," August 20, 2020, nytimes.com.

Helling, Steve. "Suspect in Killing of Ark. Jogger Allegedly Saw Her While Driving, Then Doubled Back to Abduct Her," August 25, 2020, people.com.

Hilkert, Mary Catherine. *Naming Grace: Preaching and the Sacramental Imagination*, (New York: Continuum, 1997).

Johnson, Elizabeth A. *She Who Is: The Mystery of God in Feminist Theological Discourse* (New York, NY: Crossroad, 1992).

Khadka, Jagat. "Victim's family does not wish to see her body before culprit is arrested," September 27, 2020, myrepublica.nagariknetwork.com.

King, Ursula. "Pneumatophores for Nurturing a Different Kind of Love," in *Through Us, With Us, In Us: Relational Theologies in the Twenty-First Century*, ed. Lisa Usherwood and Elaine Bellchambers (London: SCM Press, 2011).

Kobin, Billy. "Police: Louisville man charged with fatally shooting woman at Seventh and Hill streets," June 5, 2020, courier-journal.com.

Kozuch, Elliott. "HRC Mourns Brayla Stone, Black Trans Girl Killed in Arkansas," July 1, 2020, hrc.org.

Lane, Belden C. *Desert Spirituality and Cultural Resistance: From Ancient Monks To Mountain Refugees* (Eugene, Oregon: WIPF & Stock, 2011).

Lanzett, Beverly J. *Radical Wisdom: A Feminist Mystical Theology*, (Minneapolis: Fortress Press, 2005).

Leloup, Jean-Yves. *The Gospel of Mary Magdalene*, (Rochester, Vermont: Inner Traditions, 2002).

Loofbourow, Lili. "Why Do We Think 'Believing' Rape Victims Is Enough?" August 13, 2020, slate.com.

Medeiros, Zoe. "Why I Stopped," in *Not That Bad: Dispatches from Rape Culture*, ed. Roxane Gay (New York: Harper Perennial, 2018).

Pineda-Madrid, Nancy. *Suffering and Salvation in Ciudad Juarez* (Minneapolis: Fortress Press, 2011).

Russell, Diana E. H. "Introduction: The Politics of Femicide," in *Femicide in Global Perspective*, ed. Diana E. H. Russell and Roberta A. Harmes (New York: Teachers College Press, 2001).

Watterson, Meggan. *Mary Magdalene Revealed: The First Apostle, Her Feminist Gospel, & the Christianity We Haven't Tried Yet* (Carlsbad, CA: Hay House, Inc. 2019).

CHAPTER 7

Child Marriage

A War on Girls

Donna Pollard

Child marriage has devastating impacts on children resulting in intergenerational traumas and cycles of poverty and it must be stopped with common sense legislative reforms. Between 2000 and 2015, there have been over 200,000 cases of child marriage in the United States. More than 85% of these marriages are between a child bride and a much older adult male.[1] Family instability, limited educational and career opportunities, and significant diminished mental and physical health due to child marriage are evidenced by 80% of these marriages ending in divorce,[2] a 50% greater likelihood of the girl dropping out of high school,[3] psychiatric disorders three times as high as women who married as adults,[4] and a 23% greater risk of developing a serious health condition, such as diabetes, cancer, heart attack or stroke.[5] Horrifically, child marriage also places the minor in an even more vulnerable position than they may have been in prior to the marriage, as in many states, child protective services have no authority to intervene in cases of minors being abused by their spouse.[6] My direct experience as a child bride, having married a man fifteen years older than me when I was just sixteen, has driven me to fight in every corner of our nation to ensure no other child becomes the victim of legal loopholes that allow predators to hide their offenses behind a marriage license.

I was thirty-two years old when I first realized my perpetrator's crimes against me were not my shame to carry. Despite having run away over a decade

1   Tsui, Anjali, Dan Nolan, and Chris Amico. 2017. *Child Marriage in America: By The Numbers.* PBS Frontline.

2   Hamilton, Vivian E. 2012. *The Age of Marital Capacity: Reconsidering Civil Recognition of Adolescent Marriage.* Boston University Law Review.

3   Seller, Naomi. 2002. *Is Teen Marriage a Solution?.* Center for Law and Social Policy.

4   Le Strat, Yann, Caroline Dubertet, and Bernard Le Foll. 2011. *Child Marriage in the United States and Its Association with Mental Health in Women.* 128 Pediatrics.

5   Dupre, Matthew E., and Sarah O. Meadows. 2007. "Disaggregating the Effects of Marital Trajectories on Health." *Journal of Family Issues* 630–636 and 646–647.

6   Tahirih Justice Center. 2019. "Tahirih Justice Center Child Marriage Background." *Tahirih Justice Center.* 07 01. Accessed 10 15, 2020. www.tahirih.org.

before from the crippling dysfunction of my early life, I never quite shook the image of my younger self as unlovable and I blamed myself for all my pain. After all, my mother had beaten me with a belt until my flesh welted with beads of blood as far back as I could remember. Her hot breath pungent with vinegar and onions hung heavy in my face as she screamed for me to shut up when I was being too needy, too much like a child—so I must have been *bad*, *unlovable* and *to blame*.[7] And as an undesirable child, I internalized so much hate for myself that whatever actions the adults in my life took that may pained me, I always saw myself as the root of the problem. This self-loathing paved the way for me to fall prey to a predator's manipulation for many years to come.

Yet, twelve years before my big epiphany I somehow found it within myself to leave a horribly abusive, exploitive, toxic marriage to a man I had married at sixteen. It was at twenty years of age—when I had been married for four years—some glimmer of wisdom deep inside me began to softly glow beneath the cracks of my woundedness. I began questioning my husband's actions. I began standing up for myself and feeding the desire for, and belief in, my independence. This wisdom was beckoning me to realize I had value in life beyond the limitations of youth, sex, drugs, and whatever else he had cast as my identity to keep me as his slave. And so I ran, and I ran hard, pounding blood and sweat into the pavement beneath my feet a new identity that was the polar opposite of anything I had ever known. This new world would be a place where I was a stellar student and star employee out of desperation to prove to others that I was worthy.[8]

Of course, my perpetrator never counted on me being able to unearth any molecule of strength and resiliency within myself to be anything other than the malleable child he first encountered when I was fourteen. He saw me as an anxiety plagued, insecure child starved for affection and attention. The man who was fifteen years my senior, only saw my abusive past, my fear of abandonment, and all the trauma seeping forth from my young teenage pores as the perfect concoction for his manipulation and exploitation. He could sense these vulnerabilities just as a wild cat stalks, senses, and savors the weakness of its prey. My vulnerability was a sage comfort to him.[9]

7   Harris, Cathy. 2016. *Shame Expressed as Self-Blame: The Trauma Response We All Need to Understand.* Accessed 10 13, 2020. https://www.acesconnection.com/blog/shame -expressed-as-self-blame-the-trauma-response-we-all-need-to-understand.

8   Hollowood, Tia. 2018. *Complex PTSD and Perfectionism, HealthyPlace.* March 07. Accessed 10 15, 2020. https://www.healthyplace.com/blogs/traumaptsdblog/2018/03/ complex-ptsd-and-perfectionism.

9   Prevent Child Abuse Nevada. 2011. *Abusers and Grooming Tactics.* Accessed 10 13, 2020. https://nic.unlv.edu/pcan/CSA_Abusers.html.

Many studies have identified the specific characteristics of perpetrators and victims of domestic violence. Young ages, lower education levels, childhood victimization, mental illness, and pregnancy were among commonalities of those who were victimized as adults.[10] Child brides often share these vulnerabilities.

My perpetrator was smugly confident by the time he had wrung out all sense of a moral compass and dignity I had remaining, I simply would no longer be able to handle suffering through this existence any longer. "No one would blame you if you killed yourself" he told me on several occasions, sometimes coldly and other times eerily as though he were an old friend compassionately offering me a way out of my hell. But this is one act I did not fall victim to. I guess he and I both underestimated me.

To understand how I ended up marrying a person who was essentially my counselor at an inpatient behavioral health facility I was admitted to when I was fourteen, one must have full transparency into my history. Both the traumatic foundation I was born into and the archaic laws and policies that perpetuated this perverse cycle of abuse as part of a cultural (but perhaps patriarchal is a word that rings truer) norm resulted in my marriage to a pedophile. Though progress has been made on legislative reforms in multiple states,[11] the unwillingness of many legislators across our nation to address these atrocities furthers the victimization of children who are vulnerable to this gross human rights violation.

My initiation into this world came when my mother was in her mid-forties and to say having a child at that age was completely unexpected would be a severe understatement. Despite having married as a teenager herself, just two weeks shy of her fourteenth birthday, she gave birth to one other child. My sister also suffered from the dysfunction and she was a recipient of the pain our mother brought from her own unhealed wounds. But as the more compliant child, my sister was sparred some of the aggression I had to endure as the more rebellious and precocious child. This became the justification my mother would use to attempt to beat me into submission. Perhaps more potently though, it was the internalization I came to temporarily accept of myself as an identity grossly unlovable and strikingly to blame for all the wrongs in my life.

The reprieve from mother's volatility came when our father was home on weekends. As a long-distance truck driver, he was on the road more times

---

10   Nosek, M.A., Hughes, R.B., Taylor, H.B., Howland, C.A. 2004. "Violence against women with disabilities: The role of physicians in filling the treatment gap."

11   Tahirih Justice Center. 2020. "Understanding State Statutes on Minimum Marriage Age and Exceptions."

than not, yet I always felt a stronger sense of kindness and caring from him than I ever did from my mother. But his time at home was infrequent at best and my yearning for paternal love—for love in general—was never satisfied. Perpetually longing for this dream of a loving family, I fell prey to a pedophile who promised me the world and delivered the unraveling of my innocence. And the law in all three states involved in allowing my victimization remained firmly on his side.

I can still recall the energizing rush of both anticipation and dread when the CD arrived from the Department of Vital Statistics containing the data by year. Knowing in order to make any progress towards change, I had to have evidence that this was a major problem in Kentucky, I had spent months contacting the Department and following up multiple times as my requests went unanswered. When the CD finally arrived, I rushed to the library so I could download the statistics on a flash drive and review in detail the hidden crimes in the backyards of Kentucky families across the state. Nothing could have prepared me for the harsh reality of how bad the problem really was. Between the years 2000 and 2015, in Kentucky alone there were nearly 10,000 cases of child marriage.[12] The youngest child was a pregnant thirteen-year-old girl married to a thirty-three-year-old man.[13] Though her pregnancy was evidence of rape, instead of being charged with this heinous crime, her rapist was given a marriage license to hide his moral depravity. This legal marriage license also allowed him to continue raping her and it also gave him access to her child. This outrageous crime was permissible thanks to the laws in Kentucky that allowed children to wed through legal loopholes until Senate Bill 48 was passed in 2018. Prior to this legislative change, children sixteen and seventeen could marry through parental consent alone by going to the County Court Clerk—no questions asked.[14] Even if the clerk determined there was a predatory situation and feared for the child's safety, they had no authority to intervene when the parents of the minor consented to the marriage. Such was the case when a seventeen-year-old girl was married to a seventy-two-year-old man.

Furthermore, there was *no minimum age floor* as long as a pregnancy was involved.[15] In these cases, a judge would preside over the petition to give his judicial stamp of approval. Even when there was substantial age disparity, and knowing the pregnancy was evidence of rape, judges still authorize the marriages. Unfortunately, there was little concern for a female child's well-being

---

12   Kentucky Department of Vital Statistics. 2018.
13   Survivors' Corner. 2018. "Exploitation of the Married Child."
14   Survivors' Corner. 2018. "Exploitation of the Married Child."
15   Survivors' Corner. 2018. "Exploitation of the Married Child."

and with no regard for long term consequences of an early marriage and childbirth. Indeed, multiple Kentucky judges authorized the marriage of perpetrators to the little girls they raped.[16] Yes, you read that correctly. Judges authorized marriages involving children impregnated by pedophiles.

Instead of being awarded a marriage certificate, these pregnancies could have, and should have, been evidence in statutory rape cases. But because of the archaic systems that are designed to treat females as sex objects with little or no intrinsic value these legal loopholes continue to exist in the majority of states which undermine protections from these crimes against humanity. To allow child marriage is essentially giving a child rapist a license to destroy a young girl's potential for a life of sovereignty and self-sufficiency. As though child marriage itself is not harmful enough, other systems in this tangled web of oppression keep girls entrapped in these vicious cycles with nearly insurmountable barriers to protective services.

I experienced these barriers in a myriad of ways, both before and after the marriage occurred. In many instances, the police could have intervened on my behalf and in others concerned citizens could have made reports. But no one did. Our society is so desensitized to predators grooming young girls with little regard for their potential or value. Both men and women turn a blind eye toward abuse, or they *blame the victim*, labeling the victim as *loose* or *asking for it* with the way the victim dresses or behaves. For example, when my perpetrator was pulled over for a defective headlight, the police did not question why a fifteen-year-old girl was in the car with him. And the hotel staff where I was taken while my mother left me alone with him for hours never raised any alarms either.

I had just turned sixteen a couple months before my mother consented to give me to my perpetrator; he was nearly 31. I was still a resident of London, Kentucky at that time and he drove down from Indiana to take me to Pigeon Forge, Tennessee where he thought we could get married without question since it's a well-known spot for quick, easy weddings. He was right. The clerk did not glance up from her computer when taking our information when she asked which one of us was the minor. It felt cold and transactional, like I was just being auctioned off to the next adult to have control over my life. I remember clearly sitting in that chair, my heart sinking into my ribcage, wondering to myself, "Is this what marriage is?" I dared not speak up—who do you disclose

---

16   Kentucky Center for Investigative Reporting. 2018. Accessed 10 13, 2020. https://kycir
      .org/2018/03/06/kentucky-child-marriage-bill-clears-senate-committee/#:~:text=
      Kentucky%E2%80%99s%20current%20statute%20allows%20children%20aged%20
      16%20and,17%20years.%20Some%20were%20as%20young%20as%2013.

your fear to when all the authorities in your life are making the horrible decisions that cause you the fear in the first place?

Later that evening, we travelled back to London, Kentucky. Though the agreement he had made with my mother was that if she would consent to the marriage, I would finish out my tenth-grade year living with her, he had other plans and was clearly dedicated to protecting himself from any legal repercussions. During that last night living with my mother, as a newlywed sixteen-year-old girl, my perpetrator told me we had to consummate the marriage (despite having already been sexually active) so she could not change her mind and file to have the marriage annulled.

This was a new concern of his, presumably because he realized he illegally took a minor across state lines for marriage while having no intention to honor the agreement made with my mother.[17] With my mother asleep across the hallway, the marriage was consummated; a condom left as evidence in the bathroom. As I trembled and cried and wondered what on earth was about to become of my life, he shoved my clothing and a few other items in a black garbage bag he tossed over the deck to load into the green Ford Explorer in preparation for taking me *home* to Indiana the next morning.

I ended up having to drop out of school before I completed the 10th grade. Upon moving into his new apartment in Clarksville, Indiana, I tried to enroll in Clarksville High School, just up the street from the apartment complex we lived in, but the assistant principal would not allow it. She said I would become pregnant quickly, and they could not have that at their school.

I had to begin working full time as a grocery store cashier to provide for my thirty-one-year-old husband who would spend his days getting high and drunk. He was violent and manipulative. I was traumatized and broken.

But I did try to fight back even though I was a married and "emancipated" minor. Unless specific, meaningful, enumerated rights are prescribed, emancipation is meaningless. Despite working full time, when I tried to escape at both sixteen and seventeen, I was refused housing by two Indiana apartment complexes because I could not enter into a contract as a minor. I was even refused refuge in a domestic violence shelter because I was not yet of legal age. I recall arguing with the woman at the front desk, telling her "you don't understand—I'm *married*. How can I be married but not qualify for shelter?" She told me to call my mom and ask to come home. This was especially deflating as I had done

---

17   United States Department of Justice. Mann Act, 18 U.S.C. § 2421 et seq. Accessed 10 13, 2020. https://www.justice.gov/archives/jm/criminal-resource-manual-2027-mann-act.

that. My mother's response was unsettling. "You made your bed and now you have to lie in it."

The police in southern Indiana did not feel it necessary to investigate further when the neighbors called because of the violent fighting in our home. The policemen would speak to my perpetrator (who they could only see as my husband) who assured them I had emotional issues that he was helping me work through. I was furious with the sense of hopelessness I felt. I had no credibility in this world of adults.

When I was sixteen, I became pregnant the first time. My doctor did not question the fact that my spouse was fifteen years older than me. When I miscarried, they performed a suction DNC at Clark Memorial Hospital, but the procedure did not successfully remove all of the placenta. I could have died two weeks later when I spiked a high fever from the toxins the remaining placenta was releasing in my body. It took two days and discharging some of remaining tissue before I could convince my perpetrator to take me back to the hospital.

I became pregnant again when I was 17. My daughter was born just about a month after I turned 18. I spent my 18th birthday, heavily pregnant, taken to a strip club by my perpetrator for his own gratification. Shortly after I gave birth, he forced me to go to work at the strip club. Again, I had no credibility and no value—and he was going to make certain I never would.

My final breaking point came when one day he was pressuring me to do something I felt horribly uncomfortable with and I stood my ground and said no. He then proceeded to choke me as my daughter, a baby at the time, looked up from her spot on the floor closely situated to where we were. She laughed. In her innocent mind, we were playing. I knew in that moment I had to get out of this situation for my sake *and hers*.

But I was in no position to take care of a baby while I was still just a kid myself, at this point living in public housing in New Albany, Indiana and collecting food stamps to feed myself, my child, and my perpetrator. The judge awarded custody of my daughter to my perpetrator, a college graduate in his thirties. And the court awarded him child support as well to be paid by me. At this point, I was a twenty-year old high school drop-out making barely above minimum wage.

Labels had become my identity: behavioral health patient, child bride, high school drop-out, stripper, deadbeat, victim. Though these were identities unsuited to the essence of who I really was or my potential, once these seemingly insurmountable obstacles were washed away, these identity labels clung to me like duct tape. It took every molecule of strength I could muster to stand against what so many institutions and laws had reinforced about my existence; at best, I was an incompetent and incapable child. At worst: my body, educational opportunities, protective rights, credibility and income belonged to my husband—like a piece of property.

Let me state the obvious. The institutions and legal system of Indiana failed both me and my child multiple times. The legal systems in Kentucky (where the marriage was consummated) and Tennessee, (where the marriage was legitimized) did as well. There are so many others like me across the nation whose humanity and value are ripped away and this process is sanctioned by the institutions and legal systems that seek to annihilate our humanity—yet, we will not be silenced.

What do I do when my credibility, my education, my body, my child, my income has been ripped away from me and given to my rapist who hid his offenses behind a marriage license? I fight to end child marriage across our nation and refuse to let this ever happen to another child. The biggest threat of disruption to an oppressive system is the marginalized who choose to no longer live in fear of discomfort, judgment, or being ostracized for defying the status quo. I choose disruption over oppression every day.

Choosing disruption is what led me to initiate the legislative initiative in Kentucky back in 2018 to end child marriage through parental consent. I partnered with a phenomenally dedicated team from a national organization—the Tahirih Justice Center—that was equal parts grace and grit. They were polished, reasonable, and tenacious. Most importantly, they were kind, compassionate and genuinely human in their advocacy for social justice.

Through numerous conversations with legislators, children's advocacy groups (such as Kentucky Youth Advocates,[18] Kentucky Child Advocacy Centers,[19] and Exploited Children's Help Organization)[20] and other stakeholders (such as Kentucky Association of Sexual Assault Programs,[21] Kentucky Coalition Against Domestic Violence,[22] and the National Association of Social Workers—Kentucky)[23] we learned very quickly that a zero tolerance policy for child marriages was not feasible. Many Kentuckians—including elected officials—were not ready to look at the narrative of child marriage through a lens that depicted the practice as a form of criminal activity, a form of child abuse and neglect. So many of our neighbors across the Commonwealth wanted to remain with a narrative that perpetuated the story line of a young

18   Kentucky Youth Advocates. https://kyyouth.org/.
19   Children's Advocacy Center of the Bluegrass. http://kykids.org/.
20   Exploited Children's Help Organization. https://echo-ky.org/Default.asp.
21   Kentucky Association of Sexual Assault Programs. https://www.kasap.org/.
22   Kentucky Coalition Against Domestic Violence. https://kcadv.org/.
23   National Association of Social Workers—KY Chapter. https://naswky.socialworkers.org/.

girl in need of a man to *take care* of her. They were also extremely resistant to an infringement on parental rights to consent to marrying their child off to a grown man who ultimately would have many more legal rights and opportunities than his underage bride.

Several conversations left me exasperated, with people (mostly white men) making comments like *well, it's better than her having a baby out of wedlock* and *if that's what the parents want, I'm sure they have their reasons—it's not for the government to decide.* In discovering the uphill battle that we were going to face in pushing for reform, we realized in order to make anything happen, we were going to have to draft legislation that would accomplish the next best thing.

We wrote the bill to set a minimum age for marriage at 17, with judicial approval and clear criteria that must be assessed before the marriage license could be granted. Some of these criteria included ensuring the age disparity between the minor and the person intended to become their spouse was not greater than four years; requiring proof of age for both parties, determining if there had been a history of domestic or sexual violence, and requiring the minor had completed either their high school diploma or GED and was capable of self-sufficiency among other high bar requirements. We also included a requirement for the minor to be interviewed independently in the judge's chambers so they may ask questions to identify if the child was being coerced. And most importantly, we made granting the marriage license simultaneous with emancipating the minor; this way, the seventeen-year-old could elect to walk out of the courthouse without legal dependence on anyone within or outside of a marriage taking place.

I met with Senator Julie Raque Adams, a full packet of information in hand, over coffee one morning to ask her to consider sponsoring the legislation. I gave her the statistics and the bill draft, information on reforms other states had adopted, and perhaps most importantly my direct testimony. She teared up while listening and said, "I can't wait to get started on this."[24]

It was not an easy feat by any means, but the bill did pass both legislatures with minimal opposition, likely attributed to the robust media coverage we were receiving on our efforts and public outcries to end child marriage. Other states have since followed suit and adopted similar variations to our bill, outlawing child marriage through parental consent and requiring criteria be assessed and met before a judge may grant the marriage license. Despite the violence, the exploitation, the economic disadvantages, the perceived lack of credibility, I refused to hang my head in fear or shame any longer. You see,

---

24   Meeting with Senator Julie Raque Adams. September 2017.

I believe the reason I have survived all these things is to use my experiences to protect other girls from being trapped in a life like I was and to show my oldest daughter, even if from afar, that I have taken a horrible situation and done the best I could to make it right for others.

Since the atrocities of my early life, I have gone on to earn my bachelor's degree in Business Administration, graduating Summa Cum Laude. I founded a nonprofit, *Survivors' Corner*, to provide a supportive network for trauma survivors looking to make social justice changes. I travel frequently as an advocate giving testimony before legislative committees and as a keynote speaker nationally and internationally. And I share this not to be self-celebrating, but to demonstrate the resiliency that comes from giving pain a purpose.

I have an inner sense that the reason I survived all the atrocities from my past is to share the process of healing my own trauma, finding self-love, and embracing the power I possess as a woman with others so they may do the same. I am confident I exist on this earth to help foster a path forward of inclusion for those of us who have spent far too long silenced on the sidelines. When we are fully alive with purpose and demonstrate living powerfully in our authenticity, we achieve the best revenge to those who would rather us shut down. After all, another's crime against us is not our shame to carry.

But before we can experience this liberation as a nation, we must change the antiquated laws that allow child marriage to continue. It is only then we will have true change to disrupt cycles of abuse and poverty and elevate the status of women to a place of equity and equality within humanity. The devastating impact of child marriage must be stopped first by implementing common sense laws that prevent predators from hiding their offenses behind a marriage license. Additionally, our society must begin to see girls as human beings with intrinsic value.

Bibliography

Dupre, Matthew E., and Sarah O. Meadows. "Disaggregating the Effects of Marital Trajectories on Health." *Journal of Family Issues* (2007) 630–647.

Hamilton, Vivian E. *The Age of Marital Capacity: Reconsidering Civil Recognition of Adolescent Marriage.* Boston University Law Review, 2012.

Harris, Cathy. *Shame Expressed as Self-Blame: The Trauma Response We All Need to Understand* (2016). Accessed 10 13, 2020. https://www.acesconnection.com/blog/shame-expressed-as-self-blame-the-trauma-response-we-all-need-to-understand.

Hollowood, Tia. *Complex PTSD and Perfectionism, HealthyPlace.* March 07, 2018. Accessed 10 15, 2020. https://www.healthyplace.com/blogs/traumaptsdblog/2018/03/complex-ptsd-and-perfectionism.

Kentucky Center for Investigative Reporting. 2018. Accessed 10 13, 2020. https://kycir .org/2018/03/06/kentucky-child-marriage-bill-clears-senate-committee/#:~:text= Kentucky%E2%80%99s%20current%20statute%20allows%20children%20 aged%2016%20and,17%20years.%20Some%20were%20as%20young%20as%20 13.

Le Strat, Yann, Caroline Dubertet, and Bernard Le Foll. *Child Marriage in the United States and Its Association with Mental Health in Women,* 2011.

Prevent Child Abuse Nevada. *Abusers and Grooming Tactics,* 2011. Accessed October 13, 2020. https://nic.unlv.edu/pcan/CSA_Abusers.html.

Seller, Naomi. *Is Teen Marriage a Solution?* Center for Law and Social Policy, 2002.

Tahirih Justice Center. "Tahirih Justice Center Child Marriage Background." *Tahirih Justice Center.* July 2019. Accessed 10 15, 2020. www.tahirih.org.

Tahirih Justice Center. "Understanding State Statutes on Minimum Marriage Age and Exceptions," 2020.

Tahirih Justice Center. "Forced Marriage Resource Toolkit" Accessed October 15, 2020. https://preventforcedmarriage.org/forced-marriage-resource-toolkit-for-service -providers/.

Tsui, Anjali, Dan Nolan, and Chris Amico. *Child Marriage in America: By The Numbers.* PBS Frontline, 2017.

United States Department of Justice. Mann Act, 18 U.S.C. § 2421 et seq. Accessed October 13, 2020. https://www.justice.gov/archives/jm/criminal-resource-manual -2027-mann-act.

CHAPTER 8

Let Me Prey Upon You

Sandy Phillips Kirkham

This is Sandy Kirkham's story.[1] She has the extraordinary ability to take you deep into the inner world of what it is like to be sexually exploited by a trusted leader. Sandy will take you along her journey of healing and being transformed by her pain into a flourishing survivor. She is a resilient fighter who has found her voice.

Her story, you will discover, is not only powerful but will ask you to examine your own understanding of clergy abuse. Her story provides validation for survivors, hope for those recovering, and exposes some of the very unhealthy ways the institution of the church covers, conceals, distorts, and often further harms survivors assaulted or abused, who have experienced complex developmental trauma.

Society is approaching a tipping point around gender discrimination and sexual violence and churches will find themselves caught in the wave. We now know religious communities can be just as oppressive and hurtful as they are helpful. Change is coming because victims are finding and using their voices to reclaim their lives, calling out injustice and evil, and working to make our churches safer for those of all ages. Sandy Kirkham is one of those people. I hope you will allow yourself to be inspired and encouraged the same way I have been after reading her story.[2]

1 Introduction

As an insecure, sixteen-year-old girl the church is where I should have felt welcome, happy, and most importantly, safe. Tragically for me, the church became a place of great harm.

In *Let Me Prey Upon You,*[3] I detail my account of how a charismatic youth minister preyed upon me by using the church, his position, and my trust in him

---

1 Absam, LLC allows Sandy Phillips Kirkham to use material originally published in *Let Me Prey Upon You,* for this collection.
2 David Pooler, PhD, Foreword in *Let Me Prey Upon You* (Cincinnati, OH: Absam, LLC, 2019), 14.
3 Sandy Phillips Kirkham, *Let Me Prey Upon You* (Cincinnati, OH: Absam, LLC, 2019).

as my pastor. This betrayal left me broken, with a shattered faith and the ultimate shame of being blamed and removed from the church I loved. From our very first meeting, the new youth minister slowly and methodically turned the sacred relationship between a trusted spiritual leader into one of abuse: sexual, emotional, and physical. Grooming, manipulation, and gaslighting, common weapons of abusers, were all used to control me during a confusing and vulnerable time in my life.

After five long years his actions were discovered by church leaders. Instead of a punishment, he was given a going away party and simply moved to another church. I, on the other hand, was left to pay the price for his deeds. During a late-night meeting with two church elders I was told because of *my* behavior, I was to leave the church and as is all too often the case, I was neither his first victim nor his last.

Often church hierarchy and church doctrine do not permit women to serve in leadership roles. Based upon misinterpretation of the scriptures, women are to be submissive. We are told not to question their authority and are not given a voice or a seat at the table. The leadership structure within the church leaves victims of clergy abuse at the mercy of the men in charge. Too often the victim, as in my case, is blamed for leading the pastor astray or causing the offender to "fall into sin."

Despite a successful and happy life as a wife, mother, and friend, I concealed my abuse from all those around me for twenty-seven years until a trigger forced me to face the truth. *Let Me Prey Upon You* details my journey of healing from innocent sixteen-year-old victim to survivor and advocate. Throughout my journey I sought justice and closure from both the pastor and my former church, despite efforts to stop me. Although I may not have found everything I was seeking, I found strength, satisfaction, and resolution through helping others. I hope my story of tenacity and courage will inspire you.

I share the following collection of excerpts initially published in my book *Let Me Prey Upon You*. I chose specific accounts to highlight the power and control an abuser has over his victim and the institution which covers up and allows the abuse to continue. Whether the abuse occurs once or over a long period of time, the consequences last a lifetime. The accounts I have chosen to share are only part of my story. Prior to each section I've written a brief introduction to provide context for each of the following narratives.

2   Queensgate—Next Exit

> I begin with a trigger factor which set me on my journey of finding jus-
> tice and healing. My story begins in 2004 on what would normally be a
> fun weekend visiting my daughter. However, this weekend would quickly
> force me to face a trigger deep within my past.

The lie had been hidden for so long, I hoped it might disappear. Some people
claim that lies grow bigger with time, small white lies spawn bigger fibs and
soon they grow to mammoth proportions, but maybe the opposite could be
true. Maybe big lies could dissipate over time. I wanted to believe if a big lie
was hidden and wasn't hurting anyone, it didn't matter, and its power was
gone. Maybe, just maybe, there was a statute of limitations for the lies he
told me.

It was a gorgeous spring day and the late afternoon sun peeked through
the smoky haze covering the Tennessee mountains. My goal was to reach the
Hampton Inn in Greeneville, Tennessee, a city I had never visited before, before
dark. It was March of 2004, before cell phones, Google maps, and GPS were
common navigational tools, and I had already made one wrong turn twenty
miles back. I headed down I-75 from Cincinnati armed with my AAA Trip Tik
and an oversized Atlas as my navigational system to reach my daughter's college golf tournament in Greeneville.

My husband and chief navigator, Bill, was unable to make the trip. I was left
on my own. In spite of having a carefully mapped-out route, fear of becoming
lost was ever present. I had never driven this route before. Throughout our
married life, in the car and in general, I always counted on him to keep me on
track. Once off I-75, the route would involve many turns, and a few back roads.
I was getting a little nervous not having Bill with me.

My daughter's golf season was going well, and I, too, was content with this
season of my life. I was 49, had a great husband, two kids in college, a suburban house, two well-behaved dogs, and good friends. Bill and I were enjoying
our life as empty nesters and I could finally begin to focus more on myself. For
years, the joys and chaos of children had taken precedent.

My CD player was loaded with my favorite songs, but I flicked on the radio
instead. Reception was still good, and the oldies station played one of my favorite Beach Boys songs, "Good Vibrations." I bellowed along, until I saw the sign.

Queensgate Exit 1 Mile.

Queensgate? Queensgate? I had not thought of this place in years. My hands
clenched the leather wrap of the steering wheel. I held on tight, trying not to
wavier an inch, to stay steady in the left lane. I focused on the semi in front of

me that was passing a maroon Buick. No matter what, I did not want to veer toward the exit lane for Queensgate.

Queensgate? Queensgate? That's where he lives. Or does he still live there? My mind spun into overdrive. How close am I to his church? To where he may live? Reminders of Queensgate flooded my head. My legs sought the grounding offered by the accelerator. Memories raced in. I could feel the car respond and surge forward. I told myself to stare straight ahead. Follow the semi. It held me in its wake. I kept repeating, "Keep going, just keep going."

Queensgate ¼ Mile.

Every muscle tightened when I saw the next sign. I felt his presence slither into the car. I felt him all around me. I felt his touch. I heard his voice. I smelled his musky aftershave. His presence smothered me. Almost as a wicked joke, The Carpenters' song, "Rainy Days and Mondays" came on the radio and took me back to 1972. I felt paralyzed, unable to turn off the radio. I felt him in the seat next to me, putting his hand on my right thigh. Tears rolled down my cheeks and onto my lap. I no longer heard the music, or had I turned it off? I didn't know.

Queensgate Next Exit.

Unable to breathe, gasping for air, I found myself in the right lane. I pulled off the expressway just prior to the exit. All I could do was sit there and sob. For the first time in almost three decades, I was consumed by pain.

My heart raced; my body shuddered with sobs as I lay my forehead on the steering wheel. I wrapped my arms around it, wishing this inanimate object would steady me and hug me back. I could not stop the waves of sorrow. I wanted the sadness, the memories, and the sound and smell of him to go away. I needed air. As I opened the car door, the rushing wind and the roar of semis brought reality to the moment. I stepped out of the car and held onto the hood to keep myself steady. Still, once I made it to the passenger's side, I collapsed next to the guardrail.

Why was this happening? Over the years there had been small reminders of him, reminders which stung like a slap on the wrist, but this was no small reminder. This was a huge reminder, a hard punch in my gut. It had been twenty-nine years since I last saw Queensgate, the place which reminded me of the Sandy I left behind, the Sandy I loathed.

I looked at my watch and realized I had to get back on the road to beat the setting sun. I forced myself to think about the golf tournament and told myself for the next forty-eight hours I would somehow put on my "mom face" and be strong. What would happen after that? Could I push these memories, these feelings, this pain back into the abyss and go on like before? Whatever this was, I was sure I couldn't ignore it any longer.

Arriving just before dark, I called Bill from the room to let him know I arrived safely. His steady voice calmed me, and I felt better. Grateful for a weekend full of activities and the joy at seeing my daughter, I managed to not let the events on the highway ruin the weekend.

Two days later I was back in the driver's seat. I desperately wanted to find a different route home, but my fear of getting lost and ending up in Queensgate, possibly in front of the church, made the known route a better option. I steeled myself as I drove along the freeway, gripping the steering wheel. For seven hours I could think of nothing other than what he had done to me. Even after I was well beyond Queensgate, the memories still closed in. I found myself quickly moving forward into my past.

For the next two weeks I was in a constant state of turmoil. I tried to keep it hidden from Bill. Whenever he left for work, I walked through the house, wringing my hands asking myself questions for which I had no answers. Why me? Why did he pick me? What did I do?

Each night Bill came home, and I would pretend everything was fine. I needed to be strong, to put on my "wife face." This was the exterior I had perfected over the years. One evening as Bill sat at the kitchen table to eat dinner, I poured him a glass of iced tea, as I did every night. I was about to join him at the table. I poured another glass of tea, then I poured another and then a fourth glass of tea. I began shaking, aware that I was losing my ability to function. Quickly, I poured the tea down the drain and set the glasses into the dishwasher. I glanced at Bill as he sat at the table reading the newspaper. He had not witnessed the four glasses of tea. Relief filled me, but I knew I needed help. I had to unload the secret threatening to crush me. I had to tell someone.

Then I heard *his* words, "Don't ever tell anyone. They will think you are lying and never believe you."

Who *would* ever believe my story? Who should I tell?

3   **Youth Group/New Youth Pastor**

As a teenager I was active and involved in my church. I had found a place of family and friendship and latched onto the relationships I found there. Just before I turned sixteen my church hired a new youth minister.

There was an unusual excitement among the adults with this new youth pastor's arrival. Hearing of the growth and enthusiasm Jeff Coulier had created in youth participation at his prior church in Tifton, Georgia, the elders were eager to have this vibrant, charismatic youth pastor on staff.

At the reception welcoming Jeff Coulier and his family after the Sunday morning service, Mr. Wilson, the senior pastor, made a point to introduce me to Jeff Coulier. "Jeff, I would like you to meet Sandy. She is one of our fine young people here and one of the leaders of our youth group. We call her Miss Sunshine because of her radiant smile." I was totally flattered by the compliments. "Miss Sunshine." I knew people saw me that way and it made me feel special and appreciated. I was touched that Mr. Wilson made the effort to single me out and introduce me to the new youth pastor. I was nervous. Reaching down, taking my hand, and smiling, Jeff Coulier said to me with just a hint of a southern drawl, "You do have a very pretty smile." Waiting for him to let go of my hand, I was surprised when he continued to hold onto it as he talked. Before he walked away Mr. Wilson said to Jeff, "She will be a big help to you in your ministry." I hoped I had made a good first impression.

From the beginning it was clear that Jeff Coulier was a different kind of pastor than our beloved Pastor Tom. Jeff was thirty years old, close to Tom's age, but he dressed and acted more youthful, wearing cutoff jeans and other current styles of the seventies. His blonde hair and sideburns were longer. We called him Jeff, instead of Pastor Jeff. He understood our jokes, kidded with us, knew our music, and talked sports with the guys. He drove his orange convertible vw to our high school football games. He introduced us to the poetry of Rod McKuen and the music of Neil Diamond.

It was not uncommon for Jeff to compliment women and girls on their appearance. A response of, "Thank You" would be followed by Jeff saying, with a smile, "Don't thank me darlin'. I had nothing to do with it." He could also be critical of someone's appearance, but usually in a disarming way. Once in a sermon he remarked, "I don't expect women to dress like the cupboard, but I don't want them dressing like Mother Hubbard either." Everyone laughed. When I came to youth group wearing my hair in pigtails, Jeff looked at me and began making oinking sounds while flapping his hands about his ears, "You look a little funny in those pigtails. Oink, oink." Several times after that, whenever he saw me, he made an oinking sound. It embarrassed me, but I laughed it off.

A few weeks after he arrived, I was at his house babysitting. After he came home, he asked me to go to his basement to listen to the song "Brother Love's Traveling Salvation Show" by Neil Diamond. After putting the record on the stereo, and in spite of the fact there were many other places to sit, he came and sat close to me on the couch. This felt odd. I sat there wondering what he wanted me to do or say? He asked me what I thought of the music. I didn't understand the lyrics. The whole thing seemed a little weird.

Jeff's behavior was so unlike anything Pastor Tom would have ever done, taking me to his basement alone and asking me about popular song lyrics.

I had not talked to any pastor about anything other than church and the Bible. This attention made me feel uneasy and unsure of myself, but it also made me feel special.

4   Sweet Sixteen

One of my responsibilities as a youth group leader was to host Youth After Church meetings at my home. These meetings consisted of prayer, devotions, and singing. It was a time for faith and friendship.

December 1971, just six months after his arrival, a youth group meeting was held in my home. The meeting was full of worship, prayer, and song and was not unlike other youth group meetings. That is until the other teens had left, and I turned to see Jeff standing in the hallway. It was now just the two of us. He walked over to me, he looked at me and told me again how great the evening was. I felt so special. I was on cloud nine. Then he cupped my face in the palm of his hands and moved my head upward toward his. With his thumbs behind my ears, he brushed my hair away and he told me how much he loved me. Then he bent down and kissed me.

My thoughts raced as I wondered, *"What is he doing?" He just kissed me and not just on the cheek! This was a real kiss.* For a moment I was stunned. It was a soft, gentle kiss, almost innocent. It didn't seem wrong. Yet it didn't seem right either. I trusted him. I stood there for a moment, but it seemed like much more. I was afraid to move. I was trying to process what happened, unsure what to think, as he continued to compliment me and tell me how much he appreciated me.

Confused, it took me a second, but then I calmed myself with the thought, "This is my minister; this is Jeff. He wouldn't do anything he shouldn't do. He's just showing me how much he loves me and how happy he is the evening went so well."

5   Number A36D

Throughout the next year I continued to babysit at his home. His wife worked evenings which provided him the perfect opportunity to gain my trust and to exploit my love of the church. After the children were in bed he wanted to sit and talk to me about the Bible. He would give me books to read to help deepen my faith. The time he spent with me was not to help me, but to groom me so he could reach his ultimate goal of having sex with me. He did, just after I turned seventeen.

I turned to walk down the hallway toward the family room when he stopped me again. Taking my arm, he led me to the living room where only light from the kitchen lit the room. There was no furniture there, with the exception of an old console stereo cabinet with four legs sitting on the thick gold shag carpeting. I wondered why we were going to the living room.

He put me on the floor near the stereo, laid on top of me and began kissing me as he put his hands beneath my blouse. Then he began undressing me. He had never done that before. It was happening so fast. I figured he would stop. *Surely, he would stop*, I told myself. He felt so heavy on top of me. No one had ever been on top of me like that. My heart raced with fear. Then I sensed he was *not* going to stop. His breath became heavy, almost as heavy as his body.

He repeatedly asked if I loved him and I answered yes, each time. I didn't know why he kept asking me that. Yes, I loved him, but was he asking me if I loved him a different way?

"You know I love you. You know that don't you?"

"Yes." It was all I could think to say.

With his head pressed against my neck, with his hot breath, he whispered, "You know I would never do anything to hurt you."

He pulled off my vest and unbuttoned my blouse. As he continued to undress me, he pushed me a little bit until my head was partially under the stereo. I tried to close my eyes and think of something else to block what was happening. I didn't know how to tell him to stop and, if I did, would he get mad? I was afraid to say anything. I didn't want to hurt him or make him mad.

Just close your eyes, I thought.

Eventually my head was almost completely under the stereo. Even though it was nearly dark in the room, I could see some of the numbers printed on the bottom of the stereo. There was an A, a 3, a 6 and then more letters. Some were hard to see but I kept trying to repeat the letters. I repeated them over and over and over again, as he pressed against me. A36DP, or was that an F? I repeated them again.

At one point as he touched me, I remember looking at those numbers and thinking, "I wonder why they call it a serial number with so many letters in it. It's really not a number." I just tried to think of anything else, anything except what he was doing to me. I don't remember how much time passed before he slid me from beneath the stereo and lifted me to my feet. I was still partially clothed and thankful for that. He took my hand and pulled me to the stairs.

In a hypnotic, monotone voice, he kept repeating, "It will be okay. You know you can trust me. I love you."

I felt powerless and too scared to tell him no. Even though my body followed him up the steps, I wasn't sure how. I felt like I was in one of those horror movies where the girl stays crouched in a fetal position in the corner of a room as an attacker with a knife slowly approaches. She could jump up and run, yet all she does is remain there crying, whimpering, saying, "please, please don't." You want to stand up and scream at the movie screen, "Run! Do something! Don't just sit there!!! Run!" but she never moves. My head was telling me to run but my body felt frozen. It was scarier to say no than to follow him.

We reached the top of the stairs. As we entered the bedroom, the light was on and I hoped he would turn it off. He didn't.

6   Playing the Field

He reassured me this was God's will and I was to help him in his ministry. In God's eyes we were married. As the relationship continued, his obsessive, controlling, violent behavior, and threats became clear.

He dictated how I was to dress, the time I spent with my friends, what movies I could see. He forbade me to see the movie the *Exorcist*. Afraid to defy him, I didn't. When my best friend Chris had tickets to see the Carpenters in concert, she asked me to go. I was so excited. Jeff insisted I attend a function at church the same night. Chris, angry with me, took another friend. He began to isolate me from my friends, and especially Chris, by demanding more of my time, fearful I would tell her about "us." I promised him I would never tell her. This Jeff was a completely different person than the caring Jeff Coulier I had come to know over the past year.

His obsessive behavior resulted in telling me who I could date, when, and for how long. I would date a guy for a short time and without warning or reason, Jeff would tell me, "You need to stop seeing him, now. Break it off." I would. This happened so many times, but I didn't dare argue. I knew arguing was pointless. I feared making Jeff angry. Once I refused his demand not to see a certain boy who lived out of town or have any more correspondence with him. I lied to him and told him I was no longer writing to Kent and I would not see him again.

7   Strike One

During one of our "meetings" came the first moment I felt hopeless and trapped. I knew the consequences I would face if I were to ever expose him.

After having sex with me, he got dressed to leave. Just before reaching the door he looked at me and asked, "You did stop writing to Kent like I told you, didn't you?"

"Yes."

With that, the back of his hand landed across my face, knocking me to the floor. Disoriented for a moment, I sat on the floor holding my face.

"*Get up*!!"[4]

I didn't move.

"How stupid do you think I am?" "*Now get up! I said to get up!*"

I remained cowering on the floor. I saw fire in his eyes and his clenched jaw, as he told me again to get up. He towered over me and his size overwhelmed me. *If I get up, he's going to hit me again.* I was both terrified and yet ashamed of myself for lying to him. I hoped he would forgive me.

Instead of getting up, I grabbed him around his legs holding onto them, begging his forgiveness.

"Jeff, I'm sorry. I am so sorry." I just kept repeating it.

"Please forgive me."

He began to walk away dragging me across the floor.

"I told you no more letters!"

Finally, he reached down and pulled me up within inches of his face, squeezing both my arms so hard I momentarily forgot about the pain in my cheek and eye. My body was limp like a Raggedy Ann doll. My feet barely touched the ground as he held me up by my arms.

"Don't you *ever* lie to me again!"

He waited.

Still crying, but petrified he might hit me again, after a few moments, with my voice quivering, I said, "I won't."

"Don't you know I know everything you do?"

He pushed me onto the bed and left. He left me alone sitting in the room, with my eye throbbing and my heart breaking.

---

4   In the original work, *Let Me Prey Upon You,* emphasis was placed on certain words and phrases by using all capital letters. To meet stylistic guidelines for this publication, those words and phrases originally emphasized in all capital letters have been changed to italics.

It was a moment of complete and utter clarity. Any hope I ever had of getting away from him was lost. Any silly fantasy I had about my prince charming whisking me away was forever gone. There was no one to rescue me. No one to tell. No one to ever really love me. This was to be my life and I had to accept it. Defeated, from now on, I would do whatever he told me. There was no point in fighting back.

Around 11:00 that evening I left the hotel. I got off the elevator in the Pogue's parking garage. It was very dark with only three cars left on the upper level where I had parked my car. I was alone in the garage with only the sound of my footsteps and a few creaking pipes. Despondently, I shuffled to my car, recognizing the danger, but not afraid. I wished someone would attack me and kill me. After what I had done and who I had become, I deserved to be found dead lying on a cold, dirty garage floor. Then the pain of these last few years and losing Kent would be gone.

The next morning, I awoke, relieved to see my eye had only a slight cut above my upper lid. With a generous amount of make-up, the discoloration was covered well enough. Looking in the mirror as I got dressed, I kept second guessing myself.

Why did I lie to him? Why did I think I could lie, and he wouldn't find out?

Why did I ever agree to go out with Kent? Why didn't I just do as he told me and not write Kent?

If I had not lied, none of this would have happened and I wouldn't be staring at a person I hated in the mirror. It was my fault. I had disobeyed and then I needed to lie. From now on, I would do as he told me. The question of how long Jeff would make me suffer for my sin of lying loomed largest in my mind. After last night, anything was possible. I would never know what lies Jeff told Kent about why I stopped writing.

I finished dressing, got in my car, and drove to church. Putting on my choir robe, I took my seat in the choir next to Cindy. She noticed something was wrong. "Are you okay?" She asked.

Lowering my head and pulling my hair over my eye, I responded, "Yeah, I just don't feel well."

I looked over as Jeff took his seat just to the right of the choir, holding his Bible and notes. No expression. As the organ began to play, he looked over at me and smiled and nodded. He then stood up and with his hands on the podium, he simply said, "Welcome to our service this morning. We are glad you are here." I then stood with the choir as we sang, "Lead On O King Eternal."

Back to normal.

8   Who Said It Was Over?

The abuse continued for five years until his actions were discovered by two members of the church. Once the elders were informed my fate was determined. He was given the opportunity to beg forgiveness. I, however, was told to remain silent. I was told not to tell my parents. I was told by the elders to behave normally, all in their effort to protect Jeff Coulier and his family. He was given a going away party and moved to the next church. I was blamed.

I received a call from Milton Crane, the head of Walnut Branch elders.

"Sandy, Mr. Hahn and I would like to meet with you."
"Okay."
"We want you to meet us in the Fellowship Hall tonight at 7:00."
"Okay, I will be there."

He gave no indication as to why they wanted to meet me, or that I might want to bring my parents or someone with me. I trusted them, like I would any church official, so I didn't ask. Mr. Crane was an older gentleman, old enough to be my grandfather. He was very well respected, not only at Walnut Branch, but throughout the Christian community. He had served on the board at Cincinnati Christian University, had published many articles in various Christian publications, and was an ordained minister. His daughter was one of my Sunday School teachers.

Mr. Hahn was the father of one of my friends in the youth group. He was chairman of the elders and Mr. Crane was chairman of the board.

On the evening I was asked to meet at the church, I pulled into the church parking lot to find only their two cars. Usually the church was a hub of activity, yet this Tuesday evening it was strangely quiet and dark. Walking down the dimly lit hallway approaching the Fellowship Hall, I couldn't help but think of all the number of times I had been in that room over the years.

As I entered the room, both men were seated in two chairs with a third chair pulled over facing them, which obviously was meant for me. I remember Mr. Crane had his Bible in his lap. Mr. Hahn stood up and asked me to have a seat. It wasn't until that moment I felt nervous and a bit concerned I was in this room with these two men and wondered what they may want to discuss.

Nothing could have prepared me for the words I was about to hear. Without hesitation and with the voice of a scolding father, Mr. Hahn looked at me and said, "You are to leave this church."

Stunned. I just sat there for a moment until the words sunk in.

You are to leave this church.
I put my hand over my mouth to stifle my crying.
You are to leave this church. You are to leave this church. You are to leave this church.
That's all I kept hearing over and over in my mind.
This church was not just any church, it was MY church and now I was being told I had to leave?
You are to leave this church.
Where would I go? What would I do?
You are to leave this church.
I loved this church. It was my whole life.
You are to leave this church.
It was the only church I knew and now I was being told to leave.
You are to leave this church.
I was sick to my stomach. I was scared.
They continued to talk but all I could hear were their words repeating over and over in my head.
You are to leave this church.

I sat there alone in this room with these two men who now decided I was no longer fit to worship in MY church. These were not just any men. They were the elders.

9   Preparation

It would be the drive to Queensgate, twenty-seven years after being told to leave the church, that would force me to face the truth about what was done to me in 1976. After much thought and discussion with close friends, I made the decision to confront him. In 2004, I hired a private investigator, Jim Simon, to locate my abuser. He was found, still ministering, in a church in Alabama. A meeting was then set for me to confront him.

The meeting was set. Now questions haunted me. What did I hope to accomplish? Will I walk into that room and be that sixteen-year-old girl again? How should I respond if he said he was sorry? Would I believe him? Should I?

From the recorded conversations with Jim Simon, I knew a little bit of how Jeff Coulier might react and respond. He had admitted he knew he hurt me, but he thought I was happy. He wanted Jim Simon to convey to me how sorry he was. But I knew he had no idea *how* he hurt me. Words are easy, particularly for a narcissist like him. Still, I wanted him to know exactly what he had done. It wasn't enough for me to say to him, "You hurt me." And it certainly wasn't enough for him to say, "I am sorry."

If I wasn't vigilant about reminding myself why I was having this meeting, I could easily have found myself listening to the part of my brain from twenty-seven years ago. I was doubting my every move. And still fearful of him after all these years, his words, "Don't ever tell," never really left me.

I was not only confronting Jeff Coulier, but also the practice of the church to keep these matters secret. Just as my former church, Walnut Branch Church, kept Jeff's sexual misconduct hidden, his current boss, Sam Fitzgerald, was now doing the same thing. Neither his congregation nor his elders knew of his past. Jeff Coulier had a long history of misconduct championed by the devil. He had served in at least three churches and in all three at least one known act of sexual abuse occurred. Any teen or vulnerable woman in his current church might well be his next victim.

I planned to meet with Sam Fitzgerald, his boss, the following day after the meeting with Jeff Coulier and express my concerns about Jeff remaining in ministry. I would also inform his elders. I would draft a letter I intended to send after the meeting. Past experiences told me elders usually don't do the right things in these situations, and with Jeff Coulier's pattern of manipulation, the elders may well not take any action, let alone inform the congregation. With that in mind, I also intended to send a letter to the president of the denomination.

10   Confrontation

One confrontation was complete but there were more meetings I needed to find answers. My meeting with Sam Fitzgerald was held October 24, 2004.

As the meeting started, Sam Fitzgerald, Jeff's boss, started to speak, "Sandy let me just say I know how difficult this is and I want you to know that Jeff ..." *Oh no you don't. You are not going to take control of this meeting.* I cut him off.

"I appreciate that, but I will tell you what *I* expect to happen here today. First, I want you to know I did not come here out of revenge or spite. I am here because I need to heal and begin the process of healing from the pain caused by Jeff Coulier; painful memories I have tried to suppress for twenty-seven years."

Looking at Jeff, I leaned forward in my chair, with my hands clasped holding a handkerchief. Keeping his eyes fixed upon me, I said:

> For the past seven months I have taken a very painful journey to get to where I am today. I could not have done it without the help of my friends and the support of my husband. In the end, after much soul searching and prayer, I knew the only way for me to resolve this was to face you and tell you what I should have said to you thirty-two years ago when you first kissed me.
>
> Your behavior and what you did to me was unethical, immoral, and illegal and you had no right to do it.
>
> I was sixteen years old. You were thirty, married with two children and the minister of my church. You took advantage of my youth and innocence and my complete trust in you as my minister.

At this point I showed him a picture of us taken together at a church retreat just before the abuse began. Without changing his expression, he quickly looked at the picture, turned it over, put it on the table and slid it back to me. I grabbed the picture, held it close to his face and demanded, *"look at this!"*

His expression did not change. I continued.

> I was just a kid. Do you remember? You violated the most sacred of relationships; that of a minister and a member of his congregation. You used your position to sexually exploit me. You were supposed to be my moral guide, love me, care for me, and protect me. I was a child of God. Instead, you twisted it and made it all perverse. But even worse, your exploitation of me was deliberate and calculated.
>
> *You knew exactly what you were doing!*
>
> The church should have been a safe place for me and because of you, it was not. My mother had every right to expect that her daughter would be safe in her own home with the minister of the church. Even now, I am afraid to be left alone with a minister.

I leaned forward and pointed my finger at him, *"That's what you did to me."*

"While I have faith in God, I have no spiritual connection to the church. It is still unbelievable to me, even after the elders found out what you had done there was still discussion about you remaining at Walnut Branch and *I was the one told to leave the church! And you stood by and let them!"*

At this point Jeff Coulier responded, "Everything she said is right on target. I probably should have been shot for what I did. I can only say I am sorry. I didn't know how to make it right. I've had a history of hurting the people I love. My behavior hurt the church. I know I don't deserve it, but for your sake, you need to forgive me." Pausing he said, "All I can say is I am sorry."

Everything he said was about him; he had an alcoholic father, he had hurt churches in his past, he had therapy, he was a sexual addict, he had taken boundary classes, he is faithful to his wife. Not once did he articulate or give any hint of understanding what he did to me. The only time I was mentioned in his response was his statement I needed to forgive him.

Then I said, again looking directly at him, "You can never give me back what you have taken from me, and there isn't enough anger in the world to make what you did to me right." I then had him read a list I had prepared describing what he had done and the effect it had upon my life. I needed him to articulate exactly how he hurt me.

Then Sam Fitzgerald spoke. "First, let me say I admire your courage, but you are describing a man I don't know. This is not the Jeff I know today."

"I don't want to discuss that. I came here to confront Jeff and I did that. I'm finished. I will meet with you tomorrow," I said with authority in my voice which even surprised me. With that we stood up and left the room.

11   Seeking Justice

I hoped my meeting with Sam Fitzgerald would bring understanding and acknowledgement of the lifelong effects of Jeff Coulier's abuse. I expected my concerns and his past pattern of multiple incidences of sexual misconduct might result in his removal, or at the very least, his congregation would be made aware of Coulier's long history of abuse.

Sam Fitzgerald began our meeting by thanking me for my discretion. Before I could say anything, he said, "I know and have seen firsthand the pain caused when a minister falls and steps out of his boundaries." I held my composure but felt fury inside.

"Fall?! Steps out of his boundaries?!" I was incredulous. He did not fall or step out of bounds. This is not a playground activity or a basketball game. He had

gravely sinned and exploited a minor, using God to do it. I let him continue. "Jeff knows he hurt you and he took away your teenage years, and he cannot give those back to you."

After all I said in that meeting, Jeff Coulier's view was that he *took away my teenage years*? He took away my spiritual life!

He continued to tell me how Jeff Coulier was no longer the same person and he was no longer a threat. He even said, "I can tell you this, I would leave my fourteen-year-old daughter alone with him."

"Unfortunately, my mother felt the same," I responded.

I then asked him, "How do you know he is changed? *You don't know that.*" Sam Fitzgerald continued defending him, saying, "I have had the privilege of seeing him and knowing him. He is sincere."

I interrupted him, "That's exactly what he wants you to believe."

"Sandy, he has done some wonderful things here. I do know he had intense therapy for his sexual addiction, and I do believe in the power of God to change people. I believe he has been transformed. He has self-imposed boundaries. He will not counsel one on one or meet at the church with anyone. He does not have a private office."

"So why," I asked, "were you not aware of the number of times he committed sexual misconduct during his ministry in the past? Why do you only have limited knowledge if you are in charge of him? How do you justify a man with such a history of sexual misconduct is permitted to have *self-imposed* boundaries?"

I continued,

> If you don't know his weaknesses and his background, and what he is capable of, how do you know he is no longer a threat or even if you have the proper safeguards in place? Are these the characteristics you want in our spiritual leaders; a man who must be watched for sexual misconduct, an admitted sexual addict, and all the while keeping this information from the congregation and putting them at risk?

With my voice rising just a bit I asked, "And don't you think Mrs. Smith or Mrs. Jones sitting in your congregation should be the ones deciding for themselves if they feel safe with him? Not you. You have no right to keep his extensive background of sexual misconduct from the congregation."

He responded, "I suppose we differ on that."

Before the meeting ended, I informed him I was going to send a letter to the eleven elders informing them of Jeff Coulier's past. Leaving the meeting I was convinced no action would be taken by Sam Fitzgerald. Three days later,

I received a letter from Sam Fitzgerald expressing concern and fear about sending the letter to the eleven elders at the church.[5]

12   Obstacles

The lack of church hierarchy allowed the perpetrator to remain hidden and made Sam Fitzgerald's response predictable. Blaming the victim and asking for silence is the norm.

In part, this was his message. The entirety of the letter can be found in the appendix of my book. Sam Fitzgerald's four-page response arrived less than a week after the meeting. He had not looked at the disciplinary file as promised. His words stung. He indicated he considered Jeff Coulier a low risk because he felt Jeff Coulier had changed dramatically. He called Jeff Coulier a father figure and asserted his life and words bear witness to the Gospel in the church where he has built the congregation to be "300 members with a beautiful new building." He feared people might leave the church if Jeff's sins were exposed.[6]

The letter ended with him asking me to not send a letter to the elders and the president of the denomination. He had the gall to write, "I would be afraid the damage done to a dynamic congregation, the damage to people's faith, the damage to their sense of security in relationship, the damage to their ability to trust, and the collapse of their spiritual dreams *would weigh upon your spirit*."[7]

In Sam Fitzgerald's exact words, "If you were to send such a letter, you would know in your heart you may single-handedly veto the experience of God's grace for many, many people. That, to me, would be quite a load to carry. I believe it would create new wounds for you." He continued, "Sandy, I have doubts sending a letter like the one you drafted will bring healing." The message once again: I would be to blame.[8]

He then reminded me again, I had a limited view of who Jeff Coulier was. I should accept the wisdom of those who are able to see more than I am able to see. He ended the letter by once again expressing concern for Jeff Coulier's past being exposed, "*My concern relates to how much information gets to whom*

---

5   Sam Fitzgerald, letter to Sandy Phillips Kirkham, October 28, 2004.

6   Ibid., 3.

7   Ibid., 4.

8   Ibid., 4.

and whether those who receive the information benefit from it. I will keep you informed."[9]

He never kept us informed. I sent the letter to the eleven elders of his church. No one responded. Not one.

I was relatively new at telling people about abuse, yet I could see in his words, in the implied threat of shame, he was employing a tool used by predators on many victims. The message is to stay quiet, sharing truth will hurt institutions and people, and it is better to hide the truth. It was classic church-response rhetoric.

13   The Elders

> It was not only the sexual abuse which affected my life but the response of the two elders who told me to leave the church. I confronted them, looking for an acknowledgement that what they did to me was wrong. Again, I would be disappointed in their responses. Of the two elders, Milton Crane agreed to meet me, the other refused. Both denied ever telling me to leave the church, despite a letter I had saved with their signatures at the bottom as the elders inviting the members to Jeff Coulier's going away party.

Four days after sending the letter requesting to meet, Milton Crane called me. "Dear, I was so glad to get your letter.[10] I have thought of you many times over the years. I have prayed for you."

We agreed to meet but the friendliness of his tone told me he did not understand the purpose of my request. Could it be he thought I was coming to him to finally confess my sins and ask for forgiveness? Should I tell him why I wanted to meet with him? The irony did not escape me. Thirty years later I was requesting *him* to meet me and he did not seem to know what the meeting was about or consider he may want to have someone in attendance with him. Our roles were now reversed.

The meeting started with introductions and his first comment to me was, "You're just as pretty as I remember you."

After reading to him the facts of what actually took place at Walnut Branch, Jeff Coulier's grooming, manipulation, and control of me, his violent behavior

---

9   Sandy Phillips Kirkham, *Let Me Prey Upon You* (Cincinnati, OH: Absam, LLC, 2019), 174.

10   Milton Crane and Ed Hahn, letter to the congregation, 1976.

and sexual abuse, I told him of my confrontation with Jeff Coulier. He seemed surprised and said, "Good for you."

I continued by saying, "It was wrong of Jeff Coulier to take away my inno-cence and my virginity, but the response of Walnut Branch Christian Church was also wrong. At the time, you were chairman of the board and Ed Hahn was chairman of the elders. That's why I am here."

"As a teenager, you'll remember, I was very active at Walnut Branch. I sang in the choir. I taught Sunday School. I led youth retreats. If Walnut Branch's doors were open, I was there spending time and energy on something I loved so much and growing in my faith and my relationship to God."

"When Jeff Coulier violated me all that changed. The church became con-taminated for me because of what he did to me. A place where I once found joy and peace, now brings me only conflict and pain. Walnut Branch's response to the situation contributed significantly to those feelings."

"Walnut Branch never held Jeff Coulier accountable or disciplined him for what he did to me, what he did to his wife, what he did to his children, or what he did to the members of Walnut Branch. To the contrary, he was sent off with a celebration including gifts and a letter signed by you and Ed saying, "How grateful many parents will be for the influence Jeff Coulier had on their young people.""

I continued with the facts about the night he and Ed asked me to leave the church. He sat straight up and looked at me and said, "Honey, I don't remember any meeting with you, and I would *never* tell anyone to leave the church."

"Well, whether you remember or not, it is *exactly* what happened. Milton, you did not take my innocence or my virginity, Jeff Coulier did that, but what you and Ed took from me in the meeting on that night in 1976 was a lifetime of love and trust of the church."

When I finished, he then went on to disparage Jeff Coulier, and how bad he was. Again, he repeated he never liked or trusted him.

"I blame him totally."

"Milton, it wasn't just Jeff Coulier to blame. Walnut Branch was wrong as well." Sitting there looking a bit stunned, he now seemed to understand the purpose of the meeting. I continued, "Even after knowing what Jeff Coulier had done, there was a vote among the elders and you as chairman, to try and keep him on staff and keep his actions hidden from the congregation!"

"Not only was Jeff Coulier not disciplined, he was given a going-away party by the congregation and invitation came to me and my mother, from you and Ed!"

He interrupted me, "Oh no! I wasn't even on the board then."

So, both Ed and Milton used the same defense. "Couldn't have been me, I wasn't on the board."

He then began to tell me how wonderful I was, what a fine young person he remembered me to be. "You were a beautiful girl and smart too. I'm trying to remember the last time I saw you."

"It was in 1976 when you told me to leave the church," I said and looked directly at him, amazed about his denial.

Again, he repeated, "Now honey, I was not a part of that. I wasn't on the board then."

Looking at him squarely in the eye, while holding the letter from 1976 inviting the congregation to Jeff Coulier's going away party, with his name at the bottom I said, "You weren't on the board at the time?"

"No, I was not."

I then handed the letter signed by him and Ed Hahn to him.[11]

"I am flabbergasted. I have never seen this letter. I did not write this letter. I did not authorize this letter."[12]

"It clearly shows you were not only on the board; you were the chairman."

"I did not authorize this letter. I have never seen I it," he said, defiantly.[13]

14   Epilogue

In 2018, we were at a friends' house sitting in her screened-in porch celebrating another friend's birthday. It was a steamy July day, and the backyard pool looked inviting. As my friends went inside to load their plates with salads and desserts, I lingered for a moment on the same porch where I told my story for the first time fourteen years ago. How grateful I felt for their love and support. It was this very spot where I started to deal with the most painful chapter in my life. It was here where I first stuttered those words, "I was sexually abused by my youth minister." It was then when and where my healing began.

With the healing came my need and passion to speak out about clergy abuse. Through the years, I've continued to work with The Hope of Survivors ministry. I now serve on the board of the Council on Child Abuse (COCA). I've spoken to many groups and churches on the topic of prevention and I have met courageous survivors. After one such presentation, several of the attendees remarked, "You should write a book."

---

11   Ibid.
12   Ibid.
13   Ibid.

I began to understand my story could have an impact. Over the years the same suggestion came from many of my friends. It took thirteen years before I felt strong enough to consider allowing a much larger audience see my pain and struggles. When I spoke to groups, I could see their faces. I was comfortable in front of a crowd. Writing a book seemed scarier. Eventually, I realized the wound I once protected was now but a fading scar. Perhaps I could share my story in a book.

Now stronger, and with a clearer understanding of clergy abuse, I realize there are things I would have done differently if I were to again begin this journey I started in 2004. But looking back, in the midst of my pain and healing, I did the best I could. At age seventy-seven, Jeff Coulier is semi-retired and remains in good standing with the Disciples of Christ denomination.

One of the most agonizing decisions in writing this book was whether to name the pastor who abused me. For years I lived with the shame caused by this man; didn't he deserve to be shamed? In keeping his identity a secret, was I complicit in keeping his actions a secret? Over the years, I never revealed his identity when lecturing, speaking with victims, or in my work with survivor networks. My goal was always to expose the horrors of clergy abuse, not to make it a personal vendetta.

Writing allowed me to tell my story. My story is backed up by hundreds of pages of materials verifying what took place: his signed confession, written correspondence with his ministry officials, letters, and taped recordings of everything from conversations, his sermons, and meetings. I am a packrat. For years, boxes of memories from church sat unopened in my basement. Once I began to search for explanations, I had the courage to look through the boxes. In this book, I have changed the names of the pastor, the church leaders, including those who allowed the abuser to continue in the ministry (and to continue to sexually abuse women) and the name of the church where the abuse occurred. I have chosen to use real names of those who were supportive and kind to me through this process.

My story is told not as much about shaming my abuser publicly, but to explain how clergy abuse happens. My story shows how a charismatic leader (and a church full of such people) can thwart the word of God and create massive harm. The church elders who hid his actions to save his reputation, while removing me from the church, deserved to be "outed." However, they are no longer living and I saw no benefit to visit the sins of the fathers on their children.

While I was writing this book, the #MeToo movement, and the lesser known, but growing, #MeTooChurch movement were born. These groups provide so many victims a voice. My hope is those who have been abused are now heard and believed, and perhaps books such as mine and organizations such as The Hope of Survivors and Survivors Network of those Abused by Priests (SNAP), will bring light and better understanding to the topic of clergy abuse. Our goal is to provide hope and healing to victims.

To my fellow survivors, you are not alone.

CHAPTER 9

Patriarchal Power and the Catholic Church

Diane Dougherty

Misogyny is a culturally inculcated hatred of women. At the same time, however, misogynists often loudly profess their love of mothers and other women
in their lives. How can this apparent contradiction arise? It occurs because
misogyny is a primarily hidden predatory behavior of dominant enculturated males and females who feel the necessity to maintain invisible stands of
division and separation. An example of this was given by U.S. Representative
Alexandria Ocasio Cortez (a Roman Catholic) in her response to a Roman
Catholic House colleague, U.S. Representative Ted Yoho who called her a
"Fuckin Bitch" on the steps of the U.S. Capitol in front of media.[1] She was
not traumatized by this language because she has seen this type of behavior in many men. Name-calling is but one aspect of misogyny. What bothered
Ocasio Cortez was Yoho's use of the women in his family to cover for him. She
bristled at the silence of his colleagues, the acceptance of this violent language against women and a structure of power that supports it in the halls of
Congress. Dehumanizing language is common and undetectable to most. She
thanked him for saying this, so that she could remind everyone that people of
great stature, holding high rank, can accost women but decent men apologize
to acknowledge the harm done.

   Patriarchal architecture founded on misogyny forms the foundation of
"conservative" and "liberal" politics as a virus mutating and reproducing itself
from one generation to the next emphasizing male superiority over women.
This false premise is the primary engine that justifies the use of man-made
laws and legalized codes of conduct that in turn promote societal illnesses and
extreme inequality.

   When feminist scholars of philosophy began examining the exclusion of
women by male historical and canonical philosophers, three aspects of misogynist beliefs were examined: explicit misogyny; gendered interpretations
(women are lesser); and synoptic interpretations where reason and objectivity
are exclusively male attributes. Under this microscope, Aristotle could be seen

---

1   Alexandria Ocasio-Cortez, July 23, 2020, https://www.youtube.com/watch?v=LI4ueUtkRQo.

as a masterful misogynist.[2] He believed that men were mentally and biologically superior to women, therefore by nature they (women) should be slaves. He wrote "women are deformed males ... without a soul," a belief that continues to resonate in the minds of many leaders today. His misogynist narratives were utilized by nations to frame social structures based on the premise that "humans are divided into two kinds, male (superior beings) and female (lesser beings)."[3] Hence, much of the world's population, governments, and religions today continue to operate under the influence of unrelenting patriarchal structures that do untold harm.[4]

1   Normalizing Misogyny

Go to any toy store, bookstore, or game store and misogyny is on full display. What is in the girl's section giving them messages about themselves? Girls are pretty, thin, queens, princesses, and they love to wear pink. Successful females are portrayed as dolls with perfect makeup and high heels that match the perfect outfit. Make-up tables, mansions, yachts, expensive clothes, all stimulate the minds of boys and girls telling them what outer image is culturally acceptable for successful females. For boys we see endless displays of guns, building gadgets, action packed toys, video games loaded with winning through violence or oppression, as well as an emphasis on aggressive competition of all sorts. Boys and girls are enculturated to believe that girls are uncompetitive, emotional, and fragile while boys are expected to be brave, aggressive, competitive, and dominant. Masculinity ideals translate into life choices opening avenues for white boys' free exploration of these violent character traits to the point that legal and oftentimes criminal offences are trivialized.[5] Kate Manne calls this *Himpathy*, excessive sympathy shown to male perpetrators. Women and men are known for showing sympathy to white men's criminal behavior because they are reluctant to ruin their lives. Victims of white male violence

2   Charlotte Witt, "Feminist History of Philosophy". In: Alanen L., Witt C. (eds), *Feminist Reflections on the History of Philosophy. The New Synthese Historical Library* (Texts and Studies in the History of Philosophy), vol 55. 2004. https://doi.org/10.1007/1-4020-2489-4_1.
3   Carrie L. Bass, "Gender Ontology and Women in Ministry in the Early Church" *Priscilla Papers, Academic Journal*, (Spring, April 30, 2011).
4   Rabbi Tirzah Firestone, "Beyond Patriarchy: What to do with the Legacy of Trauma and Fear." *Tikkun*, (Winter,2019), https://www.tikkun.org/what-to-do-with-the-legacy-of-trauma-and-fear.
5   Kate Manne, *Down Girl. The Logic of Misogyny* (New York, NY: Oxford University Press, 2018), 196–208.

are often vilified in order to support the leniency shown to perpetrators. This is particularly evident in the multitude of cases in which parents dismiss their children's accounts of sexual abuse by a trusted male relative or priest.

On the other hand, women are treated quite differently in the patriarchy. One out of every three females will be sexually molested by a trusted adult male.[6] These females are largely unprotected by the courts. Additionally, policies and practices regarding women lead to a lifetime of inadequate income. Once caught in the cycle of poverty, wealth building is not part of their future and there is a high likelihood that their children will follow the same path.[7] As a matter of fact, the poor do not believe they have a future, they can only focus on the unmet needs of the day. The question raised here directly relates to how a low-wage workforce is necessary for other people's wealth building.[8] However, if people have human rights, societies need to rework structures to provide equity in education that in turn provides a living wage and frees poor people caught in the net of poverty for profit.[9] Could this be why in America the vast majority of those living in poverty are women and their children, and why Christian leaders under patriarchy do not address it, but offer minimal services to salve their consciences?[10] Could it also be the reason that the majority of women are kept poor from one generation to the next?

Cultural misogynist behaviors are protected by the very laws and codes that misogynists design. They become the terms of relationships demanding women stay in their place while men move about freely. "Society presents women as voiceless bodies ready to serve hetero-male desires," and that has led to a multitude of ways patriarchal society practices dehumanization of women and minorities, thereby exponentially increasing gender inequality.[11]

6   National Coalition Against Domestic Violence, https://ncadv.org/.

7   US Partnership on Mobility from Poverty, https://www.urban.org/sites/default/files/
        publication/90321/escaping-poverty.pdf.

8   Camille Bureau, "How do patriarchy and capitalism jointly reinforce oppression of women."
        Committee for the Abolition of Illegitimate Debt, September 13, 2018, https://www.cadtm
        .org/How-do-patriarchy-and-capitalism-jointly-reinforce-the-oppression-of-women.

9   Universal Declaration of Human Rights, https://www.humanrights.com/what-are
        -human-rights/universal-declaration-of-human-rights/preamble.html.

10   Shailly Gupta Barnes, "Explaining the 140 million: Breaking down the numbers in the
        moral budget." Kairos Center, Undated. https://kairoscenter.org/explaining-the-140
        -million/.

11   Chris Crass, "Going to Places that Scare Me ...," Colours of Resistance Archive. Resisting
        Patriarchy, Undated. http://www.coloursofresistance.org/536/going-to-places-that-scare
        -me-personal-reflections-on-challenging-male-supremacy/.

2   Patriarchy and Trauma

Meera Atkinson writes that patriarchy perpetuates trauma to such a degree that living itself is traumatic with endless suffering and strife.[12] Prominent church leaders are encased in patriarchal teaching and promote misogynist beliefs as part of the Christian tradition.[13] These men used religion to adopt patriarchal norms throughout recorded Christian history subjugating women to men's wishes, enslaving them, and forcing them into prostitution. Today's movement in the U.S. courts to protect rapists is a prime example. A young man raped a 16-year-old girl. It was filmed and distributed. The judge, concerned about the "assailant's bright future" ruled him a minor and gave him a light sentence because he believed it did not constitute "calculated cruelty."[14] In every age, conscious laws were on the books to deny women access to justice in the courts, as well as health, education and welfare. Why? Because Christian leaders collaborate with governments that function under patriarchal rule, meaning the emphasis is more about protecting male privilege than justice under the law.

While there is a plethora of examples of patriarchal Christian leaders, we will highlight just a few of these and provide some examples of early Christian women who pushed through boundaries, and built egalitarian communities for the first 300 years, only to be forgotten and purposefully erased from history. A leader in the early Christian Church, Tertullian (160–220 C.E.) preached, "Woman is a temple built over a sewer, the gateway to the devil. Woman, you are the devil's doorway."[15] When he met a woman who was part of the noble class, his tone changed. Free-born Roman citizens could come from families of senatorial or equestrian rank, but their wealth had to remain in that class. Once converted to Christianity, a noble woman had to marry a nobleman, or give up power, status and wealth.[16] Tertullian wanted to use her wealth and

12   Meera Atkinson, "Patriarchy Perpetuates Trauma. It's Time to Face the Fact." *The Guardian,* April 29, 2018. https://www.theguardian.com/commentisfree/2018/apr/30/patriarchy-perpetuates-trauma-its-time-to-face-the-fact.

13   Miguel De La Torre, "Quotations Track Church's Anti-Woman Legacy," *Good Faith Media,* March 25, 2005.

14   Lillian House, "US Justice System Protects Rapists," *Breaking the Chains,* July 11, 2019. https://www.breakingthechainsmag.org/u-s-justice-system-protects-rapists/.

15   Miguel De La Torre, "Quotations Track Church's Anti-Woman Legacy," *Good Faith Media,* March 25, 2005.

16   Margaret Mowczko, "Wealthy Women in the First Century World" *Priscilla Papers, Academic Journal,* Summer, 2018.

influenced her and others not to marry, for the benefit of the church. If society allowed additional freedoms to women, the church hierarchy tried to take them back.

However, women were the source of the growth of the early church and believed themselves to be disciples of Christ. Margaret Mowczko tells us that at this time, women were active in public spaces as artisans, such as Priscilla, or businesswomen, such as Lydia. Some like Phoebe were independently wealthy or born into royalty that brought privileges.[17] They filled places in society and in church. They built strong networks of Christian communities that thrived around the Mediterranean. Women believed in Christ's transformative message, allowing them to cross the boundaries of womanhood to serve outside society's norms. They grew diverse communities in the homes of the wealthy leaders of the time, preaching, teaching and ministering to those in need. Their communities were egalitarian, open to all.[18] In spite of misogynist rules and strict codes of conduct regarding marriage and sex, Karen Jo Torjensen's research shows that while early Christianity lacked buildings, officials, and large congregations marked by later stages, it was a social movement, "marked by fluidity and flexibility that allowed women, slaves and artisans to assume leadership roles," within the societal codes that kept them out of public spaces.[19]

Although they were able to accomplish great things in the early church, certain misogynist practices of the time imposed painful choices. In order to serve, some women had to be non-sexual and declare themselves a widow. Women who had authority in their communities were women who had either transformed themselves into males or who wiped out femaleness in favor of androgyny or hermaphroditism ... neither male or female.[20] They accepted these societal norms for the promise, hope and experience of women living in an egalitarian community, preaching, teaching and promoting the gospel as a disciple of Christ. However, in terms of time, this experience was short lived. April De Conick, in her book *Holy Misogyny*, describes the patriarchy's noose around a God that would dare try to call a woman a disciple. She declares, "The

---

17   Deborah Sawyer, "Sisters in Christ or Daughters of Eve", in Lucinda Joy Peach, *Women and World Religions*. (Upper Saddle River, New Jersey: Prentice Hall, 2002), 215.

18   Karen Jo Torjensen, *When Women Were Priests: Women's Leadership in the Early Church and the Scandal of Their Subordination in the Rise of Christianity*, (San Francisco, Calif: Harper Publishing, 1993), 11–37.

19   Ibid, 11.

20   April DeConick, *Holy Misogyny*, (New York, NY: The Continuum International Publishing Group, 2011), 79.

real serpent in the garden is misogyny that makes the divine write the subordination of the female in her own hand."[21] The power behind the patriarchal false notions of women continued to stream through the minds of men growing stronger as women's work and creative initiatives began to flower in the early church. Like a well-greased engine, the pathogen of power, domination and wealth building became an invisible hand trying to manipulate and/or erase their work. "I am not giving permission for a woman to teach or to tell a man what to do. A woman ought not to speak, because Adam was formed first and Eve afterwards, and it was not Adam who was led astray but the woman who was led astray and fell into sin. Nevertheless, she will be saved by childbearing." (1 Ti 2:12–15).

The influential St. John Chrysostom (304–407 C.E.) joined the men of the day parroting hatred for women, "Among all savage beast none is found so harmful as woman, a woman is as sick as a hideous tapeworm, the advance post of hell."[22] Perhaps the growth of house churches during that time through women's leadership was an annoyance. Conceivably his lashing out relates to the role women were given when Christian congregations became unmanageable. These women presbyters went to rural and large urban communities. Solid evidence exists that many women led large communities, and the practice was widespread throughout Phrygia, Thera, Egypt and Sicily. Giulia Runa has a tombstone in St. Augustine's Cathedral in Hippo, noting her as *presbiterissa* soon after his death. In other words, she was commissioned on his staff and upon death, was buried in the church with her office engraved as a mosaic on the floor at the entrance of the door.[23]

For centuries women have participated in church ministries, and men of great stature and influence continue to make sure that their work is largely uncompensated and devoid of authority and power. Such was the announcement in 2000 at the Southern Baptist Convention that shook up the patriarchy as they altered the practice of some branches of the convention that had ordained women, allowing them to preach, teach and lead congregations. "While both men and women are gifted for service in the church, the office of pastor is limited to men as qualified by Scripture,"[24] assuring higher salaries for

---

21   Ibid,149.

22   Miguel De La Torre, "Quotations Track Church's Anti-Woman Legacy," *Good Faith Media,* March 25, 2005.

23   *National Catholic Reporter,* Staff, January 13, 2013, https://www.ncronline.org/news/ theology/early-women-leaders-heads-house-churches-presbyters.

24   Southern Baptist Convention. "Resolution On Ordination And The Role Of Women In Ministry" (June 1, 1984) https://www.sbc.net/resource-library/resolutions/resolution-on -ordination-and-the-role-of-women-in-ministry/.

men and more work for women. An account of an ordained woman chaplain in a women's prison highlighted the impact this conflict produced. Because her job was dependent on further endorsement by her Baptist denomination, she and many other women would have lost their jobs. Eventually they decided not to ordain women in the future and her status did not change. It was during this time that Jimmy Carter left the Southern Baptist Convention and with a group of Elders began proclaiming worldwide that he lost his religion for equality.[25] No voice, or man of influence or denomination has been more influential in broadcasting the reality of the impact of gender inequality under patriarchy than Jimmy Carter.[26] His book, *A Call to Action, Women, Religion, Violence and Power*, is a call to spread egalitarianism in all sectors of governance, rather than patriarchal rule.

Misogynist principles continue to build wealth through systems that keep people poor. There is no room for partnership—only domination and power building. This model is responsible for continued poverty. It is the leading cause for social divisions, as well as the deconstruction of systems that take food from people and allow governments to cull their own populations by distributing health care to a select few. Christian churches today have had select armies of official clerics, lay men and women, trained to build and maintain patriarchal rule. Seen as ministers for the building of the Kingdom of God, a kingdom itself is being built on the misuse of power by domination over people. Christian missionaries of all denominations seeking to bring a gospel of good news to the poor in hindsight have come to realize they were simply used as an arm of the government to build colonial rule—the product of their colonized mind.[27] Living within the toxic culture of patriarchy, their efforts actually helped create structures that promoted patriarchal slavocracy worldwide.[28] Even today, there is not clarity within Christianity about the role of patriarchy and the practice of patriarchal rule. But a glance at the societies impacted show hierarchies of male domination, female submission, property

25   Jimmy Carter, "Losing my Religion for Equality", *The Age*, July 15, 2009, https://www.theage
      .com.au/politics/federal/losing-my-religion-for-equality-20090714dkov.html?page=-1.
26   Emilina Guimont, *"A Call to Action: Women, Religion, Violence and Power"*, review of *A
      Call to Action: Women, Religion, Violence and Power*, by Jimmy Carter, *Christians for Biblical
      Equality*, 2017, https://www.cbeinternational.org/sites/default/files/Call%20to%20
      Action%20Drupal.pdf.
27   Kaitlin Curtice, "Missions: Is it love or colonization?" *Religion News Service*, November 27,
      2018. https://religionnews.com/2018/11/27/missions-is-it-love-or-colonization.
28   Rosemary Radford Ruether, "Ecofeminism-The Challenge of Theology," *Deported, Exiles,
      Refugees*, n.20, 2012. p. 27. https://www.unive.it/pag/fileadmin/user_upload/dipartimenti/
      DSLCC/documenti/DEP/numeri/n20/06_20_-Ruether_Ecofeminism.pdf.

ownership and wealth building that left large portions of one culture poor while a small portion of another was enriched.

3   The Society of Jesus

Three major armies of global patriarchy significantly influence the identity of the Catholic Church today. The oldest, the Society of Jesus (also known as the Jesuits), has begun the process of examining the intergenerational trauma and harm they have done under the influence of patriarchy, beginning a process for restitution, restructuring and change in their policies toward women in their institutions. They have also examined their complicity in racism that was exhibited in their past treatment of slaves, making steps toward restitution. The other two, The Legion of Christ and *Opus Dei*, are using Catholicism to return to patriarchal rule in their institutions and in American society itself. They could be considered free market agents in this iteration of the global economies of power.

The Jesuits, a highly educated community established in reaction to the Protestant Reformation, began intense examination of their role in the discrimination of women in 1995 that led to significant changes in their operating procedures.[29] In an effort to stand in solidarity with women moving forward, they proposed eight action items for immediate change within all institutions, including teaching equality for women in ministry, opposing movements steeped in the exploitation of women, and the promotion of women's education at their university campuses.[30] In 2018, they came to the aid of a group of women in immediate need of a conference venue. When a woman's group called "Voices of Faith" heard they were ejected from Vatican property the day clerics realized the topic addressed was *Misogyny in Christianity*, the Jesuits offered their Conference Center. Mary McAlesse proclaimed: "We don't have trumpets, but we have voices, voices of faith and we are here to shout, to bring down our Church's walls of misogyny. We have been circling these walls for 55 years since John XXIII's encyclical *Pacem in*

---

29   Rachel I. Swarns. "Georgetown University Plans Steps to Atone for Slave Past", *The New York Times*, September 1, 2016. https://www.nytimes.com/2016/09/02/us/slavesgeorgetown -university.html.

30   Portal to Jesuit Studies. Decree 14: "Jesuits and the Situation of Women in Church and Civil Society," General Congregation 34 (1995), https://jesuitportal.bc.edu/research/ documents/1995_decree14gc34/.

Terris first pointed to the advancement of women as one of the most important 'signs of the times.' "[31]

In 2017, coming to understand their role in patriarchal slavocracy, the Jesuits also began working to change leadership patterns from practices of domination to partnership.[32] In keeping with their reformation agenda, the Jesuits apologized for the ownership and selling of slaves at Georgetown University, making restitution to the descendants they could identify.

4   Legion of Christ

The second group answering directly to the Pope is the Legion of Christ, known for the toxic influence of its cultish drug-dealing leader, Marcial Marciel Delegado, a recognized pedophile who fathered children by two women. Despite his obvious illegal activities, Pope John Paul II admired Delegado because of the money and vocations he brought to the church.[33] Delegado's community has a clerical branch of 'Orthodox' soldiers formed in cult-like fashion to the head. In addition to their obedience to the Pope, his followers take an additional vow of obedience to their leader. Their formation is a clear indication of how dehumanization is used to develop the domination/submission model of compliance to the authority of headship. The engine operating the Legion throughout the United States is the lay group, *Regnum Christi*.[34] These unordained men and women insert themselves into dioceses and start up 'private' schools in parishes of great wealth, using undue influence to siphon off the children of the wealthy, and eventually pull wealth out of the parish for their own benefit. They use the term *conservative orthodoxy* to legitimize their role. Jason Berry argues that they participate in "religious mercantilism," selling "wealth-as-virtue that triumphed over liberation theology's idealism."[35] The Gospel of Prosperity became the Vatican's clarion call.

31   Mary McAlleese, "The time is now for change in the Catholic Church", *Voices of Faith*, March 8, 2018, https://www.youtube.com/watch?v=X9Q9VqkrfCw.

32   Daniel Burke, "In emotional service, Jesuits and Georgetown repent for slave trading," CNN, April 18, 2017, https://www.cnn.com/2017/04/1/living/georgetown-slavery-service/index.html.

33   Jason Berry, "Legion of Christ's deception, unearthed in new documents, indicates wider cover-up" *National Catholic Reporter*, February 18, 2013, https://www.ncronline.org/news/accountability/legion-christs-deception-unearthed-new-documents-indicates-wider-cover.

34   Regnum Christi, https://www.regnumchristi.org/en/mission-2/.

35   Jason Berry, *Render Unto Rome: The Secret Life of Money in the Catholic Church.* (New York, NY: Crown Publishing Group, 2011) 159–196.

Archbishop Harry Flynn of St. Paul, Minneapolis refused to let the Legion into his diocese saying they develop parallel churches and schools and cut parishioners off.[36] Some called them millionaires of Christ due to their efforts to get the wealthy to invest in their schools of orthodoxy, appealing to an elite class of Catholics hoping to consolidate power. An egregious example of this was the undue influence they placed on a wealthy heiress, Gabrielle Mee (89 years old), changed her will leaving all assets to the Legion. After years of court battles, the estate was returned to the family, with a portion left to the Legion.[37] Members are actually tentacles of patriarchal rule in Catholicism with an eye on 'wealth building,' and influencing domination/submission models of governance that use the force and fear for compliance. Former members, John Lennon and Genvieve Kineke, left the cult after seeing the operations of the Legion as a pyramid scheme.[38] Their introduction into dioceses erased the 40 years of collaborative work the dedicated men and women willingly gave to build progressive Vatican II institutions. It is astounding to watch the ease with which a series of these so called 'conservative' appointments could collapse those efforts, replacing them with a patriarchal architecture for the purpose of furthering the goals of power, domination and wealth building.

Today women are addressing issues related to those who, consciously or unconsciously, collaborate in patriarchal rule. Ana Marie Cox calls white women supporting patriarchy "foot soldiers."[39] Like members of *Regnum Christi*, women congratulate themselves for their active engagement in reinstating patriarchal rule.[40] Kate Manne coined the word, *Himpathy* to describe these women.[41] Coming from long lines of patriarchal foot soldiers, it is understandable how an element within male domination controls their belief system and how the cultural surroundings cement those beliefs. However, it is incomprehensible when their actions become confused with the actual gospel Christianity is called to promote. There is no compatibility here.

---

36   Jerry Filteau, "Legionnaires of Christ Banned in 2nd Catholic Diocese." *Cult Education Institute,* January 2, 2005, https://forum.culteducation.com/read.php?12,8412.

37   Jason Berry, *Render Unto Rome: The Secret Life of Money in the Catholic Church.* (New York, NY: Crown Publishing Group, 2011) 166–168.

38   Ibid. 190.

39   Ana Marie Cox, "White Women: Foot Soldiers of the Patriarchy", *I Told You So,* February 11, 2019, http://www.anamariecox.com/with-friends-like-these/2019/2/11/white-women-foot-soldiers-of-the-patriarchy.

40   Mona Elthahawy, *The Seven Necessary Sins for Women and Girls,* (Boston, MA: Beacon Press, 2019), 16.

41   Kate Manne, *Down Girl. The Logic of Misogyny.* (New York, NY: Oxford University Press, 2018), 196–208.

Mind manipulation of the masses is an intergenerational traumatic mark of patriarchy. Whether you are at the top of the Christian hierarchy or the bottom, some Christians are encased in a lifetime of judgment, guilt, shame, fear of God, fear of the priest, fear of hell and compliance to church norms. Choices and actions of Catholic feminists within the church's framework are not understood or tolerated. However, a growing number of Catholics are beginning to see themselves as foot soldiers for Christ called to assist the oppressed and examine oppressive structures to bring about sustainable change that promotes healing. They are at odds with a multitude of believers that stand as oppressors of their very own people, falsely believing that race and gender discrimination is God's will.

5   Opus Dei

In another attempt to further tether the Catholic church to patriarchal roots after the reforms of Vatican II, Pope John Paul II made *Opus Dei* (Latin for 'God's Work') a "personal prelature," designating it as a "floating diocese" that he could dispatch across the globe.[42] This action literally cut off the systemic renewal promised to clerics and laity alike, and returned the church to patriarchal rule. Born in the fascist society of Spain in 1928, *Opus Dei* believes it is the Church's mission to "return the Catholic Church to the Center of society as in medieval times," reporting its successes directly to the Pope.[43] At its inception, its founder, Josemaria Escriva de Balaguer, understood that "no institution with a bunch of street sweepers as members could influence key public sectors, nor pull in the kind of income needed to achieve all he had in mind."[44] His political strategist taught him early on that the only "way to make a mark on society, state or institution was by dominating its summit."[45] These two principles guided the formation of the order.

Opus Dei has developed a multitude of systems that makes them a global super-spreader of patriarchy working directly to diminish democratic structures that promote equality in any form. Their undue religious influence is

---

42   Americans United for the Separation of Church and State., "Breaking the Opus Dei Code," May 2006, https://www.au.org/church-state/may-2006-church-state/featured/breaking-the-opus-dei-code.

43   Robert Hutchinson, "The Vatican's Own Cult," *The Guardian*, September 10, 1997, https://culteducation.com/group/1086-opus-dei/15639-the-vaticans-own-cult.html.

44   Robert Hutchinson, *Their Kingdom Come,* St. Martin's Press, 1999, 2006. p. 108.

45   Ibid. p.109.

transmitted through two tentacles. The first is *Corporate Works* found in systems of education, banking, financing, foundations and non-profits.[46] Under the secretive hands of unidentified members, they gain access to monies in institutions, governments and corporations to shore up their social architecture as seen in various South and Central American countries, where their institutional influence is felt nationwide to such an extent they are named a Catholic country.[47] With the appointment by the Vatican of *Opus Dei* bishops, and archbishops, entire dioceses are delivered to Vatican control bypassing the local community. The people of a diocese have no say in appointments.

The second tentacle of *Common Works* promotes the use of members' money and money from institutions manipulated by *Opus Dei* members to promote their goals. The purpose is to initiate their broad influence through media, print, broadcasting, education, and halls of governance to create an outer image of how Catholics are to identify themselves in society according to their right-wing conservative norms. For members, this means becoming active in the daily prayer life of the church as well as supporting policies that promote gender discrimination under *Religious Liberty* laws. The formula itself, based on false notions of domination, keeps people poor and women subjugated, as the organization gains access to wealth and power in the name of God.[48]

Beginning in the mid 1970s, *Opus Dei* influenced the Vatican at a time of grave financial losses for the hierarchy, leading the organization to plant the seed that it could become the Pope's Prelature and a floating diocese from which the Vatican would benefit, as it continued to spread its message throughout Europe and the Americas.[49] By building a network of private schools and universities, *Opus Dei* was assured of future vocations as well as connections with the moneyed elite. With Vatican approbation, they could claim dioceses with the appointments of *Opus Dei* bishops and archbishops, which gave the Vatican access to a new source of wealth and control over orthodoxy. For instance, in Chile, the pope's strategy was to "purge its soft bishops and replace them with Opus Dei." In addition, Liberation Theology, a theology that promotes a more viable option for the poor of Latin America, was eliminated from Catholic university studies.[50] But real societal changes came with appointments of *Opus Dei* members to elected and appointed strategic positions in all

---

46   Opus Dei Awareness Network, "Opus Dei Affiliated Foundations," https://odan.org/
       foundations.

47   Hutchinson, *Their Kingdom Come*, p. 261.

48   Ibid. pp.164–167.

49   Ibid. pp. 220–223.

50   Ibid. p. 214.

branches of national as well as state and local governments. Their campaigns were financed by these unregulated multinational Catholic capitalists and as they won offices, *Opus Dei* right-wing conservative members sought to limit the rights of women and LGBTQ community members, while shifting funds from local and state budgets to their coffers. Their members were taught international business, banking and financing in their universities. They understand how to set up shell holding companies with no paper trails as well as how to avoid state and federal taxes by setting up their own systems of intercontinental banks.[51] They insist that piety "never interferes in politics—only daily life" while they are a global mega-church, using members deeply invested in the political lives of nation-states, and diminishing the distance that connects the church to the Vatican as a sovereign state.

In the absence of international finance laws, the Vatican turns a blind eye from limiting their immoral activities because their 'works' have taken the Vatican finances from the red to the black in less than half a century. The hierarchy is aware of their practice of using the finances of nefarious people and institutions to gain access to markets, only to discard them when they achieve their goal. For *Opus Dei*, the end always justifies the means. An example would be *Esfina*, a bank under the illegal control of *Opus Dei*, that was operated through offshore trusts. They justify their actions with assertions such as "We take money from unholy souls to finance holy works."[52]

In the United States, *Opus Dei* is known for spreading its wealth and influence strategically throughout Washington, D.C., and in places where patriarchal power can be supported at the highest levels of institutions and governments. Not unlike South and Central America, their network of schools has been unduly influenced by the appointments of bishops and archbishops nationwide, an action that immediately turns the offices of Religious Education toward ultra-conservative orthodoxy, complicating the lines of local clerical authority and obedience as well as diocesan finances, as funds now go to support the "floating diocese."[53] In the era of a movement to privatize public education in America, as well as a united effort to gain access to public funds for private schools, this is most concerning in that all Catholic schools under the influence of *Opus Dei* hierarchy could come under their tutelage. "It is part of Opus Dei's modus operandi never to spend—except as a last resort—its own money to finance 'good works', but always to dig into someone else's resources,

51   Ibid. p. 164.

52   Ibid. p.167.

53   Universities, Institutions and Centers, http://www.mgr.org/ODSomeInstitutions.html.

public or private."[54] Concerns about the flow of funding is one issue, but honest communication with fellow clergy is another. Reluctant clergy under *Opus Dei* bishops are forced into the silence of becoming obedient or simply "advisors" whose advice is discarded.[55]

These changes have had a devastating impact on the collaborative structures built during Vatican II where Catholic institutions of higher learning developed programs for lay men and women who would take their place in the shared mission of the church. At one time, women were earning Master of Divinity and Theology degrees in seminaries, highlighting the changes in the American church on notice at the Vatican. Concerned about the growth of laity in ministry and the overt movement to ordain women, Pope John Paul II issued, *The Application of Ex corde Ecclesiae for the United States*, in 1999 clarifying that all Catholic institutions were to follow magisterial teaching. This *mandatum* went directly to most Catholic educational institutions and trickled down to theologians in seminaries, universities, schools, parishes, hospitals and the printed word, impeding the growth of Vatican II theology as well as the number of men and women in ministry.[56] The pope's appointment of bishops was contingent on signing an agreement to "follow this *mandatum*" strengthening his authority in terms of "magisterial teaching" and gaining access to finances. By taking vows of obedience to the head, all ordained clerics were then obliged to adhere to both doctrine and dogma without question, to finance and build social structures to support the pope's social agenda; namely, no birth control, no abortion, no same-sex marriage, no women's ordination. They would hire only people who supported this agenda, namely *Opus Dei* members, those who agreed with the Pope, and those who graduated from universities who signed the *mandatum*. The resulting impact set up a conflict because individual Catholics would now have to oppose American laws that expanded the civil rights and equality for American citizens. Under this influence, all appointed to these positions have no voice or vote to speak in opposition. These patriarchal frameworks promote race and gender discrimination as the *Work of God*. Others view their work as patriarchy in Christianity. In essence, this platform

---

54   Robert Hutchinson, "The Vatican's Own Cult," The Guardian, September 10, 1997, https://culteducation.com/group/1086-opus-dei/15639-the-vaticans-own-cult.html.

55   Daniel Morris-Young, "San Francisco Priests Voice Frustrations with Cordileone at Convocation," *National Catholic Reporter,* October 19, 2019 https://www.ncronline.org/news/parish/san-francisco-priests-voice-frustrations-cordileone-convocation.

56   United States Catholic Conference of Bishops, "The Application of Ex corde Ecclesiae for the United States," June 15, 2001, https://www.usccb.org/committees/catholiceducation/guidelines-concerning-academic-mandatum.

stands in direct contrast to the work of democracy. With the death of Justice Ruth Bader Ginsburg, a wide variety of advances in American law that would never have come under fire, are now jeopardized.[57]

Known for their undue influence in judicial circles, many lay *Opus Dei* members and affiliates in judicial branches of government as well as our Supreme Court, and the Office of the Attorney General, stand ready to use their undue influence in our judicial system overturning U.S. laws on health care, same-sex marriage, abortion rights for women, and even *Brown vs Board of Education*. Moreover, they strive to gain access to tax monies to shore up Catholic schools through vouchers and tax credits which will directly impact their influence on generations of Catholics and U.S. citizens.[58]

Notably, the United States Conference of Catholic Bishops is now headed by an *Opus Dei* bishop. In reality, the hierarchical governance of U.S. Catholicism has become a visual representation of this agenda making people believe that Catholicism aligns itself with this brand of patriarchal architecture. For instance, some Catholics believed that if they voted for the Catholic Democratic candidate Joe Biden (a Roman Catholic) in the 2020 presidential election, then they were not really Catholic (due to the Democrats' support of *Roe vs Wade*).[59] Catholic Identity under the influence of the hierarchy promotes gender discrimination believing these divisions are a part of the natural order. In essence, the hierarchy's call is to maintain these divisions, puts it at odds with a democracy that promotes equality for all people under the law. Patriarchal leadership is strategically appointed within church structures to promote the overturning of laws that give reproductive choices to women, and marriage rights to the LGBTQ community, while securing funds for Catholic/private schools.

Lay advocates of the hierarchical agenda are now appointed to lifetime positions in courts, and as they use their power to reverse U.S. law, the oppressive divide between genders will increase. Federal funds flowing to religious institutions weaken the boundary between church and state leading to undue influence in democracy by religious institutions. Should this undue influence in policy become law, Catholics will deny gays' adoption rights because of new

---

57   Tom McCarthy, "What Does Ruth Bader Ginsburg death mean for the Supreme Court." *The Guardian,* September 18, 2020, https://www.theguardian.com/us-news/2020/sep/18/ruth-bader-ginsburg-supreme-court-faq-explainer.

58   Betty Clermont, "Opus Dei's Influence is Felt in All of Washington's Corridors of Power," *The Open Tabernacle,* January 22, 2019, https://opentabernacle.wordpress.com/2019/01/22/opus-deis-influence-is-felt-in-all-of-washingtons-corridors-of-power/.

59   John-Henry Westen, "No Catholic Can Vote for Joe Biden." https://www.youtube.com/watch?v=bccOn_i94qA.

loopholes permitting discrimination. If employees are gay and married, their employment in Catholic institutions will be discontinued. The same holds true if the gay and gender non-conforming community want to enroll their children in Christian schools. They will be turned away. There will be *de facto* segregation based on a gender binary and a racial framework. This is intensified by many Catholic schools being located in elite neighborhoods. A grand transfer of government subsidy from poorer schools to wealthy Catholic private schools will flow through vouchers, making public district schools even poorer. Women employed in any Catholic institution will be denied birth control as well as an abortion if one is needed. Patriarchal architecture will dominate the social networks of American society through this version of *Catholicism* under the influence of patriarchal rule, putting a knee on the neck of American Catholics and society itself, crushing democracy.

In post-modern Christianity, many are becoming cognizant that they have little voice in the operation much less ownership of our churches and governments under patriarchal rule. Understanding patriarchy means understanding how soft violence and oppression operate for the maintenance of its very structures. Think about the ease whereby women from first-century Christianity were erased from scriptures and history, as well as their contributions to the spiritual and moral climate forgotten. This has happened today as the invisible hands of male dominance is working stealthily to erase the monumental work of the multitudes of women religious who built and served in our parishes, schools and hospitals.

6   Erasing Women in Ministry

A real insight into this maneuvering is exposed by Kenneth Briggs in his book, *Double Crossed: Uncovering the Catholic Church's Betrayal of American Nuns*. His work is a guide through the vast networks of women religious and the trauma they experienced at the hands of the hierarchy as they stepped out in renewal. Just changing their 'habit' to wear the ordinary dress of the day brought out the hierarchy's unseen fists sending shock waves throughout the world. In 1970, Cardinal McIntyre of Los Angeles, demanded, under obedience, that a community return to their habit. When the women refused, their IHM community of 600 sisters disbanded leaving only a remnant in his Archdiocese.[60]

---

60   Kenneth Briggs. *Double Crossed: Uncovering the Catholic Church's Betrayal of American Nuns* (Doubleday Broadway Inc. New York, NY 2006), 112–115.

Never before had there been such an overt power play. Younger sisters began to leave communities, causing those who remained to re-structure in protection of their elderly and most vulnerable.[61] Awareness of their plight arose in the media and a retirement fund for the sisters was begun. Rita Hoffbauer, executive director of Support Our Aging Religious, SOAR, noted, "It was so hard for the church when women got more vocal!"[62]

While the hierarchy lived in mansions with great pensions, the sisters were facing abject poverty. In the end, religious women are who were given the power to build institutions had that power removed without thought. They were becoming a footnote in history, with their accomplishments, leadership and contributions to generations of Catholics demeaned and washed over. The hierarchy believed that there would be plenty of women left behind who would step up. That was, until the laws of a nation changed, furthering the cause of equality under the law. Women chose equality leaving a church that was still holding tenaciously to patriarchal rule.

Patriarchal rule is an unnatural form of governance within all Christian sects, governments, and institutions, most particularly because its operating principle is power and authority over people, and its primary purpose promotes using and/or abusing populations as property to build wealth for itself. Misogyny is endemic in its form and function constituting a sin against humanity. Because it separates us from each other and undermines the liberating message of Christ, those who follow Christ become cognizant of its invisible chains.

Masculinity under patriarchy deafens the ears so that men cannot hear much less understand what people, most particularly women, are saying.[63] Those obedient men who are appointed to positions on the hierarchal ladder, are poorly educated, making their need to support the hierarchy more likely. Not only is patriarchy's function in society an impediment to the practice of Christianity, but its maintenance also demands the use of all political tools necessary to diminish equality. An example of societal predators aligning themselves for the purpose of recapturing the courts, can be seen in the fight to add a sixth practicing Roman Catholic to the U.S. Supreme Court following the death of Justice Ruth Bader Ginsburg in 2020. Tom McCarthy of *The Guardian*

61   Ibid.172–203.

62   Ibid. 207.

63   Chris Crass, "Going Places that Scare Me: Personal Reflections on Challenging Male Supremacy," *Colours of Resistance Archive. Resisting Male Supremacy,* http://www.coloursofresistance.org/536/going-to-places-that-scare-me-personal-reflections-on-challenging-male-supremacy/.

captured succinctly what is at stake, "Reproductive rights, voting rights, protections from discrimination, the future of criminal justice, the power of the
presidency, the rights of immigrants, tax rules and laws, and healthcare for
millions of vulnerable Americans, to name a few issues."[64] All of these rights
gained through the law have dismantled patriarchal structures, expanding
the notion that *We the people* means the inclusion of all Americans under
U.S. law.

7   Dismantling Patriarchy

The realization that patriarchy is not the men of the Old Testament we honored as precursors of the Messiah, but an invasive form of all-male governance
seeking power, domination and wealth was the ah-ha moment that begs the
question, "Where are Christian leaders?" Christian denominational leadership
today is imploding, collapsing by the weight of hierarchical leaders disputably
saving the church by keeping 'Christ in chains.' In the latest Pew Research study,
Catholicism's decline in America was matched by the rise of the "NONES,"
those claiming no religion.[65]

Increasingly, moral leaders today are not church officials. They are mobile
and flexible. They are living in a conglomerate of societies with a diverse number of power bases that do not rise from the top, their eyes pointing the way
toward innovations in governance that comprise new diverse, fluid and inclusive social networks.[66] They are in the home, in the streets and in the states
fighting for equality in laws and codes that extend the boundaries of citizen-
ship to all in the nation. Their voices advocate for fair housing, and for funding
to support laws that will make society fairer and more just.

As a serious pathogen, patriarchy must be dismantled because of the harm
it does to humanity. Mary AcAleese asks, "How long can the hierarchy sustain
the credibility of a God who wants things this way, who wants a Church where
women are invisible and voiceless in Church leadership, legal and doctrinal

64   Tom McCarthy, "What Does Ruth Bader Ginsburg death mean for the Supreme Court."
        The Guardian, September 18, 2020, https://www.theguardian.com/us-news/2020/sep/18/
        ruth-bader-ginsburg-supreme-court-faq-explainer.
65   Pew Research Center, "In U.S., Decline of Christianity Continues at Rapid Pace" 10/17/2019
        https://www.pewforum.org/2019/10/17/in-u-s-decline-of-christianity-continues-at-rapid
        -pace/.
66   Stanley Grenz, *A Primer on Post Modernism.* (Grand Rapids, MI: William B. Eerdmans
        Publishing Company, 1996), 19–20.

discernment and decision-making?"[67] Many are working to minimize and shed the virus of misogyny in patriarchal rule, actively focusing to shift the culture toward a new paradigm that offers gender justice and equality under the law. Some are claiming that by adopting the principles of radical feminism, their lives can be transformed. Men say they must become First Responders in the attack against misogyny. Men like Chris Crass have taken up this call for more than thirty years, as an activist, community organizer and author.[68] He says, "my work is dedicated to building powerful working, class-based, feminist, multiracial movements for collective liberation." He believes the work feminists have done will lead to collective liberation for men. Among his many powerful essays is one published in *On the Road to Healing: An Anthology for Men Ending Sexism* in which he outlines fourteen steps for men as they become aware of the mental grip of sexism, offering practices to change it.[69] When Australian writer Tim Winton faced criticism about the undue male focus of his book, he says he was moved "to examine my own misogyny and the toxicity of patriarchy for men and boys."[70] Robert Jensen, a professor of journalism at the University of Texas wrote a *Radical Feminist Critique of Patriarchy* because his understanding has changed his life.[71] He consistently makes the connection between men's sexual exploitation of women and the buying and selling of their bodies. These systems within patriarchy are primary networks that give men an authority to exploit people based in laws and codes of their own making. The influence is deadly for all in the gender binary and non-conforming community. In the pathology of patriarchy, he says, "the feminism we fear, is in reality a gift to us all" because it begins the movement to reorder and reconnect with the social/emotional networks in our own lives until male supremacy is eliminated.[72]

The virus of patriarchy will never be removed as it is endemic in our global society, but like all viruses it can be minimized and contained as individuals

67   Mary McAllese, "The time is now for change in the Catholic Church," https://www .womensordination.org/wp-content/uploads/2018/03/McAleese-Voices-of-Faith-Text-1.pdf.
68   Chris Crass, *Towards the Other America*. (Chalice Press, St. Louis, MO, 2015).
69   Chris Crass, "Tools for White Guys Working for Social Change," in Basil Shadid, *On the Road to Healing: An Anthology for Men Ending Sexism*. (Dual Power Press, Seattle, WA, 2009), 119–121.
70   Tim Winton, "Being called a misogynist stings a bit." Interview by Gay Alcorn. *The Guardian*, June 25, 2018. https://www.theguardian.com/books/2018/jun/26/tim -winton-most-of-the-men-in-my-books-are-doing-badly.
71   Robert Jensen, "Radical feminism is a gift to men," https://www.youtube.com/ watch?v=Mi5TG3E4rnE.
72   Ibid.

and cultures demand change. Seen as a cultural infectious disease that emerges and re-emerges to harm people for the benefit of the wealthy, four major sources of patriarchy can be clearly identified: governments, religions, institutions and corporations, that are powered by three engines.

1.   An undue desire for power that exploits.
2.   Domination that maintains power over people, resources and property.
3.   Wealth building through the development of slavocracies (Profit from prisons, human trafficking, low wage work, privatization of schools, health care, military, etc.)

In terms of undue influence, domination is also secured by altering the laws, rules and codes of conduct for the nation, state, city and home through judicial practices that pass authority to the male by appointment, assignment or undue interference in elections.[73] This form of violence is endemic to patriarchal architecture. Gender-binary in hierarchy maintains this framework, making it easy to control the development of dualities, male domination-female submission, white supremacy over people of color, and cleric over laity. Dualities make domination by force and fear, oppression and violence legitimate as the un-wanteds are shed. Once identified, this group can become a low wage or free workforce from which profits can be made by those in power.

We do not have to accept this framework in our society. We can condemn it and can fight against it until it is dismantled. Radical feminists, like Justice Ruth Bader Ginsberg, have led the way through changing the legal structures of our institutions.[74] She and many others are intersectional pioneers that have pushed the boundaries of patriarchal social structures directing activism through full access to the vote, creating legislation, and demanding and protecting our rights and privileges. By using our collective consciousness to identify and map areas steeped in patriarchy, steps can be taken to mitigate the oppressions and violence of its impact, most importantly with the help of male radical feminists, reclaiming their place in this cultural liberation. All of these efforts are being done-slowly and with great initiative.

However, the initiatives above do not compare with the invasive well-financed worldwide impact of dual religious/political organizations like *Opus Dei*, the Legion of Christ and other Patriarchal Institutions that work to impede equality and justice within democracy. Now is the time to study

---

73   Jose Cabezas, "147 women sentenced to 40 years in prison after stillbirths," *NBC News*, (July 10, 2017), https://www.nbcnews.com/news/latino/anti-abortion-el-salvador-woman-faces-second-homicide-trial-after-n1038726.

74   Sandra Pullman, *ACLU*, "Tribute: The Legacy of Ruth Bader Ginsburg and WRP Staff." Undated, https//www.aclu.org/other/tribute-legacy-ruth-bader-ginsburg-and-wrp-staff.

their playbook and slowly, systematically enlist numbers of experts to turn it on themselves. This can only be done through worldwide collaboration in the disciplines of political science, religion and business. In concert with these efforts, women, the LGBTQ community, and all minorities must continue standing up and claiming equal rights demanding fairness through the laws of their country.

Universities teaching International Finance and Political Science should invest in collaborating with governments to identify loopholes in practices that allow for financial malfeasance that leads to human rights violations. They should urge the development of updated international criminal laws and courts that will prosecute perpetrators regardless of their country of origin. But the most urgent initiative would be to look at how a country's destabilization can be connected to sects or cults within a religion that infiltrate a nation's democratic processes at the top levels of governance. How, as a multicellular global community, do we join forces to support and help countries deal with that impact because in a global village, their problem becomes our problem.

If Christianity is to survive, it must make an enormous paradigm shift in terms of full examination of its use of power, dominance and wealth building. It must make a determined effort to dismantle patriarchal architecture by developing systems of checks and balances in which power is shared. Remember, Christianity is a religion of great importance. Patriarchy is a virus, acting as a parasite that attaches itself to all forms of governance. Such systems would automatically leave parasitical political groups like *Opus Dei* and the ultra-religious right, out of the reach of Vatican influence. Just as Catholicism has been a super spreader of patriarchal rule, it could become a central figure in bringing about the transformation of Christianity itself, as women and those supporting a renewed church, the 'street sweepers,' use their power to push away patriarchal thought and their imposed structures. Following the lead of the Jesuits, a call for repentance for these sins against humanity coupled with work to repair the harm it has done to the multitudes under its influence, would be a first step. Balancing power in governance from the top down to the bottom up would open up ministries to diverse groups of qualified men and women who understand how to structure legalized forms of gender justice and equality within the fabrics of institutions. These are essential elements in reclaiming a Christianity in which Christ's liberating and transformative message will offer hope as a healthy expression of a 21st century church, unravelling the centuries-long stranglehold that patriarchy has held on the neck of our Christian traditions.

Bibliography

Atkinson, Meera. *Traumata.* New York, NY: Bloomsbury Academic, 2017.

Atkinson, Meera. "Patriarchy Perpetuates Trauma. It's Time to Face the Fact." *The Guardian*, April 29, 2018. https://www.theguardian.com/commentisfree/2018/apr/30/patriarchy-perpetuates-trauma-its-time-to-face-the-fact.

Barnes, Shailly Gupta, "Explaining the 140 million: Breaking Down the Numbers behind the moral budget." *Kairos Center for Religions, Rights and Social Justice.* Undated. https://kairoscenter.org/explaining-the-140-million/.

Barrett, Michelle. "Ideology of and the Cultural Production of Gender," in *Feminist Criticism and Social Change.* Ed. Judith Newton and Deborah Rosenfelt. New York: Methuen, 1985.

Bass, Carrie L. "Gender Ontology and Women in Ministry in the Early Church." *Priscilla Papers*, Academic Journal, Spring, April 30, 2011.

Berry, Jason. *Render unto Rome: The Secret Life of Money in the Catholic Church.* New York, NY: Crown Publishing Group, 2011.

Berry, Jason. "Legion of Christ's deception, unearthed in new documents, indicates wider cover-up," *National Catholic Reporter,* February 18, 2013. https://www.ncronline.org/news/accountability/legion-christs-deception-unearthed-new-documents-indicates-wider-cover.

Briggs, Kenneth. *Double Crossed: Uncovering the Catholic Church's Betrayal of American Nuns.* New York, NY: Doubleday Broadway Inc, 2006.

Bruneau, Camille. "How do patriarchy and capitalism jointly reinforce the oppression of women?" *Committee for the Abolition of Illegitimate Debt,* September 13, 2018. https://www.cadtm.org/How-do-patriarchy-and-capitalism-jointly-reinforce-the-oppression-of-women.

Burke, Daniel. "In emotional service, Jesuits and Georgetown repent for slave trading" *CNN,* April 18, 2017. https://www..cnn.com/2017/04/18/living/georgetown-slavery-service/index.html.

Cabezas, Jose. "147 women sentenced to 40 years in prison after Stillbirths", *NBC,* July 10, 2017. https://www.nbcnews.com/news/latino/anti-abortion-el-salvador-woman-faces-second-homicide-trial-after-n1038726.

Carter, Jimmy. "Losing my Religion for Equality," *The Age,* July 15, 2009. https://www.theage.com.au/politics/federal/losing-my-religion-for-equality-20090714-dkov.html?page=-1.

Carter, Jimmy. *A Call to Action. Women, Religion, Violence, and Power.* New York, NY: Simon & Schuster, 2014.

Clermont, Betty. "Opus Dei's Influence is Felt in All of Washington's Corridors of Power" *The Open Tabernacle,* January 22, 2019. https://opentabernacle.wordpress.com/2019/01/22/opus-deis-influence-is-felt-in-all-of-washingtons-corridors-of-power/.

Cox, Ana Marie. "White Women: Foot Soldiers of the Patriarchy", *I Told You So,* February 11, 2019. http://www.anamariecox.com/with-friends-like-these/2019/2/11/white-women-foot-soldiers-of-the-patriarchy.

Crass, Chris. *Towards the Other America.* St. Louis, MO: Chalice Press, 2015.

Crass, Chris. "Tools for White Guys Working for Social Change," in Basil Shadid, *On the Road to Healing: An Anthology for Men Ending Sexism.* Seattle, WA: Dual Power Press, 2009.

Crass, Chris. "Going Places that Scare Me: Personal Reflections on Challenging Male Supremacy." *Colours of Resistance Archive. Resisting Patriarchy.* Undated http://www.coloursofresistance.org/536/going-to-places-that-scare-me-personal-reflections-on-challenging-male-supremacy/.

Curtice, Kaitlin. "Missions: Is it love or colonization?", *Religion News Service.* November 27, 2018. https://religionnews.com/2018/11/27/missions-is-it-love-or-colonization/.

DeConick, April D. *Holy Misogyny.* New York, NY: The Continuum International Publishing Group, 2011.

De La Torre, Miguel. "Quotations Track Church's Anti-Woman Legacy" *Good Faith Media,* March 25, 2005.

Ebojo, Edgar Battad. "Sex, scribes and scriptures: engendering the texts of the new testament" *The Phillippine Bible Society,* undated.

Eltahawy, Mona. *The Seven Necessary Sins for Women and Girls.* Boston, MA: Beacon Press, 2019.

Filteau, Jerry. "Legionaires of Christ Banned in 2nd Catholic Diocese." *Cult Education Institute,* January 2, 2005. https://forum.culteducation.com/read.php?12,8412.

Firestone, Rabbi Tirzah. "Beyond Patriarchy: What to do with the Legacy of Trauma and Fear." *Tikkun,* Winter, 2019. https://www.tikkun.org/what-to-do-with-the-legacy-of-trauma-and-fear.

Gilligan, Carol and Naomi Snider. *Why Does Patriarchy Persist?* Medford, MA: Polity Press, 2018.

Grenz, Stanley J. *A Primer on Post Modernism.* Grand Rapids, MI: William B. Eerdmans Publishing Company, 1996.

House, Lillian. "US Justice System Protects Rapists," *Breaking the Chains,* July 11, 2019. https://www.breakingthechainsmag.org/u-s-justice-system-protects-rapists/.

Hutchinson, Robert A. *Their Kingdom Come.* New York, NY; St. Martin's Press, 1999, 2006.

Jensen, Robert. *The End of Patriarchy: Radical Feminism for Men.* North Melbourne, Victoria, Australia: Spinifex Press Pty Ltd, 2017.

Jensen, Robert. "Radical feminism is a gift to men" https://www.youtube.com/watch?v=Mi5TG3E4rnE.

Lerner, Gerda, PhD. "The Creation of Patriarchy Summary." Salem State University, 1987. http://w3.salemstate.edu/~hbenne/pdfs/patriarchy_creation.pdf.

Manne, Kate. *Down Girl. The Logic of Misogyny*. New York, NY: Oxford University Press, 2018.

McAleese, Mary. "The time is not for change in the Catholic Church." *Voices of Faith*. March 8, 2018. https://www.youtube.com/watch?v=X9Q9VqkrfCw.

McCarthy, Tom. "What Does Ruth Bader Ginsburg death mean for the Supreme Court." *The Guardian*, September 18, 2020. https://www.theguardian.com/us-news/2020/sep/18/ruth-bader-ginsburg-supreme-court-faq-explainer.

Mowczko. Margaret. "Wealthy Women in the First Century World", *Priscilla Papers*, Academic Journal, Summer, 2018. https://www.cbeinternational.org/resource/article/priscillapapers-academic-journal/wealthy-women-first-century-roman-world.

National Catholic Reporter. Staff, January 8, 2013. https://www.ncronline.org/news/theology/early-women-leaders-heads-house-churches-presbyters.

National Coalition Against Domestic Violence. https://ncadv.org/.

Ocasio-Cortez, Alexandria. https://www.youtube.com/watch?v=LI4ueUtkRQo.

Peach, Lucinda Joy. *Women and World Religions*. Upper Saddle River, New Jersey: Prentice Hall, 2002.

Pew Research Center. "In U.S., Decline of Christianity Continues at Rapid Pace" October 17, 2019. https://www.pewforum.org/2019/10/17/in-u-s-decline-of-christianity-continues-at-rapid-pace/.

Portal to Jesuit Studies. Decree 14: "Jesuits and the Situation of Women in Church and Civil Society," General Congregation 34, 1995. https://jesuitportal.bc.edu/research/documents/1995_decree14gc34/.

Pullman, Sandra. *ACLU*, "Tribute: The Legacy of Ruth Bader Ginsburg and WRP Staff" Undated. https//www.aclu.org/other/tribute-legacy-ruth-bader-ginsburg-and-wrp-staff.

Regnum Christi. https://www.regnumchristi.org/en/mission-2/.

Ruether, Rosemary Radford. "Ecofeminism-The Challenge of Theology". *Deported, Exiles, Refugees*, n.20, 2012. https://www.unive.it/pag/fileadmin/user_upload/dipartimenti/DSLCC/documenti/DEP/nmeri/n20/06_20_-Ruether_Ecofeminism.pdf.

Southern Baptist Convention. "Resolution on Ordination and The Role Of Women In Ministry" June 1, 1984. https://www.sbc.net/resource-library/resolutions/resolution-on-ordination-and-the-role-of-women-in-ministry/.

Swarns, Rachel. "Georgetown University Plans Steps to Atone for Slave Past" *The New York Times*. September 1, 2016. https://www.nytimes.com/2016/09/02/us/slaves-georgetown-university.html.

Torjensen, Karen Jo. *When Women Were Priests*. San Francisco, CA: Harper, 1993.

United States Catholic Conference of Bishops. "The Application of Ex Corde Ecclesiae for the United States," June 15, 2001. https://www.usccb.org/committees/catholic-education/guidelines-concerning-academic-mandatum.

US Partnership on Mobility from Poverty. https://www.urban.org/sites/default/files/publication/90321/escaping-poverty.pdf.

Universal Declaration of Human Rights. https://www.humanrights.com/what-are-human-rights/universal-declaration-of-human-rights/preamble.html.

Westen, John-Henry. "No Catholic Can Vote for Joe Biden" https://www.youtube.com/watch?v=bccOn_i94qA.

Winton, Tim. "About the boys: Tim Winton on how toxic Masculinity is shackling men to misogyny." *The Guardian,* April 8, 2018. https://www.theguardian.com/books/2018/apr/09/about-the-boys-tim-winton-on-how-toxic-masculinity-is-shackling-men-to-misogyny.

Witt, Charlotte. "Feminist History of Philosophy". In: Alanen L., Witt C. (eds). *Feminist Reflections on the History of Philosophy. The New Synthese Historical Library* (Texts and Studies in the History of Philosophy), vol 55. Springer, Dordrecht, 2004. https://doi.org/10.1007/1-4020-2489-4_1.

CHAPTER 10

African-American Pan-Methodist, Baptist and Pentecostal Women Preachers

Angela Cowser

Patriarchy is a system in which males are privileged over females. Women are routinely and systematically subordinated and disadvantaged in contrast to their male peers. Patriarchal societies have strong male divinities. As such, masculinity is associated with divinity, strength, control, and divine right, whereas femininity is associated with humanity, weakness, fallibility, obedience, and the need to be controlled. The idea of female inferiority is thereby given divine sanction, making it much harder to combat in environments where patriarchal monotheism is a significant factor.[1]

This chapter traces the history of enslaved and free African-American women called by God to preach the gospel of Jesus Christ as they labor against patriarchal norms to achieve full recognition as powerful policy-makers and ministry leaders in historically African-American Protestant denominations, which include Black Methodist, Baptist, and Pentecostal churches. I have also included Spiritualist and Independent church movements in this designation because of the militant insistence, at their founding, of the full inclusion of female religiopolitical leaders in their communions. I begin by delineating the most common New Testament scriptures used to both support and deny Black women full power in the church. I then deliver a selective history of Black women's clerical achievements in the AME, AME Zion, CME, Baptist, and Pentecostal denominations. I argue that while there have been remarkable achievements of singular women who have realized clerical success in offices of ministerial and executive leadership, the larger field in which Black women labor, from 1750 to the present, is one that is thoroughly male-dominated, male-identified, and male-centered.

The presence of female leadership and representation in historically Black Protestant clerical ranks is important because Black women tend to be more

---

1 Deborah W. Rooke. "Patriarchy/Kyriarchy." In *Oxford Encyclopedia of the Bible and Gender Studies*. Article published 2014. https://www.oxfordreference.com/view/10.1093/acref:obso/9780199836994.001.0001/acref-9780199836994.

collaborative, more results-oriented, and more likely to emphasize achievement over ego than their male counterparts. Moreover, Black women tend to be more concerned with influencing policy outcomes rather than receiving publicity or credit. Symbolically and substantively, seeing women in positions of executive leadership is important because women (may) bring distinctive perspectives to the work by placing issues related to women's lives to the fore. Women also tend to employ a gender lens and to bring their life experiences to bear on a wide variety of policy issues. Women provide perspectives, priorities, and agendas that are missing if women are not there to represent women and bring voice to members left out of policymaking spaces. These are reasons why the presence of female leaders and representation are critical in African-American religiopolitical leadership.[2]

The absence of female leadership and representation in Black Protestant clerical ranks negatively impacts girls and women and perpetuates the gender bias that persists in organizations and in society, disrupting the learning cycle at the heart of becoming a female leader. Girls and women become leaders by internalizing a leadership identity and developing a sense of purpose. An absence of affirmation diminishes self-confidence and discourages girls and women from seeking developmental opportunities or experimenting. Leadership identity eventually withers away, along with opportunities to grow through new assignments and real achievements.[3]

While there are notable exceptions, the African-American Protestant church is an arena in which most women consent, through their presence, money, and labor, to a male monopoly of the ministry as a profession. When majorities of Black women change their minds and withdraw support of the patriarchy, the situation for Black clergywomen will change. Until then, women labor, not in vain, but labor they do.

1   Preaching Women

Christians who support a moratorium on preaching women cite Pauline scripture, all written between 50–70 AD, to justify barring women from the upper

---

2   Kelly Dittmar, Kira Sanbonmatsu, Susan J. Carroll, Debbie Walsh, and Catherine Wineinger. "Representation Matters: Women in the U.S. Congress." Preprint, November 16, 2020. https://cawp.rutgers.edu/sites/default/files/resources/representationmatters.pdf.   Religiopolitical pertains to both religion and politics.

3   Herminia Ibarra, Robin J. Ely, and Deborah M. Kolb, "Women Rising: The Unseen Barriers." *Harvard Business Review,* September 2013, 1–7.

echelons of the religiopolitical hierarchy. These misogynists cite two sections from Paul's letter to the Corinthians: "Now I want you to realize that the head of every man is Christ, and the head of the woman is man, and the head of Christ is God" (*1 Corinthians 11:3*), "As in all the congregations of the saints, women should remain silent in the churches. They are not allowed to speak, but must be in submission, as the Law says. If they want to inquire about something, they should ask their own husbands at home; for it is disgraceful for a woman to speak in the church" (*1 Corinthians 14:33b-35*). From Ephesians they cite "Wives, submit to your husbands as to the Lord. For the husband is the head of the wife as Christ is the head of the church, his body, of which he is the Savior. Now as the church submits to Christ, so also wives should submit to their husbands in everything" (*Eph 5: 22–24*). And finally from Timothy, "A woman should learn in quietness and full submission. I do not permit a woman to teach or to have authority over a man; she must be silent. For Adam was formed first, then Eve. And Adam was not the one deceived; it was the woman who was deceived and became a sinner. But women will be saved through childbearing if they continue in faith, love and holiness with propriety" (*1 Tim. 2:11–15*).[4]

Christians who disavow the prohibition on preaching women cite from Paul's letter to the Galatians: "You are all sons (and daughters) of God through faith in Christ Jesus, for all of you who were baptized into Christ have clothed yourselves with Christ. There is neither Jew nor Greek, slave nor free, male nor female, for you are all one in Christ Jesus. If you belong to Christ, then you are Abraham's seed, and heirs according to the promise" (*Gal 3:26–29*). Supporters of women preachers also point to the first preacher Jesus sent to spread the good news, the Samaritan woman in *John 4: 39*.[5]

In addition to scriptural justification for misogynistic patriarchy, male-focused monotheism reinforces the social hierarchy of patriarchal rule through religious symbols and systems. The deepest roots of patriarchal domination, misogynistic violence, and androcentric selfishness are found in whom we believe and proclaim God to be, such as using the terms God the Father, Lord, King, and He. Finally, African philosopher and theologian St. Augustine (354–430 AD) helped instantiate male monotheism[6] and a male monopoly on

---

4   1 Corinthians 11:3, 14:33b-35, Ephesians 5:22–24, 1 Timothy 2:11–15 (New International Version).

5   Galatians 3:26–29, John 4:39 (Life Application Study Bible New International Version).

6   Christianity features a single, powerful, patriarchal male god with primarily masculine symbolism and imagery. Males are prophets, disciples, and leaders (with some notable exceptions). Realistic female roles models are difficult to find (with some notable exceptions), with female passivity, for the most part, the road to salvation. In some of the communions studied here, notably some Pentecostal and Methodist denominations, women have achieved the highest ranks of clerical leadership. Conversely, in most Pentecostal

the ministry by writing that "the subordination of women is intrinsic to original creation. Men possess the capacity for dominion, but women, representing nature or the body, are to be under dominion. Women, therefore, lack the image of God and are related to God's image only by their inclusion under male headship."[7] The working presumption of male domination of clerical leadership is that the 1st-century male social structure remain the will of God for all people, for all time. We turn now to the first stirrings and callings of enslaved and free Black Protestant women who challenged religious patriarchy by evangelizing and leading congregations.

2   Women in the African Methodist Episcopal Church

Conversions are defined as recognizable changes of heart which make possible a person's ultimate salvation by the grace of God. Implicit in this definition is that conversions also result in a change of life. Enslaved Black women Mother Suma and Aunt Hester in the eighteenth century preached, prayed, and converted other enslaved persons, as well as slave holding white women in their respective communities. A substantial number of enslaved African women in America converted and became Christian through revivals and camp meetings. Drawing images of freedom on earth and in heaven, they enjoined dramatic deliveries in call and response patterns, and created spirituals[8] to reshape ideas about identity, community, and freedom. For many Black women, conversions meant forgiveness by God, the hope of salvation, increased self-esteem, and a personal worth and dignity rooted in God's validation of their humanity.[9] It was also a way for untold numbers of Black women "to face and control the debilitating repressed anger and fear provoked by living with white racism."[10]

---

and Baptist denominations women are generally prevented from assuming leadership positions and are segregated into women's associations.

7   Simon Blackburn, "Augustine of Hippo" in *Oxford Dictionary of Philosophy*. Article published 2016. Current online version 2016. https://www-oxfordreference-com.turing.library .northwestern.edu/view/10.1093/acref/9780198735304.001.0001/acref-9780198735304-e -290?rskey=FDVPfr&result=6. Augustine was a North African theologian and philosopher who led the Christian faith in the transition from paganism to Christian philosophy. Augustine affirmed the reality of the Fall, and of original sin as the hereditary moral disease that we all bear, only curable by God's grace.

8   The spiritual *Go Down Moses* was created @ 1800 CE.

9   Susan Hill Lindley, *"You Have Stept Out of Your Place": A History of Women and Religion in America* (Louisville: Westminster John Knox Press, 1996), 179–196.

10   Ibid, 180.

In response to the racism experienced at the white St. George's Methodist Episcopal Church of Philadelphia in 1816, the African Methodist Episcopal (AME) Church was founded by Rev. Richard Allen. Methodists generally placed primary emphasis on Christian living; namely, putting faith and love into action. This is what Methodism's founder Rev. John Wesley referred to as practical divinity. From the outset, the AME Church aimed to free members from racial discrimination, and yet, AME Church leaders applied the hegemonic patterns of the patriarchal power and exclusive male leadership found in white churches to the AME Church. Women were denied entry into the upper echelons of the religiopolitical hierarchy in Black Methodism; namely positions as Elder, Presiding Elder, and Bishop. Given the reality of limited financial and political power for Black males in slavery and the threat to Black male identity, Black women may have been supportive of placing (and keeping) formal church leadership in male hands. Nevertheless, Jarena Lee (1784–1864) became the first woman authorized to preach in the AME Church. Despite being called by God, men denied her an appointment to pastor Mother Bethel AME Church in Philadelphia because of her gender. Lee became an itinerant (traveling) preacher, travelling over 1,600 miles to preach in schoolhouses, homes, churches, and camp meetings in Pennsylvania, New York, New Jersey, Virginia, and Maryland. By 1836, Lee had published her autobiography, arguing that "for as unseemly as it may appear now-a-days for a woman to preach, it should be remembered that nothing is impossible with God. And why should it be thought impossible, heterodox, or improper for a woman to preach seeing the Savior died for the woman as well as for the man?"[11]

Similar problems occurred in New York. In 1821 the African Methodist Episcopal Zion Church[12] (AME Zion) was organized in New York City. The impetus for the formation of a second Black Methodist denomination was racial discrimination suffered by Blacks at the John Street Methodist Church (1796) in New York City. And again, a moratorium on ordaining females called to ordained ministry was established. The unresolvable contradiction of prioritizing racial discrimination over gender subordination was set from the beginning. The cultural justification for a male monopoly on ministry was in part a response to the destructive cultural messages that portrayed Black women as Jezebels—intent on seducing white males—and Black men as hypersexual, fixated on raping white women. Black women were supportive of formal

11   "Jarena Lee, The First Woman African American Autobiographer," JStor Daily, December 15, 2018, https://daily.jstor.org/jarena-lee-the-first-woman-african-american-autobiographer/.
12   The AME Zion name was adopted in 1848.

church leadership in male hands because, at that time, the ministry was a limited path to financial and political power for Black males. Many Black women did not want to jeopardize this positive expression of Black male identity.

Regardless of the obstacles they faced, many women carved out leadership spaces for themselves. Laywomen organized most church activities and took on the financial responsibility for the maintenance of these programs. For example, in 1824 AME laywomen formed the Dorcas Missionary Society (named for a notable disciple of Jesus) to benefit AME ministers. Missionary work also provided Black women with leadership opportunities. Women missionaries served the church abroad and in the United States in designated projects. For Black AME women, missions were an alternative sphere of religious work in which to exert female control and power. Women raised money, developed their own programs, and provided oversight for their own initiatives.

Free Black Methodist laywomen were also deeply involved in the antislavery and abolitionist movements. For example, from 1849 to 1853, members of Bethel AME Church in Springtown, New Jersey provided food, clothing, and shelter to Underground Railroad passengers. By the time AME Zion laywoman Harriet Ross Tubman became Chief Conductor of the Underground Railroad (1861–1865), the Railroad was fully operational in the Midwest, Upper South, Texas, and Mexico due in large part to the hard work of free Black churchwomen. Tubman's courage was based in part on her conviction that she was an instrument of divine Providence, literally, the embodiment of God's hand in the escape from white violence, and that a guardian angel accompanied her on her trips.[13] Tubman created and presided over her own congregations of enslaved people, embodying in her work the gospel of freedom and liberation from oppression and tyranny. Unencumbered by patriarchal church authorities, she took up the call given by God to free enslaved people.

Within the AME church, the female struggle for full inclusion and ordination continued while female missionaries and philanthropists led in church and community. As a means of placation in 1868, the AME church created the non-ordainable office of stewardess for women.[14] Nominated by the pastor

---

13   Lindley, 180.

14   "The Stewardess and Deaconess Boards," First Community A.M.E. Church (website), accessed November 11, 2020, https://www.fcame.org/stewardess-and-deaconess.html. Members of the Stewardess Board prepare the Communion elements for the service of Holy Communion and Holy Baptism; assist with special services (weddings, funerals, candlelight services as requested), to care for the altar and the space in the sanctuary which is enclosed within the chancel area, and to care for and change the paraments to the proper seasonal color, linens, and all items associated with worship and special services as needed.

and then approved by the Board of Stewards, stewardesses prepared the elements for Holy Communion and Holy Baptism. And in 1870, a second Black Methodist denomination, the Christian Methodist Episcopal Church (CME) was founded in Jackson, Tennessee. Like the AME and AME Zion churches before them, the CME church adopted the patriarchal polities, ideologies, hierarchies, and customs of white Methodist churches, especially regarding the Black male monopoly of the pastorate. By 1872, midwife, nurse, philanthropist, real estate investor, and formerly enslaved woman, Biddy Mason (1818–1891),[15] helped found First AME Church in Los Angeles (with a twenty-first century roster of 19,000+ members). Mason also used her wealth, estimated in 1872 at $3 million, to feed and shelter the poor, visit prisoners, and educate children and travelers.

Meanwhile on the missionary front, the AME Home and Foreign Society continued to cultivate and promote female leadership. In 1879, AME Amanda Berry Smith sailed for Calcutta, India to labor as a missionary preacher. Although not officially ordained, Bishop James Thoburn wrote, "I have never known anyone who could draw and hold so large an audience as Mrs. Smith. Her faith was of a standard and purity rarely witnessed in our world."[16] By 1882, Smith relocated to Liberia and Sierra Leone where she evangelized, established Sunday Schools, and promoted holiness and temperance. Eventually Smith returned to the United States where she founded a Chicago-based school and orphanage.

Because women were excluded by custom and practice from pulpit leadership, the missionary profession was appealing as women could pursue leadership and preaching roles overseas denied to them in the United States. For example, in 1900 Sarah Hatcher Duncan was elected President of the AME Women's Home and Foreign Missionary Society which at that time was the pinnacle of women's power in the church. In addition to serving as teachers, evangelists and missionaries, the AME General Conference sanctioned another official but subordinate role for women as deaconess in 1900.[17] And yet since the founding of the AME church in 1816, Black women have striven for ordained

---

15   "Bridget Biddy Mason," United States National Park Service (website), accessed November 20, 2020, https://www.nps.gov/people/biddymason.htm.

16   Lindley, 180–187.

17   "The Stewardess and Deaconess Boards," First Community A.M.E. Church (website), accessed November 11, 2020, https://www.fcame.org/stewardess-and-deaconess.html. Deaconesses are set apart and consecrated by the bishop of the district after selection by the pastor and the Official Board. Deaconesses encourage, foster and improve the general interests of the church; promote the comfort and solicit the friendship and sympathy of the general public; cheer the fallen; feed the hungry; clothe the naked; seek out the homeless; encourage thrift; visit mental health institutions and prisons, and save the lost.

orders in the church. Ordination is the process by which persons are invested with the function and office of minister, pastor, priest, or rabbi. Finally, the first Black female ordained Elder was in 1948 when Rebecca Glover (1913–2012) was ordained in the AME church. For most of her years in full-time ministry, Rev. Glover served as Assistant Pastor of Metropolitan AME Church in Washington, DC. Women would have to wait until 2000 to see a woman ordained as bishop in the AME church.[18] The first female bishop, the Rev. Dr. Vashti McKenzie, was elected President of the Council of Bishops in 2004.[19] Since then, two additional American AME clergywomen were consecrated as bishops in 2004; namely, Carolyn Tyler Guidry in Los Angeles and Sarah Francis Davis in San Antonio. While it took nearly 200 years for a Black clergywoman to be ordained bishop, the AME church has evolved in its position on ordaining women.

3   The African Methodist Episcopal Zion Church

The AME Zion and CME churches would follow with a similarly slow pattern of ordaining women and appointing them to the highest levels of religiopolitical leadership in their respective denominations.[20] In 1894, AME Zion laywoman Julia A.J. Foote (1823–1901) was ordained deacon in Poughkeepsie, New York, and three years later Mary Small became the first woman ordained elder in the AME Zion church. Small won the battle to preach and ushered in new opportunities for women to advance in AME Zion church polity. Deacon Foote in 1900 became the second woman ordained elder in the church. Elders Foote and Small became the first women of any race in the Methodist denominations to achieve full rights as ordained elders. For over 50 years, Rev. Foote continued

---

18   Methodist bishops provide spiritual leadership in a broad range of settings in the United States and globally. Clergy are elected and consecrated to the office of bishops (also called the bishopric), who are charged with ordering the life of the church and helping set the direction to fulfill its mission in the world. All bishops share in teaching, equipping, and encouraging mission and service. They serve as shepherds of the entire church but are assigned to preside over the work of a regional area.

19   "Bishops of the Church," African Methodist Episcopal Church (website), accessed November 20, 2020, https://www.ame-church.com/leadership/bishops-of-the-church/.

20   Elders are clergy (called Reverend) who are ordained to a ministry of Word, Sacrament, Order, and Service. Elders preach and teach the Word of God, provide pastoral care and counsel, administer the sacraments of Baptism and Holy Communion, and order the life of the church for service in mission and ministry. Traveling elders itinerate serve in multiple ministry settings (appointments) where the bishop assigns them. "Elders," General Board of Higher Education and Ministry of the United Methodist Church (website), accessed November 11, 2020, https://www.gbhem.org/clergy/elders/.

to evangelize as a pioneering Black Methodist holiness preacher, and in 1879 Foote published an autobiographical sketch entitled *A Brand Plucked from the Fire.*

And in 1897, AME Zion evangelist Florence Spearing Randolph was licensed to preach and ordained a deacon in 1900. A year later, she served as a delegate to the Third Methodist Ecumenical Conference in London. She finally achieved her ultimate goal as elder in 1903. As an elder, Rev. Randolph pastored five small, poor churches in New Jersey, working without a salary from 1897 to 1909.[21] Once her congregations reached solvency with the promise of compensation for her efforts, Randolph was replaced by a "nice young man" and reassigned to another problem church. The bishop assigned the miracle worker, Rev. Randolph, to Wallace Chapel AME Zion church in Summit, New Jersey (1925 to 1946). She grew the 35-member mission church and built a red brick chapel that is still used today. Upon her retirement in 1946, she left the church debt-free.[22] Rev. Randolph also organized the New Jersey State Federation of Colored Women's Clubs and served as their president for twelve years. She also sat on the Executive Committee of New Jersey's Suffrage Association whose work culminated in the ratification of the 19th Amendment in 1920. Eighty-three years after Rev. Randolph was licensed to preach, in 2008, the Rev. Mildred Hines was consecrated as the first female bishop of the AME Zion church.[23]

4   The Christian Methodist Episcopal Church

The CME church was founded in 1870 in Jackson, Tennessee. By 1902, CME women had organized the Women's Home Missionary Society, but it would take sixteen years for the General Conference to approve the Missionary Society as an official organization. Commenting on the delay in approving the Society, church historians opined that "the bishops and the General Conference would allow the women of the church to have their own connectional organization to run as long as they did not conflict or interfere with the church itself."[24] In

---

21   "NJ Suffragists—Reverend Florence Spearing Randolph (1866–1951)," Online Biographical Dictionary of the Woman Suffrage Movement in the United States, accessed November 11, 2020, https://discovernjhistory.org/njsuffragists-reverend-florence-spearing-randolph/.
22   Ibid.
23   "Board of Bishops," African Methodist Episcopal Church (website), accessed November 20, 2020, https://amez.org/board-of-bishops/.
24   Larry G. Murphy, ed. *Down by the Riverside: Readings in African American Religion* (New York: New York University Press, 2000) 368.

1987, the Rev. Verse P. Easter became the first woman in the CME church to be elected Presiding Elder[25] and in 2010, the Rev. Teresa Snorton[26] became the first woman consecrated as a bishop in the church.

All three Pan-Methodist denominations (AME, AME Zion, and CME) now ordain women as deacons, elders, and presiding elders, and consecrate women as bishops. As of 2020, the AME church had three female bishops, while the AME Zion and CME churches, respectively, had one female bishop each. Between the three denominations, the full inclusion of women to elder orders and the bishopric office has taken 170 years to accomplish. This slow progression for Black women in the Pan-Methodist churches has not been replicated in the Baptist church.

5   Black Baptist Women

In 1880, Black Baptists organized the National Baptist Convention USA in Nashville, Tennessee.[27] At its founding, white, male-biased traditions and rules of decorum sought to mute Black women's voices and accentuate their subordinate status vis-à-vis Black men. Thus, tainted by the values of the larger American society, the Black Baptist church sought to provide men with full manhood rights, while offering women a separate and unequal status.[28] The distinction between speaking and teaching as female roles, and preaching as a male role was and is still the established norm.

Black Baptist women have faced a near total prohibition of female preachers along with the conspicuous absence of female leaders at the executive level of denominational leadership. In a remarkable story of extraordinary achievement under Jim Crow, racial terrorism, lynching, and widespread poverty, Baptist women created their own institutions inside a larger institutional

---

25   "Presiding Elders," McClintock and Strong Biblical Cyclopedia (website), accessed November 20, 2020. A presiding elder is an officer whose functions are those of a superintendent within a limited jurisdiction. Presiding elders serve under bishops and together with them constitute a cabinet, in which resides the appointing power over itinerant preachers. https://www.biblicalcyclopedia.com/P/presiding-elder.html.

26   "The College of Bishops," The Christian Methodist Episcopal Church (website), accessed November 20, 2020, https://www.thecmechurch.org/bishops/.

27   For Baptists, the sermon is the central element of the worship service, the minister's task is to preach the gospel, and the hearer is to respond by making an inward, then outward, commitment to faith in Jesus Christ. Baptism is a second, outward marker of inward faith.

28   Evelyn Brooks Higginbotham. *Righteous Discontent: The Women's Movement in the Black Baptist Church, 1880–1920* (Cambridge: Harvard University Press, 1993), 3.

construction. However, Baptist women's innovative institutional creations ultimately crippled their ability to fully express their female leadership and power. The following is a brief history of how this unusual development unfolded.

Early on, Women's Convention leader Mary Cook (1862–1945) and American National Baptist Convention historian and professor Lucy Wilmot Smith (1861–1889) both challenged gender orthodoxy theologically, but not congregationally. They used Scripture to argue for their full rights and in so doing, they challenged essentialist and popular conceptions regarding *a woman's place* in church and society. They challenged the silent helpmate image of women's church work and set out to convince the men that women were equally obliged to advance not only their race and denomination but themselves. They valued women's roles in the family but also insisted on the importance of public activity for women, defining themselves as both homemakers and militant soldiers. Simultaneously traditional and radical, Smith and Cook challenged gendered stereotypes and developed their own female spheres for significant action without repudiating traditional female roles.[29] Thus, Black Baptist women developed a theology inclusive of equal gender participation. What the women did not do, however, was question a male's sole right to the clergy.[30]

In 1892, Mary Church Terrell and others helped found the Black Women's Club movement in the Baptist church. The purpose of the Club was to shape broader American culture in the areas of racial progress, leadership development, benevolence, and respectability with an emphasis on instilling manners and morals. The *politics of respectability* they adopted meant embracing white cultural values including the male clerical monopoly; adhering to the ideology of female subordination to men; accepting women's primary role as educators of children; and espousing conservative sexual mores. It also meant protesting structural racism, encouraging self-esteem and achievement for Black people, cooperating with white women reformers where possible, and countering the false image of Black women as morally loose and carnal.[31] Club women organized to address both internal church and external societal issues. Black women used the Club movement to create Black settlement houses, Black branches of the Young Women's Christian Association (YWCA), the National Association for the Advancement of Colored People (NAACP), and the National Urban League (NUL), which the women saw as extensions of the church.

---

29   Lindley, 194.
30   "Servant Leadership Team & Structure," The National Baptist Convention, USA, Inc (website), accessed November 20, 2020, https://www.nationalbaptist.com/departments/auxiliaries/moderators/leadership.
31   Ibid, 194.

By 1900 the Baptist Women's Convention, with one million members, mediated between church and society using newspapers, schools, social welfare agencies, jobs and recreational facilities while mitigating white society's denial of these resources to Black communities.[32] The Convention movement enabled women to share and distribute information through periodic statewide and national meetings where thousands gathered and discussed issues of civic concern. Historian Evelyn Brooks Higginbotham acknowledges the important role these Black women assumed. She wrote: "in the closed society of Jim Crow, the church afforded African American women an interstitial space in which to critique and contest white America's racial domination. In addition, the church offered Black women a forum through which to articulate a public discourse critical of women's subordination. The Black church was a deliberative, social space for discussion of public concerns."[33]

Nannie Helen Burroughs (1897–1961) continues to be recognized as the most significant Black laywomen in National Baptist Church history. Burroughs founded the first Girls' Literary Society in public high schools as well as the National Training School for Women and Girls (Washington, DC). She was a campaigner for Black voting rights, a 50-year corresponding secretary of the NBC's Women's Convention, and the creator of Women's Day observances, which are significant because female preachers in the NBC would preach on Women's Day. Burroughs designed the day to expand the ranks of Black church women thereby "raising women by raising money."[34] During the 1960s, 70s, and 80s, it became more common to invite any ordained or licensed woman minister, who was frequently referred to as "a lady preacher," to Women's Day celebrations.[35] For Burroughs and many other Black women educators including Mary McLeod Bethune, Mary Craft Laney, Fanny Jackson Coppin, and Anna Julia Cooper, their work was rooted in a greater hope that if Black people adopted middle-class white norms and proved themselves respectable, then Blacks would be accepted by white society as equals.

---

32   Higginbotham, 8–10.

33   Ibid, 8–10.

34   Delores C. Carpenter, "Black Women in Religious Institutions: A Historical Summary from Slavery to the 1960s," in *Down by the Riverside: Readings in African American Religion,* ed. Larry G. Murphy, (New York: New York University Press, 2000), 97–108.

35   Ibid, 103.

6   The Progressive National Baptist Convention

In 1919, the National Baptist Convention USA (NBCUSA) split over charter issues and the ownership of the National Baptist Publishing Board. The new denomination was titled the National Baptist Convention in America.[36] In 1961, the NBCUSA suffered a second schism, this time over the issue of civil rights, and a third denomination, the Progressive National Baptist Convention (PNBC), was born. PNBC's founding platform included calls for full voter registration, education and participation, affirmative action against all forms of racism and bigotry, Black economic power and development, and equal educational opportunities. Despite their progressive agenda, women experienced the same subordinations and limitations in the PNBC as in the NBCUSA. For example, of thirty-three PNBC committees formed in 1963, only one of thirty-three was led by a woman. As of 2011, fifty years after the denomination's founding, there are only three women in the online historical record who had been ordained pastor in the PNBC: Rev. Uvee Arbouin ordained (1969) to co-pastor Zion Temple Baptist Church; the late Rev. Janet Tate ordained in 1991; and the Rev. Rosemarie Green ordained in 1997.[37] In recent years, a small minority of Black clergymen have sponsored women candidates for ordination in their associations; notably, Revs. Tate and Green were sponsored by the male clergy of Second Baptist Church, Evanston, Illinois.[38]

In February 2015, PNBC leaders implemented the Women in Ministry (WIM) initiative to mentor and support female preachers, pastors, and ministers in leadership. The WIM program was created as a mechanism "to biblically affirm women who are in governance roles, while offering a support system to enhance and nurture their skills, in church planting, training, and perfecting the gift of preaching."[39] As of April 16, 2019, the written policy regarding female ministers was that "the Convention does not make official positions on its member congregations, state conventions and institutions." There are many

36   "Executive Cabinet," The National Baptist Convention of America International, Inc (website), accessed November 20, 2020, https://nbcainc.com/executive-cabinet/.

37   Pamela A. Smoot. "Hear the Call: The Women's Auxiliary of the Progressive National Baptist Convention, Inc." *Baptist History and Heritage* 46, issue 1 (Spring 2011): 1–7. https://go-gale-com.turing.library.northwestern.edu/ps/i.do?p=AONE&u=northwestern&id=-GALE%7CA267973779&v=2.1&it=r (accessed November 20, 2020).

38   Jacquelyn Grant. *Black Theology and the Black Woman.* (New York: Orbis Books, 1993) 148.

39   "Women in Ministry Get Key Support from Progressive National Baptist Convention, Inc.," Black Christian News (website), accessed November 21, 2020, https://blackchristiannews.com/2015/02/women-in-ministry-get-key-support-from-progressive-national-baptist-convention-inc/.

women ordained and/or licensed to serve in the convention's affiliated congregations. A number of women serve as pastors of congregations and as trustees to the boards of American Baptist colleges. Some congregations do not ordain or license women as ministers at all, while some congregations have women deacons. The climate in the PNBC has not been supportive of women preaching and pastoring churches and according to their website there has been little progress on the WIM initiative since its inception.[40]

As of 2017, in Black Baptist churches, women accounted for between 50–75% of church members, but less than 10% of church leadership and only 1% of ordained pastors.[41] The ban on women pastors in Baptist churches increased the popularity of the Pentecostal, Holiness, and Spiritualist churches where motivated women could rise to the top. Many of the female converts from the COGIC (Church of God in Christ) to the Spiritualist church would eventually leave because they were "stifled in COGIC churches and were seeking greater avenues of expression and authority."[42] It is to Pentecostal-Sanctified churches that we now turn.

7   Pentecostal-Sanctified Church

In 1897, the largest Black Pentecostal[43] denomination in the United States, the Church of God in Christ (COGIC), was founded in Memphis, Tennessee. From the beginning, COGIC polity (governance) both embraced and excluded women. Women could establish congregations, but did not then, and generally still do not receive ordination in order to pastor those congregations. Men permit women to be evangelists, missionaries, and Mothers of the church (an honored position of authority, respect, and influence). Women could not *and still cannot* serve as superintendents of church districts. Women cannot receive ordination as bishops. They are also not permitted to chair the General Assembly or serve as Chief Apostle of the denomination.[44] And, unless they

---

40   "Official Roster of the PNBC Officers," Progressive National Baptist Convention (website), accessed November 20, 2020, https://www.pnbc.org/about/officers.

41   Eileen Campbell-Reed. State of Clergywomen: Women in the U.S.: A Statistical Update, https://eileencampbellreed.org/state-of-clergy/ (accessed November 20, 2020).

42   Hans A. Baer, "The Limited Empowerment of Women in Black Spiritual Churches: An Alternative Vehicle to Religious Leadership," *Sociology of Religion* 54, no. 1 (Spring 1993) (accessed November 20, 2020).

43   Pentecostalism is a branch of Protestant Christianity which emphasizes the activity of the Holy Spirit, stresses a strict morality and seeks emotional spiritual experiences in worship rituals.

44   Felton O. Best, ed. *Black Religious Leadership from the Slave Community to the Million Man March.* (Lewiston: The Edwin Mellen Press, 1998), 154.

are spouses of deceased male COGIC ministers, women hold no pastoral-policymaking leadership positions in the COGIC.

While the COGIC acknowledges that devout women are "talented, spirit-filled, and dedicated and well informed" and that they are capable of "conducting the affairs of the church both administratively and spiritually," the New Testament and the writings of the Apostolic Fathers prevent them from ordaining women. The COGIC recognizes that women in the early Christian church were "assigned official duties in the conduct and ministration of the early church." And "The Church of God in Christ recognizes the scriptural importance of women in the Christian ministry." However, there is no scriptural "mandate to ordain women to be an Elder, Bishop, or Pastor. Women may teach the gospel to others, have charge of a church in the absence of its pastor, if the pastor so wishes, without adopting the title of Elder, Reverend, Bishop, or Pastors. Therefore, the COGIC cannot accept the following scriptures as a mandate to ordain women preachers: Joel 2.28; Gal. 3.28–29; Matt. 28:9–11."[45] The presumption here is that the first-century male dominated social structure remains the will of God for all people, for all time.[46]

In lieu of full inclusion, the COGIC women's department, like the National Baptist and Progressive Baptist Convention women's departments, is organized in the following units: business and professional women's federation; Christian women's council; church mother's board; deacon's wives' circle; international nurses' unit; overcomer's unit prayer and bible board; purity class; sewing circle; sunshine band; and the young women's Christian council. COGIC women preach to other COGIC women at the Annual Women's International Conferences, and preach they do, with power and authority.[47] Some COGIC widows, under very circumscribed circumstances, also exercise their calls to preach and lead. For example, church mother and evangelist Mable McMurry Smith (b. 1918) and her COGIC-pastor husband Ornell Smith evangelized in Greensboro, North Carolina beginning in 1959 using tent services, houses, warehouses, radio programs, and street ministries.[48] Together, the Smiths purchased COGIC churches in their own names to prevent church

45   Ibid,164–170.

46   "The Presidium of the Church of God in Christ," The Church of God in Christ (website), accessed November 20, 2020, https://www.cogic.org/about-company/the-executive-branch/general-board/.

47   60th COGIC International Women's Convention Thursday Night Service!, video file, posted October 15, 2020, https://www.youtube.com/watch?v=uCEsWtWUIjc.

48   "Mother Mable Smith," Rescue Temple #1 COGIC (website), accessed November 13, 2020. www.rescuetemple1.com/our_founder.html.

leaders from taking church property from Mother Smith when her husband died. Mother Smith said this about her work: "my ministry has not been certified by man, but it has been sanctioned by God. God has used me to pray for the sick and see them recover, and I have conducted numerous revivals in convention halls with hundreds of people in attendance." She added, "After all, God places no restrictions on women, only men do. After God has removed the yokes from our necks, men have tried to put them back on us. Which is better, to be appointed by a man to do a work or to be anointed by God to do it?" Mother Smith assures us that "the scriptures clearly tell us that there is neither Jew nor Greek, bond nor free, male nor female. There is not a separate Spirit for men and women. A woman receives the same Spirit as a man; therefore, she can do any work in the church that a man can do."[49]

8   The Holiness-Pentecostal Denominations

While Black women struggled to achieve full clerical orders in Methodist and Baptist denominations, another group of women began their own churches and denominations where the entire religious leadership was female. Many COGIC women called to preach refused to stay with COGIC, which denied them ordained ministerial opportunities at all levels. They migrated, in many instances to denominations such as the Mt. Sinai Holy Church of America (420 churches), the Church of the Living God founded by Bishop Lillian Tate (268 churches),[50] and the House of God founded by Bishop Mary Daniels (412 churches).[51] However, all of the above-mentioned female-founded Holiness-Pentecostal churches are currently dominated by males in the executive leadership ranks.

In Philadelphia, Pennsylvania Bishop Ada Robinson founded the Mt. Sinai Holy Church of America (MSHCA) in 1924. From the beginning, Bishop Robinson, who personally established 84 of the 420 MSHCA congregations, ordained women as elders, ministers, and administrators. Robinson established Monday night as "Women Preachers Night" and allowed various "loosed" women to be released from the bondage of religious male domination and to minister the gospel so that the women could share their gifts. In 1925, Bishop Robinson organized the First Convocation and expanded the church's reach to Cuba and British Guyana. MSHCA's Office of the Bishop remained female

---

49   Best, 167.
50   "General Assembly 2020," Church of the Living God International (website), accessed November 22, 2020. https://www.clgi.org/general-assembly/.
51   Best, 168.

until 2001, when Rev. Joseph Bell was elected bishop. The Mt. Sinai Holiness Church that began auspiciously in 1923 with all-female leadership team, and which maintained female executive leadership for 77 years, is currently 80% male and 20% female.[52]

9   (Independent) Spiritualist Churches

Sexism also caused many Black women to start their own Independent churches. Spiritual churches often blend and borrow elements of African-American Protestantism, American Spiritualism, Roman Catholicism, Voodoo, and Black ethno-medicine, as well as aspects of Judaism, New Thought, and Ethiopianism.[53] Spiritualism has probably served as the most forceful vehicle for the assertion of women's religious leadership in American society because Spiritual churches accept women's legitimate role as religious authorities without question and embrace female power through its modification of the conventional identity of women. Just like their white sisters, many Black women turned to Spiritualism as a vehicle to meet their goals. While the Methodists and Baptists tended to attract middle-class Black women, the Spiritualist movement generally appealed to low-income Black Americans.

Mother Leafy Anderson, a Black Spiritualist, established one of the first Spiritualist churches in 1913, the Eternal Life Christian Spiritualist church in Chicago, Illinois. Sometime between 1918–1921, Mother Anderson started the first Black Spiritualist church in New Orleans where she trained several other women who established congregations of their own. Eventually, Mother Anderson became the overseer of an association that included New Orleans congregations as well as others in Chicago, Little Rock, Memphis, Pensacola, Biloxi, and Houston as well as some smaller cities.[54] In the 1920s Sister Moore established the Redeeming Christian Spiritualist church, probably the first Black Spiritualist congregation in Nashville, while Sister Wilma Stewart (1940s-1950s) established St. Joseph's Spiritual church, which was likely the largest Spiritual congregation in Nashville.[55] Many Spiritualist women also attained positions as pastors, ministers, elders, evangelists, deacons, and trustees. Women could also access other highly influential positions as mediums,

52   "College of Bishops," Mt. Sinai Holy Church of America Inc. (website), accessed November
       20, 2020, https://mtsinaiholychurch.org/.
53   Baer, 4.
54   Ibid.
55   Ibid, 5.

spiritual advisors, and prophetesses. In sum, Spiritualist churches provided women with much greater access to positions of religious leadership than did the Black Methodist, Baptist, and Pentecostal-Sanctified denominations.[56]

10   (Independent) New Thought Churches

New Thought, a mind-healing movement that originated in the United States in the 19th century, ascribes to the idea that truth is a matter of continuing revelation and recognizes that no one leader or institution can declare with finality what the nature of truth is. The first Black female to organize an African-American New Thought Christian church, the Rev. Johnnie Colemon (1920–1994), began in 1956 with the founding of Christ Unity Center and Christ Universal Temple. Not only did the Temple grow to become the largest church in Chicago, but Rev. Colemon also established her own denomination, the Universal Foundation for Better Living, which, at its peak, counted 20,000 adherents in the United States. In 1971, the Rev. Barbara King founded a second African-American New Thought Christian Church and Hillside International Truth Center in Atlanta, Georgia. And in 1977, King founded the Barbara King School of Ministry where Christology, metaphysics, Bible studies, meditation, and prosperity theology were taught.

Despite the strong female leadership of these New Thought Churches, the movement has fractured. In Atlanta, the New Thought Christian Church and Truth Center have closed. And the Nashville-based Spiritualist churches, founded in the 1940s by entrepreneurial women, have all closed.

We now turn to the twenty-first century to point to some possible paths forward with the emergence of Womanism, Black Protestant women's adaptation of Liberation Theology.

11   Womanism: Founders and Foundations

In the 21st century, Black Protestant feminists confront patriarchy, misogyny, sexism, racism, homophobia, and classism through womanist theologies. In 1983, novelist Alice Walker (b. 1944) coined the term *womanist* in her collection *In Search of Our Mother's Gardens* to define Black feminists or feminists of color. Womanism unites women of color and broader feminist

---

56   Ibid, 8.

movements around intersecting issues of race, class, and gender, focusing specifically on Black women's experiences of racism, sexism, misogyny, and economic exploitation. Building on these ideas in 1984, Audre Lorde (1934–1992) published an influential collection of essays entitled *Sister Outsider*. Reflecting upon Black male sexism targeted against Black females, Lorde wrote that "Black male consciousness must be raised to the realization that sexism and woman-hating are critically dysfunctional to his liberation as a Black man because they arise out of the same constellation that engenders racism and homophobia." Lorde warned that "Until that consciousness is developed, Black men will view sexism and the destruction of Black women as tangential to Black liberation rather than as central to that struggle. So long as this occurs, we will never be able to embark upon that dialogue between Black women and Black men that is so essential to our survival as a people." The self-described warrior added, "This continued blindness between us can only serve the oppressive system within which we live. In this country, Black women traditionally have had compassion for everybody else except ourselves. We need to learn to have care and compassion for ourselves." Significantly Lorde pointed to the culpability of the traditional male religious hierarchy in the oppression of Black women. She wrote: "Care and compassion for ourselves means that *the passive acceptance of abuse and misogynistic treatment in the Black Church in order to perform solidarity with Black men needs to end* (emphasis added)."[57]

Similarly in 1988, Presbyterian Church in the United States (PCUS) pastor and theologian Rev. Dr. Katie Geneva Cannon (1950–2018) published the seminal womanist text *Black Womanist Ethics*. Cannon defines womanist theology as a theology of survival which attends to the day-to-day efforts of Black women to preserve Black life in a society that devalues Black life. Cannon adds that womanist theology is a liberation theology forged by Black women focused on the power dynamics between Black women and Black men especially around issues of abuse, exploitation, and oppression. Moreover, Cannon argues that womanist theology is a global theology positing that African Americans "are part of a global community of oppressed peoples struggling for survival and freedom." At its very core, womanist theology is a prophetic theology that focuses on the dignity of persons and as such the eradication of all forms of oppression by exposing unjust, oppressive systems, a refusal to

---

57   Audre Lorde, *Sister Outsider: Essays and Speeches by Audre Lord* (Trumansburg, NY: Crossing Press, 1984), 58.

passively accept wrongdoing, and the imperative to confront wrongdoing in order to create communities of justice.[58]

Correspondingly in 1993, PCUS pastor and theologian Delores Williams (b. 1937) published *Sisters in the Wilderness: The Challenge of Womanist God-Talk*. Williams posits that Black women must listen first to their own voices and experiences in Christian faith rather than anything said or decided by males. She argues that "black theology will have to deal with women as integral parts of the whole community" since Black women represent more than half of Black population and nearly three-fourths of the Black church members. Williams points to the double oppression that Black women face with both racism and sexism inside and outside of their communities. Consequently, Black women's theology should exercise its prophetic function and serve as a "self-test" in the Black church characterized by the sins of racism, sexism, and other forms of oppression.[59] Black men intrinsically invested in the patriarchal structure of white-male dominated society must "realize that if Jesus is liberator of the oppressed, all of the oppressed must be liberated. If liberation is not human enough to include the liberation of women, it will not be liberation."[60] Likewise in 1993, American Baptist pastor and theologian Emilie Townes (b. 1955) penned *Womanist Justice, Womanist Hope*. In this text, Townes criticizes white female racism and white feminists' failure to acknowledge and take seriously Black women's experiences. She also underscores the sexism, heterosexism, and misogyny of men, as a problem intrinsic to all groups.[61]

Along with the larger canon of global liberation theologies, womanist theology, has over time, become a predominant mode of theological reflection within most mainline seminaries in the United States. It has been taken up by many theologians who have been trained in traditional denominational seminaries and divinity schools and by pastors who serve in mainline congregations, especially in Presbyterian, Methodist, Lutheran, Episcopal, Congregationalist, and American Baptist communions. Alternatively, womanism and the larger cannon of Black liberation theologies have not, however, embedded themselves in most Pentecostal and National Baptist congre.

---

58   Rufus Burrow, Jr. "Development of Womanist Theology: Some Chief Characteristics." *The Asbury Theological Journal* 54, no. 1 (Spring 1999): 41–57.

59   Grant, 148.

60   Ibid, 148.

61   Burrow, 45.

12   Significance and Conclusion

In a 1990 nationwide survey of Black clergy representing 2,150 churches in the United States, only 3.7% of respondents were female. The majority of those female clergy were found in storefront or independent churches. Young people under thirty with at least some college education tend to support women in ministry. Conversely, senior citizens with less than a high school education are the most resistant to women clergy. Not surprisingly, the three Baptist denominations and the Pentecostals tended to be highly negative in their attitudes toward women as pastors with 73% of COGIC respondents disapproving of women pastors.[62]

We are left wondering why so many Black women consent to Black male clerical domination in so many historically Black churches. Daphne Wiggins posits several reasons for this perplexing attitude given some of the major inroads women have achieved in traditionally Black churches. First, Wiggins suggests that many Black women desire male ministers because they provide a father and husband-like figure in environments where Black men are victims of early deaths, incarceration, and marginal education. Second, she argues that Black women frequently have to go to church to hear a Black male in a position of authority. Third, Wiggins posits that many women have been inculcated from a very young age that a father should be the head of the household *and* the church. Fourth, she suggests that little discourse on sexism in the historically Black churches occurs, adding to the problem. Fifth, she suggests that there is a reluctance to apply affirmative action strategies in a religious context. And finally, Wiggins proposes that women are generally satisfied with the benefits of church participation and the church's fulfillment of its mission. Combined, these elements form a sacred context that makes the current state of affairs acceptable while at the same time impeding a comprehensive critique or discourse on gender relations in Black churches, of which the role of clergy women would be one facet. In the end, especially among Baptists and COGIC, there is little to no agitation for women's ordination among Black laywomen of the magnitude found among mainline Protestants and Roman Catholics.[63]

---

62   C. Eric Lincoln and Lawrence H. Mamiya, *The Black Church in the African American Experience.* (Durham, N.C.: Duke University Press, 1990). This treatise contains survey results of a ten-year longitudinal study of 1,800 Black pastors and church members.

63   Daphne C. Wiggins, *Righteous Content: Black Women's Perspectives of Church and Faith.* (New York: New York University Press, 2005), 131–135.

Embedded patriarchy in the systems and institutions that impact the values and dogma of religious groups tend to produce in adherents a false consciousness. This false consciousness can manifest itself in continued refusals to even consider the ordination of females, including questioning the authenticity of a woman's call. On the other hand, males typically are not asked to defend their calls, or the unjust, unfair treatment of women ministers. As a general rule, Black women are not taking an active role in instituting structural and value changes concerning sexism and gender discrimination, especially in National Baptist and COGIC circles, because the issue of female clergy is neither important nor urgent. Generally speaking laywomen are not conversant with womanist and feminist theologies of liberation, and for many women, sexism is a lesser evil than racism. And perhaps most significantly, women are typically not conversant in the politics and practices of hiring new pastors.

In COGIC, the position of National Mother corresponds to the Presiding Bishop of the denomination. Women speak but do not preach. The presence of strong missionary associations, women's departments, and the financial and organizational presence and power of women in historically Black churches is undeniable. Women have voice, but they exercise, depending on the denomination, limited, circumscribed power. In the end, there is still a distinction between prescribed support positions of evangelist, missionary, deaconess, stewardess, exhorter, church mother, and religiopolitical leadership positions in Black churches. Black male ministers, in their understandable fixation on the supremacy of whiteness and anti-black racism tend to subordinate other forms of oppression and injustice to the issue of racism.[64] But "women need full humanization, clothed in an ontological identity that is grounded in the Triune life of God and that frees them to be full persons in Christ."[65]

With the notable exceptions of the early and mid-20th century Spiritualists and the women-led Holiness-Pentecostal denominations, Black males then and now continue to monopolize the ministry as a profession. The ordination of women has always been and continues to be controversial, as is evidenced by the fact that in all of the churches and denominations researched in this study, including the Spiritualists and Holiness-Pentecostals, 100% currently have a Black male as the head of their respective communions (2021). Extraordinary Black clergywomen in Black Protestant denominations have

64   Theresa Green. "A Gendered Spirit: Race, Class, and Sex in the African American Church." *Race, Gender & Class Journal* 10, no. 1 (2003): 115–129.

65   Cheryl Bridges Johns, "Spirited Vestments: or, Why the Anointing is Not Enough," in *Philip's Daughters: Women in Pentecostal-Charismatic Leadership*, eds. Estrelda Alexander and Amos Yong, (Eugene: Pickwick Publications, 2009), 170–171.

labored near and far for almost 300 years to preach the gospel and to exercise the full complement of gifts God has given them for the healing of creation and the salvation of humankind. Black women have labored, and still labor in a culture that is male dominant, male centered, and male identified. Nevertheless, the gains, especially in Methodist churches, are impressive and progressive. The militant lack of progress in National Baptist and most Pentecostal communions is distressing, and regressive. And yet, women who make up 50–75% of the membership of male-dominated denominations for the most part consent to these patterns. Many women called to lead the church will labor within conservative, oppressive structures that are deeply resistant to change; others will leave the denomination, while still others will leave the church entirely. Because women constitute the overwhelming majority of the membership in historically Black denominations, if and when enough women withdraw their consent represented in the denial of money, time, resources, and labor, the institutions will change. In the end, the power to change these circumstances is in in women's hands.

Bibliography

African Methodist Episcopal Church (website). "Bishops of the Church." Accessed November 20, 2020. https://www.ame-church.com/leadership/bishops-of-the-church/.

African Methodist Episcopal Church Zion (website). "Board of Bishops." Accessed November 20, 2020. https://www.amez.org/board-of-bishops/.

Alexander, Estrelda and Amos Yong, eds. *Philip's Daughters: Women in Pentecostal-Charismatic Leadership.* Eugene: Pickwick Publications, 2009.

Baer, Hans A., "The Limited Empowerment of Women in Black Spiritual Churches: An Alternative Vehicle to Religious Leadership," *Sociology of Religion* 54, no. 1 (Spring 1993): 1–10.

Beecher, Amanda. "NJ Suffragists-Reverend Florence Spearing Randolph (1866–1951)." Accessed November 11, 2020. https://discoverynjhistory.org/njsuffragists-reverend -florence-spearing-randolph/.

Best, Felton O., ed. *Black Religious Leadership from the Slave Community to the Million Man March.* Lewiston: The Edwin Mellen Press, 1998.

Blackburn, Simon. "Augustine of Hippo." In *Oxford Dictionary of Philosophy.* Article published 2016. Current online version 2016. https://www-oxfordreference-com .turing.library.northwestern.edu/view/10.1093/acref/9780198735304.001.0001/ acref-9780198735304-e-290?rskey=FDVPfr&result=6.

Black Christian News (website). "Women in Ministry Get Key Support from Progressive National Baptist Convention, Inc." Accessed November 21, 2020.

https://blackchristiannews.com/2015/02/women-in-ministry-get-key-support
-from-progressive-national-baptist-convention-inc/.

Burrow, Rufus, Jr. "Development of Womanist Theology: Some Chief Characteristics." *The Asbury Theological Journal* 54, no. 1 (Spring 1999): 41–57.

Campbell-Reed, Eileen. *State of Clergywomen in the U.S.: A Statistical Update.* https://eileencampbellreed.org/state-of-clergy/.

Christian Methodist Episcopal Church (website). "The College of Bishops." Accessed November 20, 2020. https://www.thecmechurch.org/bishops/.

Church of God in Christ (website). "The Presidium of the Church of God in Christ." Accessed November 20, 2020. https://www.cogic.org/about-company/the-executive-branch/general-board/.

Church of the Living God International (website). "General Assembly 2020." Accessed November 28, 2020. https://www.clgi.org/general-assembly/.

Dittmar, Kelly, Kira Sanbonmatsu, Susan J. Carroll, Debbie Walsh, and Catherine Wineinger. "Representation Matters: Women in the U.S. Congress." Preprint, November 16, 2020. https://cawp.rutgers.edu/sites/default/files/resources/representationmatters.pdf.

First Community Church A.M.E. Church (website). "The Stewardess and Deaconess Boards." Accessed November 11, 2020. https://www.fcame.org/stewardess-and-deaconess.html.

General Board of Higher Education and Ministry of the United Methodist Church (website). "Elders." Accessed November 11, 2020. https://www.gbhem.org/clergy/elders/.

Grant, Jacquelyn. *Black Theology and the Black Woman.* New York: Orbis Books, 1993.

Green, Theresa. "A Gendered Spirit: Race, Class, and Sex in the African American Church." *Race, Gender & Class Journal* 10, no. 1 (2003): 115–129.

Higginbotham, Evelyn Brooks. *Righteous Discontent: The Women's Movement in the Black Baptist Church, 1880–1920.* Cambridge: Harvard University Press, 1993.

Ibarra, Herminia, Robin J. Ely, and Deborah M. Kolb. "Women Rising: The Unseen Barriers." *Harvard Business Review,* September 2013, 1–10.

Life Application Study Bible New International Version. Wheaton: Tyndale House Publishers and Zondervan Publishing House, 1991.

Lindley, Susan Hill. *"You Have Stept Out of Your Place": A History of Women and Religion in America.* Louisville: Westminster John Knox Press, 1996.

Lorde, Audre. *Sister Outsider: Essays and Speeches by Audre Lord.* Trumansburg, NY: Crossing Press, 1984.

Luders-Manuel, Shannon. "Jarena Lee, The First Woman African American Autobiographer." *JStor Daily,* December 15, 2018, 1–4.

Mount Sinai Holy Church of America Inc. (website). "College of Bishops." Accessed November 20, 2020. https://www.mtsinaiholychurch.org/.

Murphy, Larry G., ed. *Down by the Riverside: Readings in African American Religion.* New York: New York University Press, 2000.

National Baptist Convention of America International (website). "Executive Cabinet." Accessed November 20, 2020. https://www.nbcainc.com/executive-cabinet/.

National Baptist Convention United States of America (website). "Servant Leadership Team and Structure." Accessed November 20, 2020. https://www.nationalbaptist .com?departments/auxiliaries/moderators/leadership.

Progressive National Baptist Convention (website). "Official Roster of the PNBC Officers." Accessed November 20, 2020. https://www.pnbc.org/about/officers.

Rescue Temple #1 COGIC (website). "Mother Mabel Smith." Accessed November 13, 2020. https://www.rescuetemple1.com/our_founder.html.

Rooke, Deborah W. "Patriarchy/Kyriarchy." In *the Oxford Encyclopedia of the Bible and Gender Studies.* Article published 2014. https://www.oxfordreference.com/view/ 10.1093/acref:obso/9780199836994.001.0001/acref-9780199836994.

Sixtieth COGIC International Women's Convention Thursday Night Service. YouTube video file. Posted October 15, 2020. https://www.youtube.com/watch? v=uCEsWtWUIjc&t=5007s.

Smoot, Pamela A. "Hear the Call: The Women's Auxiliary of the Progressive National Baptist Convention, Inc." *Baptist History and Heritage* 46, issue 1 (Spring 2011): 1–7. https://go-gale-com.turing.library.northwestern.edu/ps/ i.do?p=AONE&u=northwestern&id=GALE%7CA267973779&v=2.1&it=r.

Strong, James and John McClintock. "Presiding Elder." In *Cyclopedia of Biblical, Theological, and Ecclesiastical Literature.* Article published 1880. http:// https:// www.biblicalcyclopedia.com/P/presiding-elder.html.

United States Park Service (website). "Bridget Biddy Mason." Accessed November 20, 2020. https://www..nps.gov/people/biddymason.htm.

Wiggins, Daphne C. *Righteous Content: Black Women's Perspectives of Church and Faith.* New York: New York University Press, 2005.

CHAPTER 11

Black Christian Methodist Episcopal Church Clergywoman at the Crossroads in Ministry

Stephanie A. Welsh

She was about eight years old when God called her to preach. In those days, at that small Missouri Synod Lutheran Church in Milwaukee, the only service females rendered to the Lord was singing, shining church pews, cooking, or decorating the sanctuary for various religious holidays. A woman could clean the podium, but she could not read Scripture from it. She could polish the pulpit, but she could not pontificate God's word from the "sacred desk" because, according to Martin Luther, "the Holy Spirit excepted women"[1] from the call to preach. Luther, as do some members of clergy and laity, used Paul's first letter to the church at Corinth to justify his reasoning, *"women should keep silent in the churches. For they are not permitted to speak, but should be subordinate, as the law says"* (1 Corinthians 14:34 *NRSV*). Based on Luther's fifth mark of the church's seven external marks, seeds of inferiority planted in schoolgirls in their formative years are foundational in the Lutheran Church's identity.

Being unaware of Luther's teaching, the eight-year-old girl wondered why her male counterparts played a superordinate role in worship. Simultaneously, she and her female classmates sat on the sidelines watching the boys serve as acolytes. What was unique about the boys? Why were they allowed to walk down the church aisle with the pastor carrying the long-handled taper candle snuffer to light the candelabra? Why were girls restricted from participating in worship in a meaningful way? She and the other girls were just as capable of lighting the candelabra on the altar as the boys.

Instead of complaining, she took action. She did the only thing she could think to do. She pleaded her case to the pastor, advocating for not only her rights, but the rights of the girls who, in secret, sounded their discontent about being denied equal opportunity in service to God. Although she did not realize it back then, she was becoming an activist for the 'other'—those whose humanity was considered inferior. It was her willingness to speak out against

---

1   Martin Luther, *On the Councils and the Church,* https://wolfmueller.co/wp-content/uploads/2018/10/Work-on-Councils_100618.pdf (accessed September 27, 2020).

the injustice that sparked change. She and her friends became part of the weekly worship acolyte rotation. The girls of that Lutheran church functioned as acolytes until the church closed in the first decade of the twenty-first century. Sadly, radical reform still has not come to the pulpit of the Missouri Synod of the Lutheran Church. Women cannot teach in the sanctuary or serve in pastoral ministry. They remain silent in the church.

The eight-year-old girl in this story is me. It is the story of my formative years of activism. My early years of getting in "good trouble."[2] Today, I continue "to get in good trouble, necessary trouble"[3] as I embark upon a research study about the experiences of clergywomen in the Christian Methodist Episcopal (CME) Church.

Four foundational questions guided this study: 1) what is the vocational status of black clergywomen; 2) what are the ministerial experiences of black clergywomen; 3) what type of support do black clergywomen receive from CME Church leadership, and what is their perception of the support; and 4) what barriers do clergywomen face that impact their decision to leave or consider leaving? For those who leave, where do they go?

In the pages to follow, I will share the purpose and importance of this project. A brief overview of the Methodist church's tradition regarding women in ministry is provided, followed by the historical view and treatment of women in the CME Church. The early qualitative findings are presented through the stories of the lived ministerial experiences of three clergywomen—Miriam, Martha, and Deborah. The chapter concludes with a proposed intervention to balance the scales of justice for clergywomen in the CME Church.

1   The Purpose

This project explores and interprets the responses of African American clergywomen to patriarchy and sexism in the CME Church. The study aims to gain insight as to why some clergywomen thrive in their ministerial vocation despite injustices and barriers that impede mobility upward in ministry and pastoral leadership in the CME Church, while others leave or consider leaving the church.

---

2   Representative John Lewis, quoted in Joshua Bote, "'Get in good trouble, necessary trouble': Rep John Lewis in his own words" *USA Today*, July 18, 2020, https://www.usatoday.com/story/news/politics/2020/07/18/rep-john-lewis-most-memorable-quotes-get-good-trouble/5464148002/ (accessed September 27, 2020).

3   Ibid.

2   The Problem

Since its inception, the church has played an instrumental role in institutions, communities, families, and individuals; this is undoubtedly the case in the African American community. Historically, the Black Church has been pivotal in the lives of Black people. It has served as a place of refuge for the rejected, healing for the hurt, and hope for people tattered by a history of maltreatment, injustice, traumatization, and violence. Traditionally, the Black Church affirmed the humanity of African Americans in a world that treated them as less than human: those dehumanized and dejected by society. The Black Church contributed significantly to the cause of liberation and Civil Rights: offering the sanctuary as a gathering place for solidarity in the fight against social injustice.

Inasmuch as the Black Church has fought against discrimination and inequality, it has played a paradoxical role of purveyor of sexism in women's oppression, particularly Black clergywomen, while espousing freedom, liberty, and justice of Christ. This practice of prejudice is systemic. Despite Black women's educational achievements and professional advancements, Black clergywomen continue to face obstacles and barriers in attaining leadership roles in the church. "Organizational hurdles have placed a stained-glass ceiling"[4] in the way of clergywomen as these ordained elders are routinely denied significant appointments to serve larger, financially stable, congregations as lead pastor in the Christian Methodist Episcopal Church.

Black male clergy continue to monopolize superordinate church positions while subjugating women to inferior roles that limit their authority, prevent ministerial fulfillment, and inhibit their decision-making power as well as their voice. Mary Daly asserts that inequality "prevents (women) from genuine self-fulfillment and from active, adult-size participation in society"[5] as well as the church. Such injustice is a sin. Just as racism is sinful and viewed by both men and women as an injustice worth fighting, "sexism is a sin against creation"[6] and a "manifestation of evil."[7] Therefore, the CME Church has a responsibility to confess this sin of injustice and right the wrong of inequality against

---

4   TeResa Green, "A Gendered Spirit: Race, Class, and Sex in the African American Church," *Race, Gender & Class* 10, no. 1 (2003). http://www.jstor.org/stable/41675063 (accessed July 31, 2020).

5   Mary Daly, *The Church and the Second Sex*, 3rd ed. (Boston: Beacon Press, 1985), 53.

6   J. Deotis Roberts, *The Prophethood of Black Believers: An African American Political Theology for Ministry* (Louisville: Westminster/John Knox Press, 1994), 79.

7   Ibid., 79.

women. This requires transformational thinking about clergywomen, "decisive action,"[8] and a commitment to positive proactive change.

3   Significance of the Study

By listening to and lifting up the voices and experiences of clergywomen in the Black Church, specifically the CME Church, this project situates their experiences as authoritative and as evidence of the limits of the leadership model that prioritizes men, while Black clergywomen provide pastoral care within an oppressive system. The findings of this study illuminate the impact sexism has on the ministerial advancement of Black clergywomen in the CME Church. As such, this study advances the knowledge of leadership issues within the Black Church in general and the CME Church in particular. This research is a contribution to CME Church history, Black Church studies, Africology, and womanist studies. This study fills the void of the silenced voices of Black women clergy who lead within degraded conditions of inequality and subordination.

4   Hypothesis

Black clergywomen who stay and thrive in the CME Church are well connected and willing to tolerate high levels of patriarchy. In contrast, those who stay but do not thrive are not well connected and suffer the consequences of ministering in a system of oppression. Clergywomen who leave or consider leaving the CME Church are not well connected, refuse to tolerate the injustice of being denied the opportunity for advancement and find other religious institutions that provide opportunities to thrive.

5   Methodist Church Tradition Regarding Women in Ministry

An assessment of church tradition, particularly the Methodist tradition, is fundamental in understanding the history of the vocational status of women in the Methodist Church. This historical evaluation sheds light on the modern-day vocational status of women in the Methodist Church. An appraisal of Methodism, its beginnings and its leader, specifically John Wesley, along with

---

8 Ibid.

an assessment of the traditional tenets of the Colored Methodist Episcopal Church concerning the role of women in ministry is of paramount importance.

In his book, Paul W. Chilcote, *John Wesley and the Women Preachers of Early Methodism,* describes women's roles in the promulgation of Methodism in its foundational years. Many women and widows not only opened their homes to Methodist preachers, but "some took the initiative in the actual formation of societies with no other authority than their own determination and sense of divine calling."[9] While women significantly impacted the growth and development of Methodism, their roles continued to be subordinate to that of men in the church in formal leadership and preaching.

John Wesley, an Anglican priest, maintained the restrictive rules of the Anglican Church, which limited the activities of women.[10] When accused of allowing women and laymen to preach, John Wesley referred to the letter Paul had written to the Church at Corinth (1 Corinthians 14:34–35) in his retort regarding women. Women were to remain silent and were not to take the lead in public teaching.[11] John Wesley's views and practices regarding women preachers changed near the end of his life. By this point, women were preaching, though unofficially recognized as preachers, and sinners were accepting Christ following the proclamation of these women. As a result, "the English Methodist Conference was eventually led to officially recognize a number of these exceptional women."[12] When John Wesley was asked why he changed his mind about women preachers, he replied, "Because God owns them in the conversion of sinners, and who am I that I should withstand God."[13]

The death of John Wesley brought about significant changes to Methodist rules regarding the ordination of women; "the question of women's preaching became a point of bitter controversy."[14] Despite the prophetic gift and success of anointed women preachers, staunch criticism and wanton disapproval abounded. "Hostility to female preaching had become so strong that the Irish clergy took extreme and immediate action to suppress their activities."[15] The climate of patriarchal thinking increased significantly after the death of John Wesley, and the repression of women became so severe that "increasing

---

9   Paul W. Chilcote, *John Wesley and the Women Preachers of Early Methodism* (Metuchen, New Jersey: The American Theological Library Association and The Scarecrow Press: 1991), 50.

10   Ibid., 56.

11   Ibid., 57.

12   Ibid., 182.

13   Ibid.

14   Ibid., 222.

15   Chilcote, *John Wesley and the Women Preachers,* 232.

numbers of aspiring women preachers found it necessary to sever their ties with the parent body of Methodism."[16]

6   The CME Church's View of Women in Ministry

The CME Church is a historic Black Church with a reported membership of more than 500,000[17] according to the "The Quadrennial Reports of the Bishops of the Christian Methodist Episcopal Church" presented to the 38th Quadrennial Session and 39th General Conference held in Birmingham, Alabama in June of 2018. The history of the CME Church commences with its birth on December 16, 1870, in Jackson, Tennessee, at the 1870 General Conference of the Methodist Episcopal (ME) Church, South,[18] seven years after President Abraham Lincoln issued the Emancipation Proclamation, granting freedom to the enslaved. Although emancipated, blacks continued to face subjugation by white Methodist preachers. Due to the suppression, injustice, and repression faced by these liberated blacks, at the hands of white Methodist preachers, forty-one Black Methodists organized a separate Methodist branch: The Colored Methodist Episcopal Church.

The decision to organize a separate and independent church was due to the change in southern negroes' status and a question posed at the 1866 General Conference of the ME Church, South, about how to proceed with its negro church members. The enslaved, who, although members of the ME Church, South, had no rights or privileges in the church.[19] That is, "the social and political conditions of the plantations did not permit slaves to participate in the life of the church in any meaningful way other than attending worship."[20] In the southern ME Church, nearly thirty-nine percent of its membership according to records of the 1860 General Conference were enslaved people.[21] This southern Methodist church body not only approved of slavery, but also advocated for its continuation. The conclusion of the Civil War brought about significant changes. The ME Church, South, was ill-prepared to deal with the aftermath of

---

16   Ibid., 236.
17   The 500,000 members represent both clergy and laity in the United States, Jamaica, Haiti, and Africa: Congo, Uganda, Kenya, Tanzania, Sudan, Ghana, Togo, Nigeria, Lagos, Liberia, and Nigeria.
18   Othal Hawthorne Lakey, *The History of the CME Church,* rev. ed. (Memphis: The CME Publishing House, 1996), 24.
19   Ibid., 106.
20   Ibid.
21   Ibid., 107.

the South losing a war that ultimately granted freedom to the enslaved population. Liberation afforded choice in terms of the freed persons livelihood and their place of worship.[22] Although approximately twenty percent of the emancipated population stayed in the ME Church, South,[23] the ethos that permeated the church during slavery remained part of the fabric of the church after the emancipation: the freed Negro had no rights in the church and policies to address the issue of injustice did not exist.[24]

The church could not, or at least did not, make changes that were essential in dealing with the changing circumstances of its Black members. Though Negroes were being set free, their status as preachers remained unchanged and the right to be pastors, presiding elders, and to full ordination was not granted. Black preachers who wanted to associate with the Methodist Episcopal Church, South, could not exercise full ministry.[25]

The ME Church, South "would no longer care for her colored members."[26] Since there was no interest in allowing them full participation in the life of the church, the only plausible action for the newly emancipated negroes, who felt the call of God upon their lives to preach God's Word, was to leave the ME Church, South.[27] These individuals not only recognized their divine call, God-given gifts, graces and talents, they took decisive action by creating their own institution to carry out the mission and ministry of Jesus. Forty-one emancipated negroes, upon the encouragement of white ME Church, South pastors and being granted the authority of white bishops, determined it to be in the best interest of the remaining Negro members of the ME Church, South to form their own branch of Methodism. Thus, the Colored Methodist Episcopal Church was established and two of their own preachers were elected to serve as bishops of the CME Church: William H. Miles and Richard H. Vanderhorst.[28]

---

22   Ibid., 108.
23   Ibid.
24   Ibid., 110.
25   Lakey, *The History of the CME Church*, 110–111.
26   Ibid., 111.
27   The freedom of negroes resulted in competition between independent Black Methodist churches (African Methodist Episcopal Church and the African Methodist Episcopal Church Zion) in the North as well as the northern White Methodist church (Methodist Episcopal Church) for church membership amongst this population. The fierce competition and the confusion created amongst these Methodist churches, ultimately led the freed Negro members of the ME Church, South to establish their own separate and independent Colored Methodist Church (116–117).
28   Lakey, *The History of the CME Church*, 44.

Where were the women? What role, if any, did women play in the life of this newly formed Methodist religious institution? How would emancipated women express God's call to ministry? When could women expect to exercise their prophetic voice as the prophet Joel uttered, "your sons and daughters shall prophesy" and Luke, the gospel writer and physician, thought necessary to proclaim in the Acts of the Apostles? This new institution established by men[29] out of a desire to fully utilize the gifts bestowed upon them by God, gave no consideration to the voice or struggle of the women who labored with them as enslaved laborers and would continue to toil alongside them in the fight for justice and equality through the Jim Crow and Civil Rights eras. According to Bishop Othal Lakey, the history of the role of women in the CME Church was absent. Just as emancipated men had no rights to full participation in the ME Church, South, women in the CME Church "were denied leadership and had no role to play. They were merely members of the church ... (who) sang, prayed, shouted, and raised money. Leadership in the Church was for men."[30] The very injustices bestowed upon Black men in the ME Church, South that the freed men sought to escape befell Black women in the Black church.

Women securing official roles in the church, even at the local level, were met with resistance. Black women who had experienced the oppression of White men and women were now suffering subjugation by their Black brothers in Christ's Church. Although "the Black preacher sought by the word of God to bring healing and liberation to the broken personhood of Black men and women whose lives had been disrupted and degraded by slavery,"[31] Black women continued to suffer the evil of gender discrimination as they were denied preaching and leadership opportunities in the CME Church. Ministerial ordination was reserved for men. Black clergymen sought passages of Scripture to validate the suppression of women. They used God's Word "to deny women their rightful place in ministry."[32] Whether clergy or laity, women were not allowed to serve as delegates to the General or Annual conferences in the CME Church.[33] As a result, women had no voice, no voting rights, and no power. Just as emancipated men faced the oppressive force of racism in the ME Church, South; Black women faced the pang of patriarchy, sexism, and gender discrimination in this 'tender plant' rooted in the Methodist tradition.

---

29   Information about the role of emancipated women in the formation of the CME Church
      does not appear to exist. If women participated, their stories have been excluded.
30   Lakey, *The History of the CME Church*, 270.
31   Ibid., 287.
32   Roberts, *The Prophethood of Black Believers*, 77.
33   Lakey, *The History of the CME Church*, 404.

There were, however, women who refused to allow the sexism and patriarchy that prevailed within the CME Church to intimidate or discourage them from engaging in ministry. One such woman was Mrs. Caroline W. Poe.[34] Mrs. Poe, in her resolute determination, advocated for the recognition of women in service to the church. Twelve years after 'God's tender plant' had taken root, she visited the General Conference of 1882 hoping to persuade members of the General Conference to welcome the Women's Missionary Society into the convention.[35] Although her request at the 1882 General Conference was denied, the 1886 General Conference proved to be moderately successful for the Women's Missionary Society. The General Conference approved the "organization of a General Woman's Missionary Society throughout the denomination" at the local and annual conference levels.[36] While approval to organize at the annual conference level was granted, the women of this Society were not in control. Men were the recipients of privilege and legatees of power. The men led while women played a subservient role in the very organization they formed. Though the Woman's Missionary Society was now official, at the local and annual conference levels, the role women were to assume in its leadership was not. When the Constitution and By-Laws of the Women's Missionary Society was approved in 1890, it specified, "The officers of the Board shall be: 1st, a Male Corresponding Secretary."[37] Further, the Women's Missionary Society was to be governed by the General Missionary Board, which was led by men.[38]

Although black women could work in the church—raise funds, go on missions, and teach children—they were not permitted to serve as members of clergy. Church law proscribed the ordination of women, thereby eviscerating the promise of God's prophetic gifting upon all flesh and the liberating power of Jesus in relation to women. This was the case with many denominations, particularly Black denominations—and specifically, the CME Church. The ministerial work of women was not a priority for male leadership within the church. It wasn't until 1966, nearly 100 years after the founding of the CME Church, that women, who acknowledged the call to preach, were ordained.[39]

---

34   Mrs. Caroline W. Poe was President of the Women's Missionary Society of the East Texas Conference. The history of the formation of that particular Women's Missionary Society is not provided in *The History of the CME Church*. I have not been able to locate historical documents, to date, about the Women's Missionary Society of the CME Church.

35   Lakey, *The History of the CME Church*, 270.

36   Ibid.

37   Ibid.

38   Ibid.

39   Mark Chaves, *Ordaining Women: Culture and Conflict in Religious Organizations* (Cambridge: Harvard University Press, 1997), 17.

Two decades later, in 1987, a woman, Rev. Versie P. Easter, was appointed presiding elder. Rev. Easter was the first woman to serve in the capacity of presiding elder; an appointment made by Bishop William H. Graves.[40]

Despite the commendable achievements of the Women's Missionary Society as well as those who have garnered admirable feats within the CME Church, Bishop Lakey recognized that the church had not evolved in relation to the status of women. "Careful analysis suggests that on the whole women in Christian Methodism have not made the progress in attaining positions of authority, recognition, and influence in the decision-making of their church their history [sic] and numbers would seem to warrant. Though the occasional appointment of women to major churches is commendable, such appointments are in actuality quite rare."[41] Bishop Lakey's statement, appearing in the 1996 revised edition of *The History of the CME Church,* continues to resonate today. The first and only woman elected bishop, Rev. Dr. Teresa Snorton, in the history of the CME Church happened within months of its one hundred fortieth year of existence on June 30, 2010.

While women of color, according to the 2018, "State of Clergywomen in the US," are outpacing White women as well as Black and White men in seminary, Black clergywomen continue to be underrepresented in leadership at the general connectional and annual conference levels of the CME Church. According to the 2014 edition of *The Book of Discipline of the Christian Methodist Episcopal Church,* Black clergywomen represent less than twenty percent of key general connectional leadership roles within the church.[42] There is an even more startling statistic at the annual conference level. In reviewing the websites of the seven US CME episcopal districts reporting presiding elder data, Black clergywomen comprise only nine of forty-eight presiding elders' roles in 2020. Episcopal leaders continue to overlook women to serve in this key paid leadership position. The CME Church continues to fall short concerning the advancement of clergywomen in leadership. The scant number of clergywomen in the appointed role of presiding elder bears that out.

---

40   Lakey, *The History of the CME Church,* 661.

41   Lakey, *The History of the CME Church,* 662–63.

42   There are four clergy members who serve on the judicial council; however, no clergywomen were appointed to serve on this committee. Clergywomen made up one of three alternate judicial council positions. Of the five CME Church-related educational institutions, men are the only persons to serve as president of the institutions. There are ten elected general officer positions; only three were filled by women in 2014. Of the eighty-two general connectional board members, represented by members of clergy, clergywomen represent only seventeen percent of the board members.

Stories of experienced, gifted, and educated women who have been discouraged from looking beyond their current status in the church, yet often overlooked because of their gender, permeate the church. Clergywomen continue to be "asked to be quiet and deferential and to yield leadership to men."[43] I personally can attest to having my hopes thwarted, dreams of advancement dismissed, and being passed over for leadership opportunities not because I lacked experience or education, but because of my physiology.

7   The Importance of This Study

I am an African-American woman ordained elder in the Christian Methodist Episcopal Church with full rights and privileges. I have two master's degrees: Master of Business Administration and a Master of Divinity. Prior to fully embracing my call to pastoral ministry in the CME Church, I had a successful career in corporate America. I served in pastoral ministry from July of 2010 until December of 2018, when I decided to take a sabbatical for my own physical, emotional, psychological, and spiritual well-being. I, like a number of clergywomen with whom I have spoken, had high hopes and aspirations when commencing the process of ordination and entering the pastorate. Sadly, my optimism quickly faded as I came face-to-face with sexism, sexual harassment, discrimination, and oppression in a system that not only embraces, but champions patriarchy. I am intimately familiar with injustice. I encountered sexism, oppression, and racism throughout my professional secular career. While I expected to experience oppression in corporate America, I did not imagine it in the twenty-first century Christian Church. More specifically, it is counterintuitive that a church whose vision is "to be a transforming church for Jesus the Christ within a changing world"[44] would continue to engage in the systematic repression of clergywomen.

Like many other Black CME Church clergywomen, I love God, Methodism, and the Black Church. I have preached through the pain of being ignored and denied opportunities for advancement. I have employed the proverbial Pauline text, "We know that all things work together for good for those who love God, who are called according to his purpose" (Romans 8:28 *NRSV*). I have worn a smile in the face of disappointment, while crying a pool of tears upon

---

43   Charisse Jones and Kumea Shorter-Gooden, *Shifting: The Double Lives of Black Women in America* (New York: Harper Collins Publishers, 2003), 260.

44   "CME Mission & Beliefs," The Christian Methodist Episcopal Church, accessed May 9, 2019, http://www.thecmechurch.org/our-mission-beliefs.html.

my pillow. I have been at the crossroads of leaving the CME Church for as long
as I have served in pastoral ministry. I have listened attentively to the stories
of other women clergy who have left as well as those who are considering a
departure from the CME Church. I have encouraged my clerical sisters to fast
and pray before making an emotional decision. My personal lived experience
of injustice invoked not only the necessity to share the stories of the ministerial experiences of other clergywomen, but to serve as a clarion call to episcopal leadership of the need for change.

8   Methodology

I am a fifty-two-year-old African-American female elder, with full rights and
privileges, in the Christian Methodist Episcopal Church. I served in pastoral
ministry from July 2010 to December 2018 before taking an extended sabbatical for my own physical, emotional, psychological, and spiritual well-being. My
personal experience of oppression as a clergywoman was the desideratum for
pursuing this study.

I am a womanist theologian approaching this body of research through a
social constructivist framework as I seek to gain clarity about the experiences
and perceptions of leadership support of clergywomen in the CME Church.
The ultimate goal of the researcher is to present the findings to the episcopacy
as well as the committee on women in ministry and develop a leadership training program for clergywomen that aid the CME Church in living out its vision
of becoming a transforming church.

I have used both quantitative and qualitative research methods in this
study. The descriptive-survey research method, specifically questionnaires,[45]
was used to gather data about and assess the vocational status and ministerial
experiences of forty-one African-American CME clergywomen, respondents,
across five of the eleven episcopal districts comprising the CME Church. The
case study method, "a research approach that is used to generate an in-depth,
multi-faceted understanding of a complex issue in its real-life context,"[46] was
employed. Nine clergywomen were interviewed to capture and compare their
ministerial experiences: three who have thrived, three who left, and three who

---

45   Questionnaires were sent to one hundred twenty-five clergywomen across five episcopal
      districts.
46   Sarah Crowe *et al.* "The Case Study Approach," *BMC Medical Research Methodology*,
      11, no. 100 (2011). http://www.biomedcentral.com/1471-2288/11/100 (accessed August
      25, 2020).

were considering a departure from the CME Church at the time of the study. This chapter provides a glimpse of the experiences of three clergywomen: one who thrived (referred to as Miriam), one who stayed (referred to as Martha), and one who left (referred to as Deborah).

I conducted an initial analysis of the lived experiences of three of the nine African-American clergywomen who shared the triumphs and disappointments of their ministerial journey in the CME Church. Although a prescripted interview guide was used, participants were allowed to freely share their narrative, oftentimes providing responses to the predetermined interview questions.

The voice of one clergywoman who thrived in the CME Church is presented first, followed by the story of one clergywoman who stayed but did not thrive, and finally the voice of a clergywoman who, finding another religious institution to serve, left the CME Church. The data from each clergywoman provides insight on their vocational status in the church, their ministerial experience, the support they received from leadership, and the barriers they faced.

9   Participants

The participants for the qualitative portion of this research consisted of nine African-American clergywomen, all elders, in full connection in the CME Church. Their ages ranged from late thirty to the early seventy. All but two of the participants were born into the CME Church. Four grew up in the parsonage. Three had fathers who were pastors and one, formerly of another denomination, had a mother who served in pastoral ministry.

The nine clergywomen interviewed by the researcher hold bachelor's degrees. Most have a Master of Divinity degree; while three of the nine participants have Doctor of Ministry degrees. Two of the three participants who thrived, left professional careers to focus on ministry full-time, while the other clergywoman who thrived was appointed to serve as pastor in her early twenties. She did not have a professional career outside of pastoral ministry. Of the six clergywomen women who considered leaving or left the church, all but two were bi-vocational. Two of the three clergywomen who considered leaving at one point, but remained with the CME Church, no longer pastor: one by choice. The location of their ministries included rural communities, small towns, and major cities. The congregational size of the churches led by the participants ranged from twenty-five to one hundred seventy-five. The ages of the clergywomen who thrived ranged from fifty to just over seventy. The age range of those clergywomen who have stayed, but did not thrive in ministry, is between forty to early seventies. The three clergywomen who left, although one who left around 1995 is now in her seventies, are in the late thirties to late fifties.

The participants easily engaged in dialogue with the researcher; demonstrating their willingness to share their stories and have their voices heard. Participants were given pseudonyms, names of women in the Bible, to protect their identity. The following vignettes represents the narratives of the ministerial experiences of three clergywomen in the CME Church: one who thrived, one who stayed despite her lack of success, and one who left.

10   Miriam's Story

Miriam is in her fifties and has served in ministry in the CME Church over thirty years. She grew up in a patriarchal household. She was trained by her family to place the needs and desires of men above her own because "men mattered more than women." For Miriam, serving in a patriarchal system was normal; she had been imbued socially to believe that women were inferior. Miriam's familial and social formation was instrumental in her ability to navigate, or perhaps live into, a system that devalued women. She thrived in ministry, receiving her first pastoral appointment in her early twenties as a lay minister. Miriam did not go through the standard process of standing before the quarterly conference to be approved to receive a local preachers' license: a license all preachers were to have at least a year before commencing the process of ordination. Instead, she was thrust into the ordination process at the first annual conference she attended after serving as an unlicensed lay pastor less than a year. She received both her deacon's and elder's orders at that same annual conference at the age of twenty-one. It is important to note that at that time in the CME Church bachelor's or master's degrees were not required for pastoral leadership. Her experience was unprecedented, particularly for a woman.

While Miriam's ministerial experience, being fast-tracked in pastoral ministry and the accelerated ordination process, was unique for women in ministry, her experience of sexism and sexual harassment was typical. Miriam spoke of not only her own story, but the countless stories of women who experienced sexual harassment or made sexual compromises to move up in ministry. She spoke of how she always thought it was the clergywoman's fault when they had been silenced, sidelined, or erased from the church. Miriam confessed that it wasn't until it happened to her that she realized it was not the woman's fault. She then shared her experience of serving faithfully in the church nearly twenty years before being removed from her pastoral post and exiled after refusing the sexual advances of a bishop. The bishop used his coercive power to silence Miriam by threatening to demote any pastor or leader who gave her any opportunity to preach God's Word from a CME pulpit. The bishop upheld his promise. Miriam recalled how the bishop demoted a male presiding elder, relieving him of his leadership duties, and removed another male pastor, from a prominent church to serve a smaller congregation, who allowed her to preach.

Miriam was displaced eighteen months before receiving a call from a more senior bishop who learned of her plight. She said, "He found me. He called me and asked if I would do him a favor." The favor placed her back into pastoral ministry in the CME Church. It was the support of another episcopal leader with the ability to use legitimate power to give her another opportunity to use the gifts and graces bestowed upon her by God to preach God's Word and lead God's people. Upon her return to the CME Church at the behest of this more senior bishop, she was given opportunities to teach and preach at national CME Church conferences. The exposure catapulted her into key leadership roles within the church. She continues to receive support from key leaders in the CME Church today.

Miriam experienced both highs and lows in ministry. She attests to having considered a departure from the CME Church because of its inflexibility and resistance to clergywomen in leadership. She then expressed this reality, "The more ecumenical I've become, the more I realize women are treated the same everywhere." She expressed the need for the CME Church to be intentional about changing their views and treatment of clergywomen.

11   Martha's Story

Martha, a clergywoman in her early seventies, describes herself as being born into the CME Church. Her grandparents, who raised her, were leaders in the local church. Her grandfather was a steward, while her grandmother served as a stewardess, one of few leadership roles women were allowed to serve in those days. Martha accepted her call to preach in 1996. She was in her mid-forties. While most individuals who acknowledged their call to preach would go before the quarterly conference of their local church to be examined for a local preacher's license, she, like some other women pursing their call to ministry, received an exhorter's license. This license delayed the ordination process two years.

Although Martha maintained her professional career, her desideratum was pastoral ministry. While her desire to provide pastoral care was met, she expressed her discontent in being sent to serve churches in need of major financial support. Martha spoke of the heartbreak she experienced after getting one church she pastored on solid footing only to be appointed to another church in financial disarray and in need of major repairs. She recalls, "The church they sent me to was basically falling apart. It was one of our larger buildings, but it needed a lot of repairs. The church had no heat and I found out the electricity had been jimmy-rigged." Martha periodically received money for fuel from the congregation, but she never received a salary; nor did she receive any financial support from the episcopacy to help support the church. She lamented as she shared her harrowing story of receiving a call, during her hospitalization, from the presiding elder—a woman—seeking registration funds for the annual pastors' conference, but never a call or visit to check on her physical well-being. She spoke of the lack of care and concern leadership has for the people of the church as well as the pastors.

Ministry in the CME Church did not meet Martha's expectations. As she reflected on her ministry experience, she remarked, "I just don't think they would do a man the way they do women." She also spoke of the issue of ageism as she voiced her concern for the lack of opportunity granted to preachers over the age of forty. In this instance, Martha revealed that the gender of those over forty did not matter because the church is focused on promoting younger, less experienced, men to lead the church.

Martha did have mentors during her formative years in the church. Those mentors, primarily missionaries, focused on grooming Martha and other female gendered individuals on being "proper ladies" in the church and society. Those persons who provided her support and guidance, as she accepted her call to preach and served in pastoral ministry, were primarily from other denominations: Baptist and Church of God in Christ (COGIC). Although she talked about having one mentor who was a well-known CME pastor, his support did not garner her visibility, exposure or backing from key leaders in the CME Church. While mentors matter in the CME Church, the position and level of respect of one's mentor in ministry plays a significant role in one's upward mobility.

Martha is embittered by her experience; but because of the relationships she has formed as well as her family's historical connection to the CME Church, she never considered leaving. She did speak of retiring early. She said, "I will remain a CME, but I'm not opposed to going somewhere else." She reflected on the fact that individuals who are part of the "in crowd" are elevated in ministry. Those persons are typically men.

12   Deborah's Story

Deborah is in her late fifties. She is a daughter of the parsonage. Her father served as a CME pastor until his retirement; as such she was intimately familiar with the Methodist doctrine, the expectations of pastoral ministry, and the ethos of the church when she accepted her call to ministry in her late twenties.

Although Deborah's father was a CME pastor, she left the CME Church because she experienced the church in those days as being very traditional and lackluster in its worship. Since she grew up in an area where the Baptist church held services the first and third Sunday of the month and the Methodist church held service the second and fourth Sunday, she found a greater sense of connectedness with the Baptist church. She recalled, "The Methodist church was dead. I was the youth department. There were no other youth in the church."

While she received her salvation in the Baptist church, her heart for and desire to do ministry was in the CME Church. In her late twenties she returned to the CME Church and accepted her call to ministry. She expressed reticence in speaking with her pastor about her call, because the focus was on encouraging young men to accept God's call to preach and subsequently moving those young men through the ordination process. Once she spoke with her pastor about her call to ministry, her ordination process was accelerated. Her pastor used his influence with the bishop to ensure she received full orders immediately. The support she received from her pastor positioned her vocationally to serve in numerous leadership capacities: preacher-in-charge, the joint board of finance—a role generally reserved for "first church" pastors—young adult counselor, district finance committee, and the administrative assistant to the bishop.

Inasmuch as Deborah shattered glass ceilings in ministry advancement, she expressed displeasure with the way clergywomen treated each other in the CME Church. She described the actions and mentality of clergywomen as "crab in the barrel." Most clergywomen were not supportive of Deborah's accelerated path to ministry and accused her of participating in immoral activities with men in leadership. While she expected to receive pushback from male clergy, she was dismayed as she received admonishment rather than support from clergywoman.

Deborah spoke of her disdain for the lack of accountability within the CME Church as she shared her experience of being sent to pastor a church with an average Sunday worship attendance of thirty congregational members, a parsonage that was uninhabitable, and an annual apportionment[47] of

---

47   Apportionments in the CME Church are referred to as conference claims: fees that are assessed to the local church to support the expenses of the general church (general claims)

thirty-thousand dollars. Deborah, along with family and friends, remodeled the parsonage and led the church in achieving financial solvency. Shortly after redeeming the church, she was moved to a church with only eighty-four cents in its treasury and another parsonage in need of restoration. Deborah shared her frustration of being used to stabilize churches only to be moved to another financially failing church, while the bishop sent a male pastor to reap the harvest of her hard work. She spoke of a male pastor who had been moved to another church after he fathered a child, outside of his marriage, with a congregational member. She expressed the harsh reality of knowing that if a clergywoman were impregnated outside of her marriage or as a single woman, "She would have been sanctioned. She would have been sat down."

As the conversation with Deborah came to a close, Deborah spoke of her disappointment in being passed over for a presiding elder's role that was given to a male counterpart with fewer years of pastoral ministry experience. Deborah made it clear that she did not think she was passed over because of her gender, but because of her integrity and willingness to speak truth to power. She said, "I'm not the yes person. I'm not the person that will allow you to make an arbitrary decision and say nothing about it." Deborah reflected on the difference in treatment of clergy men and women and she could not foresee any significant change in the CME Church in the near future.

Deborah's decision to leave the CME Church was a difficult decision to make. She loves the church but could not remain in a system where leadership lacked integrity and accountability. Her call to ministry was a call to be Christ-centered, soul-minded, and community-focused, just as her male and female CME pastoral mentors instilled in her. Although Deborah left the CME Church, she did not join another religious institution. Instead, she created her own ministry with a focus on leading people to Christ.

13　　Proposed Intervention

As with many churches and institutions, the CME Church has work to do in its treatment and elevation of clergywomen into superordinate leadership roles.

---

as well as episcopal districts (annual conference claims). A portion of the claims are distributed to the general church to support the general functioning of the CME Church, the salaries and retirement funds of general officers and bishops, and to financially support CME Church colleges and the seminary. Conference claims assessed to support episcopal districts are collected to pay the salaries, housing, the retirement fund of presiding elders, the upkeep of and expenses related to the episcopal residence, the expansion of churches, and stipends paid to annual conference officers.

In order to balance the scales of leadership equality for clergywomen in the CME Church, the development and implementation of a leadership training program designed specifically for women is proposed. The program would be designed to:

- identify and invest in burgeoning high-potential clergywomen by giving them exposure at key leadership conferences;
- accelerate the development of clergywomen by providing opportunities to foster and strengthen their skills and confidence;
- increase the effectiveness of current clergywomen leaders through continued educational enrichment;
- build a gender-balanced leadership structure to support the continued growth of the CME Church; and
- create a mentorship program that aims to retain and promote clergywomen.

14   Conclusion

Decades have passed since the eight-year-old Lutheran schoolgirl charted her course of advocacy. Today, she continues to shed light on the unjust treatment of women, particularly the prejudices faced by clergywomen while engaging in their call to ministry. The voices of the three clergywomen presented here not only illuminate the pervasiveness of patriarchy within the CME Church, but confirms that the misuse of power by men in leadership continues to be commonplace. There is an opportunity within the CME Church to make profound changes that will uplift the status and increase the retention of gifted clergywomen. Change requires the collective work and determination of both clergy men and women. Women clergy can no longer simply complain about the injustices or sit on the sidelines waiting for change to come. Clergywomen must be willing to stay the course, take decisive action, and raise their voices against sexism and oppression. Male clergy must be willing to envision, embrace, and cultivate the Spirit that has been poured into their sister clerics, just as the same Spirit has been poured into them.

Bibliography

Bote, Joshua. "'Get in good trouble, necessary trouble': Rep John Lewis in his own words" *USA Today*, July 18, 2020, https://www.usatoday.com/story/news/politics/2020/07/18/rep-john-lewis-most-memorable-quotes-get-good-trouble/5464148002/ (accessed September 27, 2020).

Chaves, Mark. *Ordaining Women: Culture and Conflict in Religious Organizations* (Cambridge: Harvard University Press, 1997).

Chilcote, Paul W. *John Wesley and the Women Preachers of Early Methodism* (Metuchen, New Jersey: The American Theological Library Association and The Scarecrow Press: 1991).

Crowe, Sarah, *et al.* "The Case Study Approach," *BMC Medical Research Methodology*, 11, no. 100 (2011). http://www.biomedcentral.com/1471-2288/11/100 (accessed August 25, 2020).

Daly, Mary. *The Church and the Second Sex,* 3rd ed. (Boston: Beacon Press, 1985).

Green, TeResa. "A Gendered Spirit: Race, Class, and Sex in the African American Church," *Race, Gender & Class* 10, no. 1 (2003). http://www.jstor.org/stable/41675063 (accessed July 31, 2020).

Jones, Charisse and Kumea Shorter-Gooden, *Shifting: The Double Lives of Black Women in America* (New York: Harper Collins Publishers, 2003).

Lakey, Othal Hawthorne. *The History of the CME Church,* rev. ed. (Memphis: The CME Publishing House, 1996).

Luther, Martin. *On the Councils and the Church,* https://wolfmueller.co/wp-content/uploads/2018/10/Work-on-Councils_100618.pdf (accessed September 27, 2020).

Roberts, J. Deotis. *The Prophethood of Black Believers: An African American Political Theology for Ministry* (Louisville: Westminster/John Knox Press, 1994).

CHAPTER 12

Misogynoir and Health Inequities

Giving Voice to the Erased

Francoise Knox-Kazimierczuk and Meredith Shockley-Smith

Black women in America have long been silenced, erased, and left without voice. This *voicelessness* is a great detriment, particularly to Black women and children. For example, Black maternal and infant mortality rates are significantly higher than any other racial groups in the United States. Despite the wide racial gap and the national attention, the disparities have persisted. In this chapter, quantitative data details the problem of maternal mortality alongside qualitative data giving voice to the experience of Black women as they confront racism, sexism, and classism during pregnancy, labor, and delivery.

In September 2000 leaders from around the world met at the Millennium Summit to discuss the plight of the impoverished. The aim of the summit was to develop goals by which countries could measure and benchmark the health outcomes of their citizens. This resulted in eight Millennium Development Goals (MDGs) that focused on equitable allocation of resources and improving health.[1] Two of the eight MDGs specifically addressed maternal and infant health, aimed at improving maternal health and reducing infant mortality (MDGs 5 and 4 respectively). Significantly, MDG 5 set an explicit target of reducing maternal mortality rates by 75% within fifteen years.[2] Despite their good intentions, global data indicated that this target was not met. Developed countries showed the least amount of improvement towards the goal. In fact, developed countries only saw a 35% reduction in maternal mortality rates with one notable exception.[3] During this same time period data from the National Center for Health Statistics (HCHS) showed an *upward trend* in the United States for maternal mortality rates.[4] While the goals were specifically developed to target developing countries with extreme widespread poverty,

---

1   United Nations, *The Millennium Development Goals Report.* New York (2015).
2   Ibid.
3   Ibid.
4   L.M. Rossen, L.S. Womack, D.L. Hoyert, R.N. Anderson, S.F.G. Uddin, *The impact of the pregnancy checkbox and misclassification on maternal mortality trends in the United States, 1999–2017*, National Center for Health Statistics. Vital Health Stat 3: 44 (2020).

these goals also provide metrics by which to evaluate developed, high-income countries, such as the United States. While developed countries have significantly lower rates of maternal death than developing countries, the rates in the United States for Black women are higher than two of the World Health Organization's (WHO) listed high priority regions.[5]

Pregnancy-related maternal mortality in the United States remains one of the highest among developed countries. In fact, the United States currently ranks 64th in the world for pregnancy-related maternal mortality.[6] The Center for Disease Control & Prevention (CDC) has reported an upward trajectory over the last thirty years, between 1987 and 2017. Data from 2017 reveals that the United States' pregnancy-related maternal mortality ratios (PRMRs) (defined as the number of maternal deaths per 100,000 live births) was 17.3 deaths per 100,000 live births. Black women have experienced the highest rates of PRMRs of any racial/ethnic group in the United States. The PRMRs for Black women between 2014 and 2017 were 41.7 deaths per 100,000 live births. During the same timeframe, white women experienced 13.4 maternal deaths per 100,000 live births.[7] The disparity between Black and white women in the United States is significant, with Black women experiencing maternal death 3.1 times more often in birth.

Numerous factors can contribute to pregnancy-related deaths in women as data from the CDC demonstrates. During 2014–2017, the most frequent cause of pregnancy-related death was cardiovascular conditions (15.5%). Cardiovascular conditions, such as cardiomyopathy (11.5%), hemorrhage (10.7%), thrombotic pulmonary or other embolism (9.6%), cerebrovascular accident (8.2%), hypertensive disorders of pregnancy (6.6%), and amniotic fluid embolism (5.5%) comprised the vast majority of causes of pregnancy-related deaths in the United States.[8] Many of these conditions are related to obesity, hypertension, diabetes, and chronic heart disease. Black women are disproportionately affected by obesity and chronic disease. Many reasons for the higher rates have been posited.[9] K.M. Flegal and colleagues, for instance,

---

5 United Nations, *The Millennium Development Goals Report*.

6 Centers for Disease Control and Prevention, *Pregnancy Mortality Surveillance System*, (2017) https://www.cdc.gov/reproductivehealth/maternal-mortality/pregnancy-mortality-surveillance-system.htm#:~:text=Since%20the%20Pregnancy%20Mortality%20Surveillance,100%2C000%20live%20births%20in%20 (Accessed November 2020).

7 Ibid.

8 Ibid.

9 K.M. Flegal, M.D. Carroll, C.L. Ogden, and L.R. Curtin, "Prevalence and Trends in Obesity Among US Adults, 1999–2008," *The Journal of the American Medical Association*, 303, no. 3 (2010) 235–241.

examined the prevalence of obesity in the United States, using the National Health and Nutrition Examination Survey (NHANES). This important examination collects national data for a representative sample of the population. In addition to observing the increasing rates of obesity, investigators also noted the trend of disproportionate rates of obesity between Black and white people. The most striking rates of obesity were noted in Black women, prompting campaigns and interventions to address this disparity.[10] As with other interventions the focus was short-sighted and narrow, prescribing solutions to mitigate downstream health determinants such as improving access to care and creating programs that target individual health behaviors. However, these interventions lacked the incorporation of methodologies to address racism as a significant determinant of health and thus did not yield the results witnessed in controlled clinical studies.[11] Many disciplines (e.g. public health, psychiatry, psychology, and education) have expressed concern with transitioning clinical-based interventions to real-world settings in an attempt to identify confounding factors.[12] The problem with the intervention lies with the basic understanding of etiology (the causes of disease) within the field of medicine and health. Most often, physiological explanations are frequently cited as the cause of these medical conditions and chronic diseases. However, the development of a chronic disease or medical condition is far more complicated and involves numerous external inputs, related to an individual's race, societal structure, political system, and history.

Race/ethnicity is of particular interest in examining PRMRs, as the construct of race further complicates health and the delivery of care.[13] Race/ethnicity is linked to social disparities, that can adversely impact health.[14] Racial differences in health risks and outcomes can be attributed to a number of factors that reflect differences in socioeconomic status, housing, and social positionality/strata.[15] Additionally, individuals minoritized due to not being

---

10   Ibid.

11   H. Yoshikawa, "Placing Community Psychology in the Context of the Social, Health and Educational Sciences: Directions for Interdisciplinary Research and Action," *American Journal of Community Psychology, 38* (2006) 31–34.

12   Ibid.

13   D. R. Williams, "Race and health: Basic questions, emerging directions," *Annals of Epidemiology,* 7, no. 5 (1997) 322–333.

14   P. Braveman, S. Egerter, and D.R. Williams, "The Social Determinants of Health: Coming of Age," *Annual Review of Public Health,* 32 (2001) 381–98.

15   B. Smedley, A. Stith, and A. Nelson, eds., "Committee on Understanding and Eliminating Racial and Ethnic Disparities in Health Care" in *Unequal treatment: confronting racial and ethnic disparities in healthcare.* Washington D.C.: The National Academies Press (2003). https://doi.org/10.17226/10260.

part of the dominant cultural reference group may face individual racism as well as systemic racism. Ford and Airhihenbuwa (2010), in their commentary in the *American Journal of Public Health*, introduced Critical Race Theory (CRT), as a framework by which public health and healthcare professionals can understand the embedded nature of racism in the United States.[16] In CRT, the first premise is the centrality of racism. Race theorists posit that racism is an ingrained feature, which due to its ordinariness becomes almost unrecognizable. This inability of whites to be able to identify racism leaves them blind to the marginalization of nonwhites and to the privileges afforded them due to their whiteness.

The construct of race has always been rooted in white supremacy. In America race has been structured in a way to create a binary opposition, bifurcating whiteness from otherness. This division promulgated a narrative of superiority and inferiority, which positioned the other into the role of deviant. This notion of a deviant/underclass conjures specific imagery, which for African American women has been depicted by two iterative representations, the mammy and the jezebel. The mammy with her black face and rotund body nurtured the household of the master. She was self-sacrificing and obedient, while the jezebel was a temptress, exposing her breasts and acting in lewd ways to lure men to her.[17] Black women were forced into one of the two roles that the dominant culture had constructed for her, placing her in a position to be demonized. The mammy and the jezebel have appeared in media and in social text as early as the 1800's and both were misrepresentations of Black womanhood which stripped away the humanity of Black women. This dehumanization means that the individual is devoid of agency and power, allowing other actors to dictate the circumstances of one's existence. Whiteness, in conjunction with maleness, has privileged these two characteristics and established them as the standard by which to measure individual value.[18] The privileging of these specific characteristics means those embodying these traits get to create the narratives for and about those occupying a positionality perceived as inferior. In the case of Black women, being doubly minoritized, the ability to effect change in their lives is limited by the power exerted on them by the

---

16   C.L. Ford and C.O. Airhihenbuwa, "Critical Race Theory, race equity, and public health: toward antiracism praxis," *American journal of public health*, 100 Suppl 1(2010) S30–S35. https://doi.org/10.2105/AJPH.2009.1710581.2.

17   Patricia Hill Collins, *Black sexual politics: African Americans, gender, and the new racism.* New York: Routledge (2003).

18   A.K. Sesko, and M. Biernat, "Prototypes of race and gender: The invisibility of Black women," *Journal of Experimental Social Psychology*, 46, no. 2 (2010) 356–360.

White male esthetic. This esthetic reifies Blackness in women as hypersexual and depraved or subservient and docile. However, the cultural reproduction of these images and narratives has conflated these two constructs into the *welfare queen*, a misrepresentation coined by late President Ronald Reagan. This construct when evoked allowed for the reform of federal aid programs, shifting millions of dollars from programs established to assist in feeding and housing families in poverty to the military and governmental pet projects. Through the construction and reproduction of social text, whiteness is able to maintain supremacy and assert control over Black bodies.[19] The process of control is insidious, due to the entrenchment of images and narratives. These images and narratives do not only operate at a personal level, but also through institutions and systems.

Racism in healthcare can manifest itself through two primary means. In addition, it can exert its impact via several mechanisms. Dr. Camara Jones, former president of the American Public Health Association (APHA), identified institutional racism and personal mediate racism as determinants of health for African Americans and a factor in health disparities. Likewise, Dr. David R. Williams, chair of the Department of Social and Behavioral Sciences at the Harvard T.H. Chan School of Public Health, cited institutional/structural racism and cultural racism (referring to racial ideology of Black inferiority) as contributing factors of adverse health outcomes for African Americans/Blacks.[20] Institutional racism informs the material conditions of the lived experiences of African Americans/Blacks through policies, laws, and practices embedded in society, which can impact the physical environment and access to services. Both personal mediated and cultural racism can result in implicit bias and/or discrimination. Williams and Mohamed (2013) link racism to stress and physiological responses which impact morbidity and mortality.[21] Several models exist linking racial stress due to discrimination and institutional racism to adverse health. Additionally, co-occurring societal factors—such as socioeconomic status, geographical location, neighborhood/community cohesion—can have an additive effect upon racism. For example, racial housing segregation (institutional racism) which presents several mechanisms by which it acts on health

19 Hill Collins, *Black sexual politics.*

20 D.R. Williams, J.A. Lawrence, B.A. Davis, "Racism and Health: Evidence and Needed Research," *Annual Review of Public Health*, 40, no. 1 (2019)105–125. doi:10.1146/annurev-publhealth-040218-043750.

21 D.R. Williams, S.A. Mohammed, "Racism and Health," *American Behavioral Scientist*, 57, no. 8 (2013)1152–1173. doi:10.1177/0002764213487340.

has been linked to increases in adult and infant mortality.[22] Likewise, personal mediated and cultural racism, can manifest as dismissing a patient's request for pain management, due to the belief that they have a higher pain threshold or that they are more likely to be a drug addict because of stereotypical narratives assigned to Black bodies.[23]

Racism remains a persistent and pervasive risk factor for Black women giving birth.[24] C. Prather and colleagues conducted a literature review to examine the historical events related to the reproductive health of African American women. Their researchchronicled the mistreatment and abuse of Black women, during four distinct periods: slavery; Jim Crow; civil rights era; and post-civil rights era.[25] During all four time periods Black women endured racist assaults and structural barriers due to the color of their skin, resulting in deleterious impacts on maternal health. Over the last couple of years there have been dozens of news stories reporting the death or near-death experience of Black women giving birth in the United States. The issue of maternal mortality disparities was often linked to the expectant mother's education and income. This perspective, however, totally disregards racism and racial bias as significant factors of analysis. Yet, when Beyoncé and Serena Williams shared their birthing experiences, it facilitated a national conversation about the willful negation of agency and presence of Black women. In the case of Beyoncé and Serena, their money and social position should have offered them protection and both of their births should have been unremarkable. However, their race placed them in situations that are common and so familiar to other Black women. Being educated, articulate, or well-to-do does not provide protection from racial bias. All Black women are at risk of a medical crisis during birth.

Black women have been dying at the hands of the white medical establishment in the United States since they first disembarked from the hull of slave ships on the shores of North Carolina.[26] After an arduous journey where men, women, and children had been stacked next to and on top of each other for

22   D.R. Williams, J.A. Lawrence, B.A. Davis, "Racism and Health: Evidence and Needed Research," *Annual Review of Public Health*, 40, no. 1 (2019)105–125. doi:10.1146/annurev-publhealth-040218-043750.

23   Ibid.

24   C. Prather, T.R. Fuller, W.L. Jeffries IV, K.J. Marshall, A.V. Howell, A. Belyue-Umole, W. King, "Racism, African American women, and their sexual and reproductive health: a review of historical and contemporary evidence and implications for health equity," *Health Equity* 2:1 (2018) 249–259, DOI: 10.1089/heq.2017.0045.

25   Ibid.

26   H.A. Washington, *Medical Apartheid: The Dark History of Medical Experimentation On Black Americans From Colonial Times to the Present.* New York: Doubleday (2016).

months, with limited nourishment, slave traders cleaned up their property so that the enslaved appeared healthy with the help of physicians. Throughout the South, physicians were an integral component in the slave trade. Slave owners relied on physicians to verify the health of slaves prior to sale and to determine if slaves were malingering. The relationship provided reciprocity for the physician, as he would be allowed to experiment with new treatments, dosages of medicine, and would take possession of slaves who succumbed to their ailment or the prescribed treatment. In addition, slave owners served as the gatekeepers to medical care. As medical attention was expensive, it was often financially beneficial to withhold care to extract the maximum amount of labor from the enslaved, until they believed care was absolutely necessary.[27] Harriet Washington, in her book *Medical Apartheid*, has shown the medical neglect and abuse of the enslaved due to their lack of power.[28] Additionally, she presented modern cases exhibiting similar medical neglect due to systemic and cultural racism, which continues to leave Black women powerless.

Systemic racism in the United States has relegated Black women to an inferior social space, which often erases and leaves Black women voiceless and vulnerable. The silencing of Black women due to occupying a positionality that is deemed inferior means Black women are less likely to be heard, and medical issues that would normally be deemed non-life threatening with appropriate medical care, devolve into crisis situations which extinguish life.

As healthcare systems and providers continue to struggle with bleak maternal mortality numbers, it is clear that a paradigm shift how we address this issue needs to occur. Solutions frequently focus on developing anti-racist policies, awareness of implicit bias, and providing cultural competence training. Research on the efficacy of implicit bias and cultural competence training as a means to reduce health disparities has been mixed.[29] Policy solutions to eliminate and/or reduce disparities requires a multilevel approach targeting the social determinants of health, such as housing, income, education, and community development. While policy approaches have been successful in improving some health outcomes, they have yet to be successful in reducing racial disparities with maternal mortality.

In the case of maternal mortality, while policies need to be explored and implemented, they cannot continue to be done in a vacuum. Meeting rooms filled with the same individuals who perpetrate acts to erode the humanness

---

27   Ibid.
28   Ibid.
29   Aidan Byrne and Alessandra Tanesini, "Instilling new habits: addressing implicit bias in healthcare professionals," *Advances in Health Sciences Education* 20, no. 5 (2015) 1255–1262.

of Black women, should not have their thoughts and voices privileged as an authority on how to address the very problem they created. Positionality often places Black women on the periphery of decision-making processes, even when it relates to their lived realities. Black women must be included in envisioning, developing, and implementing any proposed solution. They must be in positions of leadership in this process. Healthcare providers and systems need to center Black women by listening, hearing, and letting them lead. In pursuit of giving voice to the birth experiences of Black women, a community-based research study was conducted using focus groups and in-depth interviews.

1 Background for Our Study

The aim of this study was to explore the labor, delivery, and post-partum experiences of Black women, with the intent of gaining insight into challenges and triumphs during pregnancy and birth. Maternal mortality rates for Black women remains significantly higher than any other racial/ethnic group in the United States. Additionally, the current rate is at a level higher than two WHO high-priority regions in developing countries without the medical and technological resources of the United States. Currently, there is limited literature examining the experiences of Black women aimed at understanding and addressing this disparity. Study procedures were approved by the University Institutional Review Board (IRB).

2 Methodology

In this study, a phenomenological qualitative research design was used to conduct focus groups and in-depth interviews. Phenomenology is a type of qualitative research rooted in both psychology and philosophy. The phenomenological approach focuses on lived experiences and meaning making.[30] Phenomenological research engages in this process by asking questions related to specific phenomena shared by a group of people. In this study, Black women eligible to receive Special Supplemental Nutrition Program for Women, Infants, and Children (WIC) and who had given birth within the last

---

30   V.E. Worthen and B.W. McNeill, *A Phenomenological Investigation of "Good" Supervision Events. In Merriam, S. Qualitative Research in Practice. Examples for Discussion and Analysis*, San Francisco, CA: Jossey-Bass (2002) 96–117.

two years were recruited to participate in several focus groups as well as in-depth interviews.

Focus groups were conducted to provide a more natural social space for participants to have a conversation about their experiences. All focus groups were led by the same two Black women group facilitators/researchers. Focus groups consisted of two to four women in a group. Multiple sessions were held over the course of the study with each participant attending two focus groups. Participants were provided several times and locations in close proximity to their residence for focus groups and interviews. In-depth interviews were used to elicit richer data by asking probing questions building upon themes that emerged from the focus groups. Focus groups and in-depth interviews were concluded after data saturation was met. Sessions were conducted between April 2017 and June 2017. Focus groups and interviews used a semi-structured format. All sessions were recorded and transcribed.

This study was conducted in the community setting, within neighborhood recreational centers, in a midwestern city. All recreational centers were located near metropolitan housing authority owned rental units and public transportation for ease of access.

3   Recruitment

Black women eligible for WIC were recruited through snowball sampling using African American and Black mothers birthing and breastfeeding Facebook Groups. A recruitment script and a recruitment video, providing study details and contact information for the primary investigator were posted on several group pages administered by local Black women groups dedicated to breast-feeding and birth experiences (see appendix). A follow-up script was posted two weeks later. Women interested in participating were instructed to contact the primary investigator. Women meeting the inclusion criteria were scheduled for small group interviews.

4   Participants

Participants included in the study met the following criteria:
- Participants were current residents of the Greater Cincinnati area.
- They must be women at least eighteen years old.
- They self-identified as African American, African, and/or part of the African diaspora.

- They self-identified as cis-gendered female.
- They spoke and read English fluently.
- They qualified for WIC subsidies.
- They initiated breastfeeding with their infant child.
- They were either currently breastfeeding or previously breastfed.
- It had been no more than two years since they gave birth.
- They were eligible, and they were willing to give informed consent.

From the cohort of volunteers, eight women who aligned with the criteria above were selected to participate in focus groups and in-depth interview sessions from April through July 2017. Each of the selected participants completed a demographic survey prior to the focus group sessions. One participant was a recent immigrant from South Africa, one was African American, and six of the participants were bi-racial (African American and European American descent). The six bi-racial women self-identified as African American. All of the women except one were married or were cohabitating with an African American partner.

5   Data Collection and Analysis

Data was collected during four small group interview sessions and eight in-depth interviews, with each participant (see appendix). All small group interviews and individual in-depth interviews were recorded via a digital record and transcribed. We analyzed the data after independently creating memos of the interview experiences that included our observations, impressions, as well as our perceptions of the overall emotions of participants during each session. The memos and the transcribed interviews were used to develop and cluster recurring themes. Additionally, data analysis software Nvivo 12 was used to perform a word and phrase query, and nodes were created by grouping the common words and phrases. Investigators compared themes and nodes for congruence. Concepts which were clustered together and reflected a specific node, but were not included, were added to the node created within Nvivo 12.

6   Results

In the Landmark text *Unequal Treatment*, B. Smedley details the pervasiveness of racial bias within the medical system.[31] Not surprisingly, all of the

---

31   B. Smedley, A. Stith and A. Nelson, eds., *Committee on Understanding and Eliminating Racial and Ethnic Disparities in Health Care* (2003). *Unequal treatment: confronting racial*

participants in our study reported having experienced racial bias and micro-aggression from their healthcare providers during various stages of pregnancy, labor, delivery, and post-partum. The racial bias experienced by the participants manifested in several ways in participant interactions with healthcare providers. Three of the participants indicated they experienced intimidation and coercion. Half of the women had experienced a traumatic birthing experience and reported the avoidance of the healthcare system subsequently. Analysis of the textual data led to the emergence of four primary themes based on the experiences of the study's participants:
- Invisibility/Disregard,
- Distrust/Fear,
- Control, and
- Cultivating Social Capital.

6.1   Theme 1: Invisibility/Disregard

> They don't listen. I tried to let them know from the beginning that I wanted to be natural and I know you are here to support me and help keep me safe, but don't tell me what I can't do.
>
> So, I remember telling the nurses um that I felt dizzy because everybody was focused on the baby no one had checked my blood pressure. I told them that they didn't check my blood pressure. Something is really off.
>
> And they were like, that's nice, but no. Here is what you are going to have to do. We should schedule a c-section and if she is not here by the 12th then we should go ahead and induce. This is at the first appointment and I literally had my birth plan right there. I was like so you didn't listen to anything I had to say.

As these participant quotes illustrate, these women reported repeatedly that they did not feel as though healthcare providers listened to them. This contributed to their belief that they were being neglected due to their invisibility. Without exception, participants indicated that during their pregnancy, labor, and/or delivery they received substandard care due to caregivers' total disregard when they expressed their questions and concerns. Often these women reported that healthcare providers went through a well-rehearsed checklist without ever acknowledging them as a person. These providers never engaged

---

and ethnic disparities in healthcare. Washington D.C.: The National Academies Press. https://doi.org/10.17226/10260.

these women in conversations concerning their care. Expectant Black mothers throughout the country have reported similar experiences. In summary, Black mothers' pain, symptoms, and inquiries are frequently minimized or ignored.[32]

6.2 Theme II: Distrust/Fear

I was like well I just don't really feel like dying when I'm giving birth to my child ... I don't trust the system that has consistently and was built to constrain black women and reproduction, so.

They kept throwing things at me and they never explained and never wanted to provide me time to look up information. Their response was always, your baby is going to die.

I had no information, and I was not provided information. I was told early in my pregnancy that I needed to have a C-section. They were really pushing it. I was told my pelvis was too small and with the weight I had gained they said he would be 10lbs. He wouldn't be able to get out. He could die. They would have to break his arm. I was so scared. I had no idea what was going on.

In the second theme, participants discussed their fear of interacting with healthcare providers and their distrust of providers due to perceived racial and class bias. Many participants discussed unethical and deleterious experiments that had been conducted historically on African Americans, for the sake of medical advancement. Significantly, many participants cited historical as well as their personal lived experiences as women of color being mistreated and victimized due to systemic racism founded on our country's practices of imperialism and colonization. Low levels of trust and difficulty in building rapport with African American patients have been cited in several studies as potential factors in the gaps in health related outcomes.

6.3 Theme III: Control

My OBGYN actually gave me the hardest time because when I went in for my 6-week checkup she told me that I was fine. I could go back to

---

32   D.C. Owens and S.M. Fett, "Black Maternal and Infant Health: Historical Legacies of Slavery," *American Journal of Public Health*, 109, no. 10 (2019) 1342–1345. doi:10.2105/AJPH.2019.305243.

work, but I said my job gives me 12 weeks. She said well are you just going to be getting paid to not be working? I was like, what business of that is yours?

I feel like doctors are so out of their place sometimes. We are coming to you for you to assist us. We are not coming for you to take over our bodies and control us.

Control emerged from the data as the third theme. Participants believed that their healthcare providers had an overwhelming need to control their bodies, the situation, and the environment. Participants reported having no options presented to them. Many indicated that birth decisions were made unilaterally by the physician without involving them in the decision-making process. Participants expressed feeling that their healthcare providers not only exerted control within the context of their pregnancy and delivery, but also imposed themselves on other aspects of their private lives. These women did not welcome these invasive intrusions.

6.4   Theme IV: Support Systems and Social Capital

I didn't have any support. Her dad backed me up with what I wanted. All the anger I had from my first baby, all the bullying. ... I refused to let it happen again.

I think the idea too of just building the sisterhood and building the trust in our community. Um to be able to say like come talk to me. Like let's go through this journey together.

The fourth theme focused on support systems and social capital. Participants shared that their birthing experiences had been difficult, and they often had to find strength and support from their partners, family, and friends. For those participants with limited contact or support, they expressed the need for Black women to form a supportive birthing community. Participants discussed relying on unconventional nonphysician providers for support and guidance. Many of the participants reported working with doulas or midwives. Additionally, several of the women after their birthing experiences sought training to become a doula or a Certified Lactation Consultant (CLC). Their experiences also prompted some participants to empower other women, so they developed blogs and social media communities to support Black expectant mothers.

7   Conclusion

Kimberlé Crenshaw argued the impact of being doubly minoritized when she coined the term *intersectionality* in her 1989 essay.[33] Crenshaw asserted that the oppression of systematic racism for Black women was different from either sexism or racism. The combination of these two oppressive forces of sexism *and* racism combined to act in a way that does not align with the categorization of either singular oppressive force. The inability to categorize the experiences of Black women to align with the sexism experienced by white women and racism experienced by Black men, leaves Black women with few remedies.

The entrenchment of whiteness in America has fostered an insidious and pervasive cultural of anti-Black racism that devalues Black bodies. The intersection of gender along with race has created a space of double stigmatization for Black women. This marginalized space often erases Black women, as their societal worth is reduced exponentially due to the intersections of sexist and racist oppression. In this study, participants experienced the double burden of being Black and a woman. Additionally, women in this study experienced triple oppression due to their low-income status. Several theories have posited that multiple subordinate identities can significantly impact one's social interactions and life experiences.

Black women operate within the margins of these two marginalized identities. This space of femaleness and Blackness means Black women do not fit the expectations for what is considered female or male. V. Purdie-Vaughns and R. Eibach (2008), hypothesized that the overlapping of subordinate-group identities leads to the invisibility of Black women, due to being non-prototypical group members.[34] Similarly, in a study conducted by A. Sesko and M. Biernat, results showed that white study participants had difficulty recognizing and distinguishing Black women's faces more often, and they noticed the presence of Black women less than other groups.[35] Additionally, this study found that Black women's voices often went unheard, due to their statements being misattributed. In healthcare, the issue of invisibility is a major theme for Black women trying to receive care, as many women report not being listened

---

33   Kimberlé Crenshaw, "Demarginalizing the Intersection of Race and Sex: A Black Feminist Critique of Antidiscrimination Doctrine, Feminist Theory, and Antiracist Politics," *University of Chicago Legal Forum* (1989) 139–67.

34   V. Purdie-Vaughns and R.P. Eibach, " Intersectional invisibility: The distinctive advantages and disadvantages of multiple subordinate-group identities," *Sex Roles*, 59 (2008) 377–391.

35   A.K. Sesko and M. Biernat, "Prototypes of race and gender: The invisibility of Black women," *Journal of Experimental Social Psychology*, 46, no.2 (2010) 356–360.

to by providers. Sesko and Bienat describe invisibility as another form of discrimination that is often directed towards Black women. Although their study did not investigate the consequences, the qualitative data collection reported in this chapter illustrates the implications of invisibility.

Additionally, the racism and sexism experienced by Black women has eroded trust in institutions in this country. The women participating in this study all expressed fear and distrust in the healthcare system. The feeling of being controlled through coercion and manipulation was a universal theme for the women. Many of the women discussed historical abuses by the medical establishment, in addition to their own stories of intimidation and mistreatment. The experiences of the women in this study have been well documented by other researchers, with results showing significant abuses against expectant mothers. Women in several other studies reported being yelled at, verbally abused, forced to accept interventions that they did not want, and provided delayed care.[36]

Black women continue to die preventable deaths during labor and delivery. Despite substantial recognition of this issue and increased funding to address maternal mortality, the rates for Black women remain high and the gap between white women is significant. In the United State, the CDC has set goals to reduce health disparities for the last thirty years but has consistently failed to meet their proposed targets. Likewise, cities and hospital systems have set agendas to reduce maternal mortality by,
- increasing funding for initiatives,
- providing implicit bias trainings,
- and recruiting diverse healthcare providers.

However, these actions are only a starting point. This cannot be the sum total of the efforts to undo over 400 years of atrocities. The racialized experiences of Black women must be centered, and an equity lens must be used to develop inclusive spaces to hear Black women. Additionally, healthcare systems and healthcare providers need to take a step back and allow Black women to lead in this work. Shifting to a community/patient-healthcare provider partnership is a departure from the status quo, but it is a needed paradigm shift that has the potential to remove the death sentence that coincides with childbirth for too many Black women.

---

36   L.P. Freedman and M.E. Kruk, "Disrespect and abuse of women in childbirth: challenging the global quality and accountability agendas," *Lancet*, 384, (2014) 42–44 and L. Rosenthal and M. Lobel, "Explaining racial disparities in adverse birth outcomes: unique sources of stress for black American women," *Social Science and Medicine*, 72, no. 6 (2011)977–83.

8   Appendix

Recruitment Advertisement

Community Health Research Study

Be a part of an important research study focused on African American Women who are or have breastfed!

– Are you African American?
– Are you 18 or over and WIC eligible?
– Have you or are you breastfeeding?
– Are you interested in sharing your experiences about that?

If you answered yes to these questions, then you could be eligible to participate in this research study.

The purpose of this research study is to assess the socio-cultural barriers and assets to help promote breastfeeding.

This study is a one-hour interview about your breastfeeding experiences. No Medications, invasive procedures, or additional information is required.

Interview Question Guide for Qualitative Data Collection

Black Women, Breastfeeding & WIC
RE: Social-Cultural Environmental Barriers
Demographics:

– Age
– Race
– Marital Status
– Number of children
– Education level
– Occupation
– Work status
– Religion/spiritual preference
– Sexual orientation
– Geographic location (urban, rural, suburban or Kentucky vs Ohio)
– How many reside in your household?
– Who resides in your household?

Discussion Questions

1. Can you tell me about your birth experience (prenatal visits, birth plan, method of delivery, length of labor, etc.)?
2. Tell me about the support you had during labor, delivery, and postpartum?

3. What was your experience/relationship with your healthcare provider?
4. What did you find most challenging about giving birth?
5. What did you find most beneficial in aiding you through giving birth?
6. Were you breastfed? (For how long?) (Did anyone else in your family/circle of friends breastfed?)
7. Were you planning to breastfed?
8. Did the type of birth (vaginal vs. C-section) impact your decision? (Explain.)
9. Did anyone help you with the decision to breastfeed? (If Yes—how did they help?)
10. Did WIC impact your decision to breastfed? (Explain. How did it impact your decision and what was the impact?)
11. How does the media represent breastfeeding? How did this representation impact your decision?
12. Are you an exclusive breastfeeder? Predominantly a breastfeeding? How did you choose your specific breastfeeding pattern?
13. How soon after birth did you initiate breastfeeding? Could you tell me about that experience?
14. How frequently did you breastfeed in a 24-hour time period? What was that experience like for you?
15. How long did you breastfeed?
16. How long did/do you intend to breastfeed?
17. When did you begin introducing complementary foods? And how frequently did you provide complementary food during a 24-hour period?
18. What do you most value about breastfeeding?
19. What do you most enjoy about breastfeeding?
20. What do you find most difficult/challenging about breastfeeding?
21. What do you find most helpful/beneficial in aiding you with breastfeeding?
22. What/who could have made breastfeeding easier for you?
23. What did your family and friends think about your decision to breastfeed?

** These questions serve as a guide for areas to probe if the participant is having a difficult time opening up about her birth and breastfeeding story. The goal is to allow the participant to share her story naturally.**

Bibliography

Braveman, P., Egerter, S. and Williams, D.R. "The Social Determinants of Health: Coming of Age," *Annual Review of Public Health*, 32 (2001) 381–98.

Byrne, Aidan and Tanesini, Alessandra. "Instilling new habits: addressing implicit bias in healthcare professionals," *Advances in Health Sciences Education* 20, no. 5 (2015) 1255–1262.

Centers for Disease Control and Prevention, *Pregnancy Mortality Surveillance System*, (2017) https://www.cdc.gov/reproductivehealth/maternal-mortality/pregnancy-mortality-surveillance-system.htm#:~:text=Since%20the%20Pregnancy%20Mortality%20Surveillance,100%2C000%20live%20births%20in%20 (Accessed November 2020).

Collins, Patricia Hill. *Black sexual politics: African Americans, gender, and the new racism.* New York: Routledge (2003).

Crenshaw, Kimberlé. "Demarginalizing the Intersection of Race and Sex: A Black Feminist Critique of Antidiscrimination Doctrine, Feminist Theory, and Antiracist Politics," *University of Chicago Legal Forum* (1989) 139–67.

Flegal, K.M., Carroll, M.D., Ogden, C.L. and Curtin, L.R. "Prevalence and Trends in Obesity Among US Adults, 1999–2008," *The Journal of the American Medical Association*, 303, no. 3 (2010) 235–241.

Ford, C.L. and Airhihenbuwa, C.O. "Critical Race Theory, race equity, and public health: toward antiracism praxis," *American journal of public health*, 100 Suppl 1(2010) S30–S35. https://doi.org/10.2105/AJPH.2009.1710581.2.

Freedman, L.P. and Kruk, M.E. "Disrespect and abuse of women in childbirth: challenging the global quality and accountability agendas," *Lancet*, 384, (2014) 42–44.

Owens, D.C. and Fett, S.M. "Black Maternal and Infant Health: Historical Legacies of Slavery," *American Journal of Public Health*, 109, no. 10 (2019) 1342–1345. doi:10.2105/AJPH.2019.305243.

Prather, C., Fuller, T.R., Jeffries IV, W.L., Marshall, K.J, Howell, A.V., Belyue-Umole, A., King, W. "Racism, African American women, and their sexual and reproductive health: a review of historical and contemporary evidence and implications for health equity," *Health Equity* 2:1 (2018) 249–259, DOI: 10.1089/heq.2017.0045.

Purdie-Vaughns, V. and Eibach, R.P. "Intersectional invisibility: The distinctive advantages and disadvantages of multiple subordinate-group identities," *Sex Roles*, 59 (2008) 377–391.

Rosenthal, L. and Lobel, M. "Explaining racial disparities in adverse birth outcomes: unique sources of stress for black American women," *Social Science and Medicine*, 72, no. 6 (2011) 977–83.

Rossen, L.M., Womack, L.S., Hoyert, D.L., Anderson, R.N., Uddin, S.F.G. *The impact of the pregnancy checkbox and misclassification on maternal mortality trends in the United States, 1999–2017*, National Center for Health Statistics. Vital Health Stat 3: 44 (2020).

Sesko, A.K. and Biernat, M. "Prototypes of race and gender: The invisibility of Black women," *Journal of Experimental Social Psychology*, 46, no. 2 (2010) 356–360.

Smedley, B., Stith, A., and Nelson, A., eds., "Committee on Understanding and Eliminating Racial and Ethnic Disparities in Health Care" in *Unequal treatment:*

confronting racial and ethnic disparities in healthcare. Washington D.C.: The National Academies Press (2003). https://doi.org/10.17226/10260.

United Nations, *The Millennium Development Goals Report.* New York (2015).

Washington, H.A. *Medical Apartheid: The Dark History of Medical Experimentation On Black Americans From Colonial Times to the Present.* New York: Doubleday (2016).

Williams, D.R. "Race and health: Basic questions, emerging directions," *Annals of Epidemiology,* 7, no. 5 (1997) 322–333.

Williams, D.R., Lawrence, J.A., Davis, B.A. "Racism and Health: Evidence and Needed Research," *Annual Review of Public Health,* 40, no. 1 (2019)105–125. doi:10.1146/annurev-publhealth-040218-043750.

Williams, D.R., Mohammed, S.A. "Racism and Health," *American Behavioral Scientist,* 57, no. 8 (2013)1152–1173. doi:10.1177/0002764213487340.

Worthen, V.E. and McNeill, B.W. *A Phenomenological Investigation of "Good" Supervision Events. In Merriam, S. Qualitative Research in Practice. Examples for Discussion and Analysis,* San Francisco, CA: Jossey-Bass (2002).

Yoshikawa, H. "Placing Community Psychology in the Context of the Social, Health and Educational Sciences: Directions for Interdisciplinary Research and Action," *American Journal of Community Psychology,* 38 (2006) 31–34.

Index

CPSIA information can be obtained
at www.ICGtesting.com
Printed in the USA
JSHW022219150522
25891JS00002B/3